Delayed Endings

Delayed Endings

Nonclosure in Novalis and Hölderlin

Alice A. Kuzniar

The University of Georgia Press
Athens and London

Paperback edition, 2008
© 1987 by the University of Georgia Press
Athens, Georgia 30602
www.ugapress.org
Set in 11 on 13 Garamond Number 3 with ITC Garamond Book
display.
Printed digitally in the United States of America

The Library of Congress has cataloged the hardcover edition of this
book as follows:
Library of Congress Cataloging-in-Publication Data

Kuzniar, Alice A.
    Delayed endings : nonclosure in Novalis and Hölderlin /
Alice A. Kuzniar.
        XIV, 249 P. ; 23 CM.
    ISBN 0-8203-0901-X
    Includes index.
    Bibliography: p. [207]-235.
    1. Novalis, 1772–1801 —Technique. 2. Hölderlin, Friedrich,
1770–1843 —Technique. 3. German literature—18th century—
History and criticism. 4. German literature—19th century—History
and criticism. 5. Romanticism—Germany. 6. Closure (Rhetoric)
I. Title.
PT363.C57 K89   1987
831'.6'09 19   86-11362

Paperback ISBN-13: 978-0-8203-3244-4
ISBN-10: 0-8203-3244-5

British Library Cataloging-in-Publication Data available

The jacket illustration is the Caspar David Fredrich sketch "Zwei
Männer in Mänteln mit Pelerine," ca. 1815–18. It is reproduced here
courtesy of the Kupferstichkabinett und Sammlung der Zeichnungen,
Nationalgalerie, East Berlin.

South Atlantic
Modern Language Association
Award Study

Contents

To my parents

Acknowledgments

The contours of the ideas herein laid forth were incipient in my dissertation, which dealt with the narration of the apocalypse around 1800. "Ihr bringt mit euch die Bilder froher Tage, / Und manche liebe Schatten steigen auf," as Goethe says in the "Dedication" to *Faust*. Once again my most affectionate thanks go to my "Doktorvater" Stanley Corngold, especially for the continued support he has shown for my work. The suggestions of my readers, Theodore Ziolkowski, Ralph Freedman, and Wilfried Barner, for transforming the dissertation into a book have served as invaluable and unfailing guidelines since I left Princeton.

New bonds of devotion have been forged, however. I would like to voice my warmest appreciation to my supportive colleagues in the German Department at the University of North Carolina at Chapel Hill—never faltering, least of all when I was floundering, in their kind encouragement of my every effort. Siegfried Mews, in particular, has patiently alerted me to various stylistic *Schönheitsfehler* in my writing. Gratitude must also be extended to the University of North Carolina Faculty Research Council for providing the funds for my assistants Joan East, Steven Lamb, and Penelope Pynes.

I would also like to take the opportunity to thank both the University of Georgia Press and the adjudicators for the SAMLA Award Competition. Ellen Harris and Nancy Holmes were sharpeyed, sensible editors. My primary readers for the award, Robert Bell and Raymond Gay-Crosier, deserve special recognition for their insightful, critical, and extensive commentary on my manuscript.

Abbreviations

Abbr.	*Reference*
Aus	Lavater, Johann Kaspar. *Aussichten in die Ewigkeit in Briefen an Herrn Joh. Georg Zimmermann, königl. Großbrittanischen Leibarzt in Hannover.* Zurich: Orell, Geßner, and Füßli, 1770–1775.
AW	Klopstock, Friedrich Gottlieb. *Ausgewählte Werke.* Munich: Hanser, 1962.
HKA	———. *Werke und Briefe: Historisch-kritische Ausgabe.* Berlin: de Gruyter, 1974–.
GS	Kant, Immanuel. *Gesammelte Schriften.* Edited by the Königlich Preußische Akademie der Wissenschaften. Berlin: Reimer, 1910–.
W	Lessing, Gotthold Ephraim. *Werke.* Munich: Hanser, 1970–.
Suphan	Herder, Johann Gottfried. *Sämmtliche Werke.* Edited by Bernhard Suphan. Berlin: Weidmann, 1877–1913.
HA	Goethe, Johann Wolfgang. *Werke.* Edited by Erich Trunz. Munich: Beck, 1978.
SW	Richter, Jean Paul. *Sämtliche Werke: Historisch-kritische Ausgabe.* Edited by Eduard Berend. Weimar: Böhlau, 1927–.
NA	Schiller, Friedrich. *Werke: Nationalausgabe.* Weimar: Böhlau, 1943–.
Fichte	Fichte, Johann Gottlieb. *Gesamtausgabe.* Stuttgart: Frommann, 1964–.
StW	Schleiermacher, Friedrich. "Ueber die Religion: Reden an die gebildeten unter ihren Verächtern." In *Sämmtliche Werke.* Part 1, vol. 1. Berlin: Reimer, 1843.

GW	Hegel, Georg Wilhelm Friedrich. *Gesammelte Werke.* Hamburg: Meiner, 1968–.
StA	Hölderlin, Friedrich. *Sämtliche Werke.* Edited by Friedrich Beißner. Stuttgart: Kohlhammer, 1943–.
FHA	――――. "Elegien und Epigramme." In *Sämtliche Werke: Frankfurter Ausgabe.* Vol. 6. Edited by D. E. Sattler and Wolfram Groddeck. Frankfurt: Roter Stern, 1976.
N	Hardenberg, Friedrich von. *Werke, Tagebücher und Briefe.* Edited by Hans-Joachim Mähl und Richard Samuel. Munich: Hanser, 1978.
KA	Schlegel, Friedrich. *Kritische Ausgabe.* Edited by Ernst Behler. Munich/Paderborn/Vienna: Schöningh, 1958–.
Schröter	Schelling, Friedrich Wilhelm Joseph von. *Werke.* Edited by Manfred Schröter. Munich: Beck, 1927–.
Kleist	Kleist, Heinrich von. *Sämtliche Werke und Briefe.* Munich: Hanser, 1977.
Reclam	Bonaventura. *Nachtwachen.* Edited by Wolfgang Paulsen. Stuttgart: Reclam, 1974.
Gü	Günderrode, Karoline von. *Der Schatten eines Traumes: Gedichte, Prosa, Briefe, Zeugnisse von Zeitgenossen.* Edited by Christa Wolf. Darmstadt: Luchterhand, 1981.
SS	Heine, Heinrich. *Sämtliche Schriften.* Munich: Hanser, 1974.

Introduction

The purpose of this book is to make more familiar to an English-speaking audience two authors who are increasingly moving into current critical ken—Hölderlin and Novalis. It focuses on a problem that makes both authors attractive to a generation of scholars that keenly reads Derrida on the erased archē, Lévinas on infinity, Deleuze on adjacencies and stratifications, and Said on beginnings. The question is that of nonclosure. It preoccupied Novalis and Hölderlin throughout the span of their creative years and found its ultimate expression in the fragmented writing of the latter author before his mental abilities dimmed.

Friedrich von Hardenberg (1772–1801), better known under the pseudonym Novalis, belonged to a group of writers called the Jena Romantics who were active around the turn of the nineteenth century. This group included Ludwig Tieck, the brothers Friedrich and August Wilhelm Schlegel, and the theologian Friedrich Schleiermacher. Together, in an exercise of what Novalis called "symphilosophizing," they contributed to a journal entitled the *Athenäum*. Novalis is most renowned for his unfinished novel, *Heinrich von Ofterdingen,* and his prose poem, *Hymnen an die Nacht.* But his oeuvre is much more extensive than is commonly appreciated. One of his many goals, uncompleted like numerous others in his short life span, was to compose an encyclopedia. A geologist by profession, Hardenberg's interests were eclectic and manifold. As his voluminous fragments testify, he avidly responded to the writings of Kant and Fichte.

Friedrich Hölderlin (1770–1843) was also steeped in the philosophy of the period. He was close friends with Schiller, Schelling, and Hegel. Hölderlin's works are primarily lyric; indeed, in German letters he is considered the poet's poet. But Hölderlin is also remembered for his novel *Hyperion,* the tragedy *Empedokles,* the theoretical essays, as well as his translations from the Greek. Although Hölderlin lived much longer than Hardenberg, he was productive at roughly the same time; by 1804 his poems had become brittle, halting utterances, symptoms of a destabilized mind, and in 1806 he was taken by force to a psychiatric clinic in Tübingen, where he was placed under strict surveillance. Yet despite what this contemporaneous literary activity of Hölderlin and Novalis might suggest, the present study does not set about to document their mutual influence or even speculate about it. For that matter, the two authors are recorded to have met on only one occasion. Instead, this work investigates a theoretical problem that was common to both men, indeed to a generation of writers known as the German Idealists: what does it mean to lose the belief in endings and ultimacies?

The question is also a preeminently current one. We can see Novalis and Hölderlin attractively foreshadowing many of today's critical thinkers. In particular, they anticipate certain Poststructuralist concerns, which their writings strikingly exemplify. Undoubtedly, the alignments about to be proposed present significant terminological problems. Before the writings of Hölderlin and Novalis can be considered, therefore, a common discourse needs to be staked out or, at least, various approaches to nonclosure brought into conjunction with one another. I mean here to essay a versatile definition of nonclosure and to give an indication of how Novalis and Hölderlin are less our ancestors than our contemporaries.

Nonclosure can be viewed as inextricably linked to a number of current theoretical concepts. The question, though, is how? The term permits a magnanimous scope, but it also threatens to become a catchall. Nonclosure can be compared to and set off from similar terms, most of which have a decidedly Derridean ring, such as *indeterminacy of meaning, supplementarity, displacement, spacing, deferral,* and *différance.* Nonclosure also relates to the reader's response to textual endings. It can furthermore pertain to purely formal considerations, as well as to the self-reflexive space a text creates. The word *nonclosure* thus evokes various resonances. Without claiming to assimilate, exhaust, or dogmatically compartmentalize, how can we chart the various intricacies of nonclosure and transform it into a flexible matrix?

First and foremost, nonclosure is narrative. It involves the avoidance of endings and whatever strategy would aim to bring a tale, a poem, or an essay to a final, synthesizing halt. On a strictly anatomical level, this means that works are left unfinished, often intentionally, or, once completed, are subject to constant correction and extension by their authors, as by the late Hölderlin. On the level of the narrative fabric itself, nonclosure arises when the reader retrospectively sees how the expectations generated by the teleological movement of the story are not met. To illustrate this formal nonclosure, we need only consider the Romantic novels written at the turn of the nineteenth century, such as Brentano's *Godwi*.[1] They are seemingly interminable. Generally speaking, when they do end, they break off abruptly, so that it would be an understatement even to say that their closure is unstable. Their endings fail to cohere with the narrative means that supposedly led to them. Their episodic plots follow no probable and inevitable sequence. Furthermore, within these Romantic novels the narrative threads are constantly being broken by interspersed poems and shorter tales. Such noncontingency leads to nonclosure in its most radicalized form. The collected laconic remarks of one or two lines called "fragments" by the Jena Romantics likewise testify to the parcelled, dispersive nature of much writing at this time.

Formal nonclosure entails a certain nonresolution and prolongation of tension; it thus contributes to a psychology of reception. This may be the case whether we refer to the actual ending of a work or to the stations along the narrative path where the promise of illumination, a turning point, restitution, or consummation wants to be kept. On the one hand, aesthetic discomfort results as expectations of pending harmony and reconciliation are not met. On the other hand, speculation, extrapolation, and even suspicion are encouraged. The fragmented text both distracts and leads us on. Awakening desire and curiosity, it offers a certain "plaisir du texte," to speak with Roland Barthes. Indeed, the Romantics mastered the arts of suggestion and suspension. They indefinitely prolonged foreplay. Yet however much these authors eschewed endings, they did set their narratives into play towards them. Trajectories, though, are rarely sustained. Whenever we encounter paradigms of fulfillment, as in Novalis's fairy tales, satisfaction is temporary; the thrust of the larger, incomplete narrative, into which these tales are set, draws us back into a state of anticipation.

Nonclosure, here signifying repeated open-endedness and a constant prying-ajar of enclosed structure, implies a criticism of integral systems, a questioning of monadic totalities and ultimacies. It betrays a mistrust of completed artifice. Indeed, the authors considered in this book pursue nonclosure rigorously. Novalis recommends systematic asystemization and cultivates chaotic form. Friedrich Schlegel's preferred image for asymmetric, discontinuous, and allocentric structure is the arabesque. Hölderlin speaks of an eccentric narrative path. Whenever repetitive structures surface in German Romanticism, they give the sense not of enclosure but of vertigo and nondirection—of what Lucien Dällenbach refers to as "mise en abyme." Writers such as Novalis and Schlegel thus advocate either a proliferation or a redundancy of structures, rather than the organic, unitary form often attributed to them, most notably by René Wellek. Indeed, their digressive works invite fewer readings of the kind performed by New Criticism than ones attuned to ironic inconsistencies.[2] The German Romantics mistrust exhaustiveness, inclusiveness, and pretensions to mastery.

Narrative nonclosure not only bears upon structural or purely textual considerations and their effect on the reader; it also gives rise to questions regarding the process of writing. In Hölderlin and Novalis, composition becomes interminable. The evasion of endings has much to do with their need to continue writing after having put the last word to the page. The open-ended text thereby bespeaks a hesitancy and self-interrogation on the part of the writer in his quest for a proper voice. Here Hölderlin serves as the prime example. He subjected the so-called authoritative versions of his poems to sustained emendation. The impression of continuity, coherence, and closure that the finished version gives is disrupted by its later marred, palimpsest-like variations. The added inscriptions and deletions indeed unsettle the reader's perception of the earlier poem as a total entity. The later work of Hölderlin thereby stages displacement and decentering of authorial intention and identity. Hölderlin's poetic voice is found in the interstices of his fragmented, ever-reformulated texts, paradoxically in his desire for the dissolution of voice.

For Novalis too—as for the author of *Le livre à venir* and *L'entretien infini,* Maurice Blanchot—the ideal form of writing is prefatory, provisional, and anonymous.[3] Writing does not relate or allude to a goal. Instead it holds its object in reserve; it submerges authorial presence, is dissociated from the identity of any particular author. Novalis's most famous embodiment of such generic fictionalizing is the female figure Fabel in *Heinrich von Ofterdingen.* She spins an unbreakable thread beyond the confines of the inset tale in which she acts as a character. Indeed, Novalis, like Mallarmé and Blanchot after him, envisaged an absolute and, thus by necessity, always incomplete book.

This nonprogressive, unending, and fragmented writing of the Romantics is premised on a particular theory of signification—of how language does or does not produce meaning. Nonclosure can refer not only to narrative but also to issues of semantics. It addresses the question of referentiality. We come here to the second rubric under which to consider nonclosure. It can be understood to mean the refusal to decide whether a word can be appointed a specific meaning; it does not let utterance be reduced to a content. Nonclosure hence takes into account the residual factor left after the noncoalescence of signified and signifier. It pertains to what Derrida coins the activity of *differance*—a term that shares distinct affinities with the theory and practice of writing in Hölderlin and Novalis.

The identity, unity, or even overlapping of signifier and signified presumably would call forth presence; it would be possible to conjure up totality and luminous meaning. The repetition and reproduction of the signified in the signifier would entail sameness. Re-presentation would thereby be accomplished. However, the line separating signifier from signified marks an unbridgeable scission. The former, barred from the latter, obliquely relays instead to other signifiers in a chain. Signification thus arises through contextual, differential positioning. Derrida calls *differance* the systematic, prolonged play and production of differences: "Differance is what makes the movement of signification possible only if each element that is said to be "present," appearing on the stage of presence, is related to something other than itself but retains the mark of a past element and already lets itself be hollowed out by the mark of its relation to a future element."[4] Here any repetition involves, rather than sameness, eccentricity and deviance. Differance thus inscribes the movement of continuous differing and deferral.

It is this element of temporality and laterality that relates to the theme of postponement in nonclosure. Differance indexes unending lateral modification, displacement, or supplementing of one signifier by the next in time. In doing so it creates spacings, intervals, distances from an unspecifiable origin.[5] A desire to compensate for the initial lack, to attempt recuperation or to anticipate it, is what drives narrative forward. Differance, however, suspends accomplishment, prolongs desire, and thus generates nonclosure. Derrida, along with Hölderlin and Novalis, focuses upon this production of intervals and interims, not upon what is absent or remains hidden. None of the three articulates a negative theology or a belief in pure absence.

At this point a few further distinctions must be made. What is not to be equated with nonclosure? Nonclosure does not imply simply unresolvability, ambiguity, or equivocality of meaning. This would involve a choice between simultaneous possibilities of meaning. Nor does nonclosure suggest polysemy—a wealth of possibilities. Nonclosure for our purposes means a deferral of decision. Yet by the same token, although language is an arbitrary, relative system, it is not absolutely nonreferential. To advocate the categorical nonreferentiality of language would be an act of closure, albeit a negative one. By contrast, nonclosure suggests ever-unresolved hesitation and indeterminacy. For Hölderlin and Novalis this does not exclude the expectation of semantic shiftings and reaffiliations. Novalis, for instance, sees signification as an ongoing, ateleological process in which the reader is very much involved. He leaves the fragment not to be completed but to be extended and extrapolated upon by the reader. For Novalis, there lives the thrill of heterogeneity, proliferation, and unchecked referral in language. Hölderlin, on the other hand, fears that the sign too restrictively and hence erroneously signifies: how can an author ever speak, for instance, about the sacred, about the coming Deity? His words threaten to be incompatible with what they attempt both to describe and descry. For Hölderlin the future is radically unpredictable: it always resists being signified and pushes its being so onto a constantly receding temporal horizon.

Narrative and semantic nonclosure thus involves a third use of the term. Nonclosure is thematically illustrated in Novalis's and Hölderlin's deferral of parousia (absolute, divine presence, or the apocalypse). The implications of this third category are metaphysical and theological. Here the pursuit of an ultimate ending to the human story is questioned.

In German Pietist circles of the eighteenth century, millenarianism came once again to the fore. In particular, the closing decades of this century witnessed numerous shifts and variations in the chiliastic belief in the coming reign of Christ on earth. Indeed, the phrase "Kingdom of God" was a catchword in the correspondence of the young Hegel and Hölderlin. The expectation of an ultimate end to secular time and entry of divine rule makes systemization, periodization, and temporal continuity possible. It authorizes present existence and endows it with a narrative purpose—whether this be at the phylogenic level of the human race or at the ontogenic level (*Bildung*) of the individual. This purposeful goal to human existence and beatific termination of temporality I shall interchangeably call *telos* or *eschaton*. The former term shares with the latter a sense of futurity. Whatever is teleological moves along a trajectory towards this absolute end.[6] As shall be seen, Hölderlin and Novalis criticized the closed narrative that structures the belief in progress towards resolution. Indeed, Hölderlin and Novalis were sceptical of anyone's attempting to write the ultimate narrative—a philosophy of history. For them, as for Adorno and Benjamin, history is composed of shards and remnants; it records the fragmentariness of existence.

Hölderlin, in particular, vigilantly resisted closure by sustaining millennial anticipation. Cognizant of the alterity of divinity and the violence of predicating it, Hölderlin deferred the parousia. He privileges infinite expectancy rather than summational totalities, to speak with the recent French philosopher, Émmanuel Lévinas.[7] Hölderlin foresees not an encounter with God but its possibility, however distant in time.

Of course, any dismantling of the notion of the telos will have repercussions for the archē. It too, Novalis says, is a willful fabrication of the imagination. By no means, then, can we draw a straight arrow from one to the other—or the Romantic author extend a narrative between the two. Instead writing becomes what Friedrich Schlegel called characteristically modern, that is to say, fragmentary. The question thus arises: what sets the Jena Romantics, Hölderlin, and their twentieth-century successors apart from "nonmodern" authors? Or has the mistrust of closure been equally strong throughout Western history? Why or why not?

To answer, one must return to a key word that has surfaced repeatedly in this discussion: *temporality*. Prolonged nonclosure engenders a sense of lived tension. Such sustained uncertainty can be attributed to the way that an author and his generation experience time transpiring. If time is no longer advancing towards a culminating point or if anticipations are continuously thwarted and expectations belied, then we are dealing with the problem of radical temporality. The process of growth and unfolding over time can be called *temporalization*—a concept antithetical to temporality, which dispenses with purposefulness. The former is a unitary concept, the latter a multiple one. Once caught in temporality, man is given over to the meaningless passage of time wherein nothing is sustained except the flow of time itself. Neither memory nor hope is redemptive. Duration marks intermittence rather than prolongation. Such is the dominant concept of time as it is registered from the 1790s on. One purpose of the present study is to see how, in the aftermath of the French Revolution, authors shift away from a rectilinear notion of time to one of discontinuous seriality.

The abruptness of this breach with former models of time sug-
gests that the vague concept of secularization can mislead. *Secu-
larization* can be defined as the assimilation, reformulation, and
reinterpretation of theological ideas in a nonreligious framework.
In particular, it has frequently been invoked to explain the reten-
tion and revision in secular literature of Christian eschatology or
salvation history (*Heilsgeschichte*), claimed above all for philosophies
of history in the late eighteenth and nineteenth centuries. Such
works underwrite the directedness of human development. They
borrow from the Christian scheme of time. Secularization, an act of
carrying-over, serves to preserve meaning and guarantee con-
tinuity. It permits its scholar to regulate diachronic shiftings, even
revolutions in Western thought, in much the same way that, on a
microcosmic scale, it lets the scholar uncover a teleological emplot-
ment in each text analyzed. In both senses of the word, the advo-
cate of secularization observes systemization. Secularization thus
represents a conservative, conserving ideology. Perhaps for this rea-
son, it has directed, almost unchallenged, the course of both
American and German studies in Romanticism and the Age of
Idealism. The present contribution wants to read against the grain
of such scholarship which claims to rediscover teleologies in works
written around 1800. It purports to trace the effects of temporality,
the relation of its writers to delayed presence, as well as the limits
to this knowledge of incalculable distance. I would like in the
pages that follow to offer to specialist and nonspecialist alike this
alternative perspective on European intellectual history.

Chapter one deals with what I have just outlined—the break
around 1800 with past temporal paradigms. Chapters two and
three then explain the ways in which Novalis and Hölderlin oper-
ate with the interlocking categories of nonclosure: the narrative,
semantic, and thematic. However, contrary to what this introduc-
tion might suggest, references to Poststructuralist terminology,
even to the global word *nonclosure,* are kept to a minimum. I would
not want to hide the eloquence of Hölderlin and Novalis by famil-
iar current critical vocabulary but instead would prefer to let the
authors themselves provide access to the new thought. In order to

let late eighteenth-century writers state their own case without encoding their turns of phrase in foreign ones, I have chosen to quote extensively.[8] I follow here the wont of German, rather than English, scholarship. Quoting is also, in part, to give the reader a more immediate familiarity with these authors. But there is another reason for not applying current terminology after having initially reviewed it. I cannot do enough in this introduction to acquaint my reader with various contexts in which terms such as *spacing, differance,* and *supplementarity* have been used. Critics such as Derrida enact the temporal, contextual sliding they describe in language. Inasmuch as their phrasings are themselves subtle displacements of one another, they are means of avoiding conceptual closure. Such shifting discourages direct appropriation. Transferral of terminology to the works of Hölderlin and Novalis would be an act of framing, of semantic reduction, of closure itself.

Notwithstanding, the motivation for writing this book is clearly to examine how Novalis and Hölderlin reproduce, indeed anticipate, modern critical thought. To be sure, the masters of enclosed systems, Kant and Hegel, have repeatedly attracted deconstructive readings by scholars such as Deleuze, Derrida, De Man, and Hamacher. However, other European critics, most notably Philippe Lacoue-Labarthe, Jean-Luc Nancy, and Manfred Frank, have documented in numerous ways that the affiliation between the two groups need not be antagonistic. These other critics perceive how Idealism can excitingly illustrate contemporary views. Indeed Lacoue-Labarthe and Nancy solved the dilemma of presenting Jena Romanticism without direct recourse to Poststructuralist vocabulary; they divided their chapters in *L'absolu littéraire* between their own commentary and translations into French from the *Athenäum.* The one intertext contributes to the other but in no way substitutes for it. The same pertains to the ties suggested in this introduction. To explain why Hölderlin and Novalis, along with other writers of their day, were preoccupied with the delay of an ending will help profile modern critical theory. Reciprocally, German writers at the turn of the nineteenth century can be approached with a heightened awareness of the theoretical repercussions of their thought.[9]

It must not be forgotten, however, that this reciprocity and enfolding are double edged throughout. If deconstruction purports to rupture acts of closure, in doing so it retraces the efforts of certain Idealists themselves: it reinscribes aspects in Hölderlin and Novalis that this book tries to illuminate. Inversely, Hölderlin and Novalis work within closure. Just as for them the unfulfillable nature of the desire for an ending necessitates nonclosure, so does the avoidance of closure arouse their desire and hope for an ending. Hölderlin and Novalis speak of the postponement of that which is constituted only through postponement. Likewise, Gayatri Spivak parenthetically remarks on the Derridean enterprise: "We must know that we are within the 'clôture' of metaphysics, even as we attempt to undo it."[10]

The procedure taken in this investigation is thus receptively hermeneutic rather than "deconstructive" of Hölderlin, Novalis, or Poststructuralism. After consideration of certain concepts in literary theory today, the framework is set in which to view nonclosure around 1800. The exemplary grappling of Hölderlin and Novalis with this problem in turn informs and inspires our own critical consciousness. My point is not that Poststructuralism is evidence of the recrudescence of Jena Romanticism but rather that all of us have inescapably inherited Kantian divisions: all are barred from transcendent certitudes and, with them, from the reassurance of any resounding closure. We can articulate our situation better by detouring back to Hölderlin and Novalis. They speak with the urgency that comes from being direct successors not only to Kant but also to the French Revolution and its destabilizing effects.

1 Scenes of Transition

The French Revolution as Preface

> Das goldne Zeitalter der Literatur würde dann sein, wenn
> keine Vorreden mehr nötig wären.
>
> —Friedrich Schlegel

In an early essay sceptically entitled "Über die Frage, ob eine Philosophie der Erfahrung, insbesondere ob eine Philosophie der Geschichte möglich sei" [On the possibility of a philosophy of experience, in particular, a philosophy of history], Schelling writes that history is composed of unendingly diverse digressions from the ideal. To the extent that we broaden the horizons of our knowledge, we foreshorten our distance from the ideal. By negative implication, however, history measures our limitations and imperfections. In other words, as we expand our knowledge, we see more clearly how limited our historical perspective is. Schelling thereby concludes that history is a product of our narrow-mindedness (*Beschränktheit*) (Schröter 1:393 and 396). It records only what is deficient, deviant, and in progress. Novalis likewise writes that the novel arose out of the shortcomings of history; the latter always must remain incomplete (N 2:829). And Friedrich Schlegel maintains that our receptivity to what is fragmentary, impulsive, and enterprising forms the transcendental part of the historical spirit (KA 2:169, no. 22). In these passages Schelling, Novalis, and Schlegel suggest that historical consciousness awakens with an awareness of imperfection and absence. The necessity to write a history or, in other words, a continuous narrative (including, according to Schelling, a philosophy of history) stems from the desire to stop the gaps and lend closure to the fragmentary. The longing for perfection propels both history and its telling.

But at the same time that Schelling, Novalis, and Schlegel recognize that disparity generates the writing of history, they also see that this is a lasting state of affairs not to be alleviated by any narrative purporting to establish continuity. Neither the empirical stuff of history nor its chronicling can respectively attain or effect closure—to which Schleiermacher would have retorted: "Die Aufgabe ist, so gestellt, eine unendliche" [So put, the task is unending].[1] Schiller, after recalling how much data either remain hidden from the historian or refute his conclusions, projects the true writing of universal history onto the most distant future (NA 17:374). In addition to the impossibility of ever gathering all the facts to begin to write a history, a temporal gap will always stretch between the disarray of human events and the efforts to order them sequentially or causally. Indeed, Schleiermacher calls the play between the historian and his object of study an only apparent (*scheinbarer*), pried-open circle.[2] The historian/writer is never present to his material—nor, as Novalis claimed, would he ever wish to be. Perhaps in order to continue writing his novel, Novalis keeps history incomplete: "Die Geschichte muß immer unvollständig bleiben."

Such references to the noncontinuous, ateleological nature of temporal progression abound in turn-of-the-nineteenth-century writings and are reflected in their narrative structures. Hölderlin, for instance, in his hymn "Patmos" calls the disparate spots of time "pinnacles." The persona longs for wings that would transport him back and forth between them (StA 2:165, ll. 14–15). Friedrich Schlegel criticizes the Enlightenment historian, Condorcet, who in his *Esquisse d'un tableau historique* claimed to discern a direct line of development from the past to the future. Schlegel refutes Condorcet by saying that historical proof of continuous progress in the past can only be partially rendered (KA 7:7). Not only is an exhaustive history impossible but the necessary laws of human progress also cannot be discerned. Similarly, in the sixth Schalttag of *Hesperus,* Jean Paul says that, with reference to historical necessity, we can speak only of the "Nothwendigkeit einer ewigen Veränderung; jedoch hier gibts nur *auf*- und *niedersteigende* Zeichen, keine Kulminazion" [necessity of eternal change; the signs, however, are only ascending and descending, without culmination] (SW 3:384). The historical evidence of relapses, divergent courses, and even out-and-out regression discredits the Kantian or prevalent Enlightenment belief in the progressive development of the species. Schlegel therefore writes:

> Das eigentliche *Problem* der Geschichte ist die Ungleichheit der Fortschritte in den verschiedenen Bestandteilen der gesamten menschlichen Bildung, besonders die große Divergenz in dem Grade der intellektuellen und der moralischen Bildung; die Rückfälle und Stillstände der Bildung. (KA 7:7)

> [The true problem of history is the disparity between advancements in the various parts of mankind's development, especially the divergency in the degree of intellectual and moral education; the setbacks and cessations of development.]

As Schelling suggests, the task of the historian would be to trace deviancies—to write only sketches and to mark, in Schlegel's words, relapses and standstills. Indeed Schlegel calls for a new and different type of historiography, one that is more precise and attends to "das vollständigste und sorgfältigste Detail" [the most complete and most careful detail] (KA 7:9).

Underlying both this notion of the deviancy of past occurrences and its rehearsal in any narrative that tries to come to grips with the past is, of course, the question of how time—Kant's subjective, pure form of the sensibility—progresses. How can continuity be assured? Can we speak of time as a linear vector? Is it composed, as Locke, Condillac, or Diderot would suggest, of isolated durations? And how would these be linked to extend into the future?

Schlegel, as we have seen, radically calls into question the efficacy of rational prognosis, which is, of course, grounded in this notion of temporal linearity. He consequently repudiates Condorcet's belief in infinite amelioration.[3] For Condorcet, the future poses no mystery:

La philosophie n'a plus rien à deviner, n'a plus de com-
binaisons hypothétiques à former; il ne lui reste qu'à
rassembler, à ordonner les faits, et à montrer les vérités utiles
qui naissent de leur enchaînement et de leur ensemble.[4]

[Philosophy no longer has anything to guess at, has no more
hypothetical combinations to formulate; it only needs to re-
order and reassemble the facts, to demonstrate the useful
truths that arise from their linkage and unity.]

But Schlegel rejects Condorcet's claim that "facts" culled from past
experience help us predict the future. Once the historian, accord-
ing to Schlegel, discerns the rupturing of temporal continuity and
causality, the future becomes radically enigmatic. Jean Paul like-
wise observes that experience teaches us that we cannot know what
is to come (SW 14:51). Coherence cannot be read where there is
none. Nor, by extrapolation, can we imagine a future point in time
when the pieces of the puzzle will fall into place. How we write
about the past implies something about how the future will come
to be. And if the past is marred by breaks and mirrored in the
discontinuous writing of the present, how can Condorcet's or any
perfect future state ever be attained? Jean Paul, for instance, can
only speak of "Klüfte der Zukunft" [chasms of the future] (SW
3:387). Nothing verifies our hopes and aspirations for the future.
Kleist therefore mistrusts speculation about the future: "[G]esetzt
ich verträumte diesen und forschte dem *zukünftigen* [Wirkung-
skreis] nach – ist denn nicht die *Zukunft* eine *kommende Gegenwart,*
und soll ich denn auch *diese* Gegenwart wieder verträumen?" [If I
were to dream away this present circle of influence and search after
a *future* one—is not the *future* a *coming present,* and would I then
dream away *this* present in addition?] (Kleist 2:318). Instead of
bringing apocatastasis, the recovery of all things, or the fruition of
the Enlightenment ideal, the future becomes nothing more than
a projection of present and past gaps. A philosophy of history—
this Janus-faced science that complements and completes his-
tory's backward-gazing glance—will thus always be a patchwork

effort. In Schelling's words of 1798, philosophy of history is an impossibility.

But if we, unlike the Romantics, may speak of effective motivation, what causes this shift between Schlegel and Condorcet? And from what, can we speculate, was Hegel far enough removed in 1807 to write the resurrection of the philosophy of history in the guise of his *Phenomenology?* Condorcet's essay was written in the midst of the Reign of Terror but looks back to and, in its systemization, culminates the Enlightenment historiographical interests of Turgot, Helvétius, Holbach, D'Alembert, and Raynal. It is ironic indeed that the author of this testament to Enlightenment optimism found himself in prison at the time of its publication. In the *Athenäum* August Wilhelm Schlegel acknowledged Condorcet's valor in the face of adversity: surrounded by mortal dangers, Condorcet envisioned man's eternal prospects, instead of depicting his finite individuality (KA 2:196). But his valor was equally a repression. Writing with the hindsight of two more years in 1795, Friedrich Schlegel, unlike Condorcet, had the direct aftermath of the French Revolution in mind when he spoke of disproportionate developments.

Schlegel sums up the force of the Revolution's effect on its generation in the *Athenäum*'s fragment number 424:

> Man kann die Französische Revolution als das größte und merkwürdigste Phänomen der Staatengeschichte betrachten, als ein fast universelles Erdbeben, eine unermeßliche Überschwemmung in der politischen Welt; oder als ein Urbild der Revolutionen, als die Revolution schlechthin. (KA 2:247–48, no. 424)

> [One can regard the French Revolution as the greatest and strangest phenomenon in state history, as an almost universal earthquake, an immeasurable inundation in the political world; or as the model for revolutions, as the Revolution itself.]

In retrospect, the year 1789 marked the ultimate, unprecedented event defying interpretation. But its advent was greeted as the resolution of historical strife. What Schlegel described in the apocalyptic image of the universal earthquake, Klopstock, for instance, earlier depicted with images of chiliastic expectancy. In his ode, "Die états généraux" (1788), Klopstock heralded the coming of the Revolution as the apocalyptic culmination of time, as the dawn of a new era. Yet as Klopstock's expectations were great, so was his disillusionment profound. In 1793 he wrote: "Ach des goldenen Traums Wonn' ist dahin, / Mich umschwebet nicht mehr sein Morgenglanz" [the glory of the golden dream has disappeared; its matinal glow no longer embraces me] ("Mein Irrtum," AW 149). For Klopstock, the years 1792 to 1794 saw the expression of disappointment in the odes entitled "Freiheitskrieg," "Die Jakobiner," "Der Eroberungskrieg," and "Die Trümmern." Klopstock's reaction was paradigmatic. Heine was later to write of the dream of the French Revolution (SS 2:655)—the dream that went unfulfilled.

According to the registerings of the German Idealists, the Revolution and the following Reign of Terror had profound effects on European man's concept of time. Fichte called the Revolution important for the entire human race (Fichte 1. Abt., 1:203), and Novalis spoke of the new times when states were being overthrown (N 2:743). Suddenly man was faced with an event that jarred with the main tenet of *Vernunftreligion*—the steadily progressive development of mankind. He was confronted with unaccountable violence, or "revolution" in its modern sense—meaning sudden overthrow, rather than return or recurrence. Furthermore, this took place within the entire European social and political structure.[5] Herder wrote in 1792 that nothing had ever occurred that was comparable to the Revolution in its strangeness and consequences (Suphan 18:314). The Revolution betokened a global watershed but did not bring the redemptive reversal expected. Radical change did not cause release from oppression or usher in the golden age. On the contrary, it proved previously cherished aspirations and the rhetoric in which they were couched to be profoundly misguided, blind, and deceptive. The language of both Enlightenment rationality and millennial rebirth had become bastardized, for example, on Robespierre's tongue, which proclaimed: "Le temps est arrivé. . . . [L]es progrès de la raison humaine ont préparé cette grande révolution" [The day has arrived. The advancements in human reason have prepared this great revolution].[6] How in the aftermath was the failure of this singular event, and with it the Enlightenment, to be accounted for? Because the past proved to be a blind alley, what could the future possibly hold? Furthermore, what language could one use to describe it?

To begin with, the Revolution did not eradicate faith in change by other, often nonviolent means. The parousia had only been deferred. Hölderlin, for instance, wrote to Ebel that he believed in a future revolution of ideas surpassing anything that had previously occurred (StA 6:229). The Revolution had to be prolonged by being imported to German soil. It did not, however, have to be political: it could occur in the realm of the imagination—as Schlegel suggested with his "aesthetic Revolution" (KA 1:269) and Schiller with his "aesthetic State" (NA 20:410).[7] The Revolution was thus incorporated into *another* teleological philosophy of history. As the French Revolution did not bring about the end of the world but in the minds of its survivors probably resembled it, apocalyptic expectations—be they cheerful or dismal—were renewed. In speaking of the contemporary scene, Novalis indeed referred to the myth of Sisyphus (N 2:743). The eschaton was projected farther into the future. Novalis spoke of the teleology of the Revolution (N 2:772, no. 153), and Friedrich Schlegel referred to an unending chain of inner revolutions (KA 2:255, no. 451). Indeed, Schlegel saw Napoleon not only as an executor of the Revolution but as the originator of *multiple* revolutions: "Buonaparte [spielt eine große Rolle in der Revolution], weil er Revolutionen schaffen und bilden, und sich selbst annihilieren kann" [Buonaparte plays a major role in the Revolution, because he can create and mould revolutions; he can annihilate himself] (KA 2:247, no. 422).

For the German Idealists then, the French Revolution began to acquire symbolic and proleptic significance. Novalis rechristened it "secular Protestantism" and on one occasion, using Lessing's image of the education of the human race, even denigrated the Revolution to the level of a puberty crisis (N 2:743; 2:279). Schlegel called it an excellent allegory (KA 2:366). In a 1793 essay entitled "Beitrag zur Berichtigung der Urtheile des Publikums über die französische Revolution" [A Contribution to a Correction of the Public Opinion on the French Revolution], Fichte alluded to another, incomparably more important revolution (Fichte Abt. 1, 1:204). Schlegel likewise referred to this "other" revolution—the discovery of Idealism—as a greater and more comprehensive revolution (KA 3:96; cf. 2:314), which, however, was still in the process of becoming (*im Werden*). Indeed one could hardly boast of its existence (KA 18:131, no. 117). Schlegel's afterthought suggests that this revolution might not prove to be different from the former. Kleist and Heine shared the same scepticism. Could the goals of 1789 ever be realized?

The insistence with which German writers of the time referred to this coming revolution or, even more so, to a series of revolutions testified to their need to erase the failure of the former one and what seemed to be the misguided longings that prompted it. They needed to break with a past that could not be fulfilled. The desire to radicalize discontinuity, though, was more a symptom of their malaise than a solution to it. According to the post-Enlightenment generation, the present no longer served as a happy model for the future, as it did for Condorcet. Instead it symbolized sheer difference. The signs of the times were disheartening, confusing, and radically unprecedented. Hölderlin wrote: "Ein Zeichen sind wir, deutungslos" [A sign are we, meaningless] (StA 2:195). Faced with a new, unpredictable future, the present appeared incomplete and lacking in interpretation. Hölderlin referred to the time in which man lives as "reißend," flüchtig," and "wandelnd" [rending, fleeting, changing] (StA 2:112; 64; 5:268). The notion of discontinuity disrupted the once-cherished belief in the teleological progress of human time.

The generation entering the nineteenth century thus felt itself cut off from its past and belonging to a new age. In the essay *Christenheit oder Europa,* Novalis diagnosed the birth pangs of a coming era (N 2:747). And in "Germanien" Hölderlin similarly heralded this imminent break in time: "Wie anders ists! und rechthin glänzt und spricht / Zukünftiges auch erfreulich aus den Fernen" [How different it is! Distances away there gladdeningly

gleams and speaks what is yet to come] (StA 2:152). Concerning
the effect of the Revolution, the German historian Reinhart
Koselleck has cogently remarked that those living in the decade
following 1789 felt they were entering a never-before-experienced
future.[8] Although this generation did not cease to make provisions
for its future, it realized that the results of prognosis could not be
guaranteed.[9] Hence the necessity arose to posit a multiplicity of
revolutions. In 1793, for example, the translator of Edmund Burke's
Reflections on the Revolution in France, Friedrich Gentz, expressed his
fear that the Revolution would promote other revolutions without
end (*ins Unendliche*); it would introduce an alternation of revolu-
tions.[10] Repeated crises and reversals were expected and indeed
experienced as French revolutionary troops moved across the
Rhine. These crises did not, however, bring freedom from political
oppression, let alone usher in the golden age.

The manner in which the post-1789 generation anticipated
change was not the same as before. With doubt about rational
forecasting, a new and pessimistic way of structuring the future
prevailed. Expectation of radical change became combined with
the expectation of permanent and repeated crises which would not
necessarily bring about desired reform. The cataclysmic experience
of the Revolution disrupted the traditional, calming belief, shared
by Pietists and Enlightenment thinkers alike, that some divine
force was benevolently directing the course of human history. One
need only compare Kant's faith in the "regelmäßigen Gang der
Verbesserung der Staatsverfassung" [regular course in the improve-
ment of state constitution] (GS 8:29) and in the "anhaltende Ent-
wickelung der reinen Vernunftreligion" [continuous development
in the pure religion of reason] (GS 6:135) with Fichte's will to-
wards unrelenting, ever-renewed striving. One then appreciates
the difference between the ways in which each writer saw history
unfolding. Hölderlin, like Fichte, writes of "dieses Weiterstreben,
dieses Aufopfern einer gewissen Gegenwart für ein Ungewisses ein
Anderes, ein Besseres und immer Besseres" [this ongoing striving,
this sacrifice of a given present for something uncertain, different,
better, and ever better] (StA 6:327). When questioning doubt

constantly undermines chiliastic expectations, the parousia is repeatedly deferred. The striving becomes an unending, sacrificing struggle (ein eifriger Wettstreit [Fichte 1. Abt., 3:41]).

Recurring mistrust of the future then forces the writer to follow a detour or, in Hölderlin's words, an eccentric course (StA 3:163). The writer's narrative will chart out the points at which it must swerve aside and resume its course. It will map a series of ateleological crises. As Friedrich Schlegel remarks, the post-revolutionary writer describes his present state as somehow significant, yet in midstream, as a "Tendenz, ohne gründliche Ausführung" [a tendency wanting thorough execution] (KA 2:198). Indeed, for Schlegel the epoch represents "das Zeitalter der Tendenzen" [the age of trends] (KA 2:367). The Revolution thus becomes a preface, but one that never comes to an end.

The question therefore arises, the question this work wants to address: how can the author at the turn of the nineteenth century write endings or write about them? It is a problem that concerned Hölderlin and Novalis—of all their contemporaries—most vigilantly, especially in reference to the possibility of one continuous world history or to what Lessing called "the education of mankind" and Kant "philosophic millenarianism." For Hölderlin and Novalis, problems of temporality, narrative form, and the philosophy of history become inextricably meshed. As they in particular discovered, if history is no longer viewed as either teleological or progressive but as discontinuous, marked by repeated crises and inexplicable interruptions, then the writer cannot conscientiously depict the future. Once the parousia is perennially postponed, a writer can no longer ask what the best utopia would be or even how he could best formulate his utopic aspirations. As we shall see, that step of projecting oneself into a future society—whether it be cast as a present utopia or as the telos of human history—categorically does not occur in Hölderlin or Novalis without immediate recantation. Given the sole certainty of radical temporality, such a projection risks error.

The question they pose is rather how to find a discourse about future possibilities that will be correct and "kundig des Wandels" [versed in change] (StA 2:64)—in other words, that will have error somehow built into its system. Hölderlin therefore draws a bar separating present and future:

> Viel hat von Morgen an,
> Seit ein Gespräch wir sind und hören voneinander,
> Erfahren der Mensch; bald sind wir aber Gesang.
>
> (StA 3:536, ll. 91–93)

[Man has experienced much, from morning onwards, since we have been a discourse and have heard from one another; soon, however, we shall be song.]

How song is to be characterized remains for Hölderlin an enigma. He can only presuppose that it will be different:

> wo aber
> Ein Gott noch auch erscheint
> Da ist doch andere Klarheit.
>
> (StA 3:533, ll. 23–24)

[Yet where a god still also appears, there shines a different clarity.]

And as Hölderlin's desperate query about the role of the poet in an age of dearth (StA 2:94, l. 122) suggests, it was difficult enough to reflect upon the present, ever-elusive use of language, let alone speculate about the future. Jean Paul speaks in this respect of prophetic modesty (SW 3:383). For what would guarantee that the future would be different? As we saw in Kleist's sobering remark, it could prove to be identical to the past.

Only the indefinable temporal space of Hölderlin's "soon" rescues him from the verdict of false prophecy. Hölderlin insures that the interim will always stretch between present discourse and future song. In other words, Hölderlin and also Novalis consistently insert the wedge "soon" or "later" to maintain that distance from a future which could prove them wrong. Their problem is how to stay within the bounds of correctness—how to keep writing a preface. They thereby render the prelude that the Revolution was for them and their generation a permanent state of affairs.

The problem of a correct, stabilized pose was one Hölderlin, it seems, had difficulty resolving precisely with regard to the French Revolution. In the years since Pierre Bertaux's studies, Hölderlin's attitude towards events in France has witnessed much critical attention. And it is conceivably Hölderlin's own ambivalent, veiled stance which has caused the debate on his Jacobinic sympathies to wax to such a pitch—more so among Germany's politicized readership than in America. Hölderlin undoubtedly cherished revolutionary expectations which he then voiced in chiliastic terminology, as, for instance, in the "Friedensfeier," written after the peace of Lunéville in 1801. On the other hand, we are confronted in the Sinclair affair with Hölderlin's alleged denial of treason. To what extent can we discuss his political leanings on the basis of his poetry? We can later take up the reasons supporting both the political and text-immanent readings of Hölderlin. But we need not take a stand on either side and thereby risk being untrue to his other voice. The point is to see what such opposition suggests. The result of this latent schism in Hölderlin, mirrored in the camps of Hölderlin criticism, is that a pattern emerges of preoccupation with and then self-distancing from what could generally be termed the phenomenon of the Revolution. For the French Revolution, as we have seen at least with Klopstock, acted as a vehicle on which to project both millennial hopes and disillusionment. Whether at this early stage in our investigation we want to trace a direct line of inheritance from Klopstock to Hölderlin, we must recall that Hölderlin did model himself on Klopstock, at least in undertaking to write his main work on the delayed Second Coming, namely, the hymn "Patmos." With the imputed protraction of the Revolution, then, the scene of oscillation promised to reenact itself repeatedly. Since the Revolution was not over, it could not be interpreted. Indeed Schleiermacher termed this exegetic gesture of unresolvable, protracted hesitancy, which was so characteristic of its age, "approximierende Oszillation" [oscillation which approximates].[11]

And Novalis defined historical progression itself as "eine Oszillation, ein Wechsel entgegengesetzter Bewegungen" [an oscillation, an alternation of juxtaposed movements] (N 2:735).[12]

What we could construe to be Hölderlin's ambivalence towards the Revolution can be translated then as his awe before the parousia, coupled with the realization that it must be postponed: "Nah ist / Und schwer zu fassen der Gott" [Near and difficult to grasp is the God] (StA 2:165). Millennial delay does not mean that millennial speculations suddenly disappear. On the contrary, the young post-1789 generation sustains a fascination with the idea of imminent change and therefore also with the possibility of a beatific future. Schlegel writes that modern history begins with the revolutionary desire to realize the Kingdom of God. This desire is the elastic axis which pulls development onward (KA 2:201, no. 222). Novalis similarly states that the notion of the future drives us to action (*zur assimilirenden Wircksamkeit* [N 2:282, no. 124]). The fact that Schlegel, Hölderlin, and Novalis constantly write about prolonged expectancy, not the future per se, proves that they are nonetheless deeply preoccupied by what is to follow. Novalis describes this play of anticipation and deception: "(Jede immer getäuschte und immer erneuerte Erwartung deutet auf ein Capitel in der Zukunftslehre hin)" [Every always-deceived and yet ever-renewed expectation points to a chapter in futurology] (N 2:530, no. 314). An extended prolegomenon never permits Hölderlin and Novalis to write the narrative that is to follow, but the future text is still the unuttered topic of their preliminary discourse—a discourse destined constantly to displace what it writes about. Their writing risks erring. But as Novalis says, even misguided expectation paradoxically *deutet hin*. Intimations tell us that our discourse will have been anticipatory—that it is part of a *Zukunftslehre* yet to be unfolded.

But why focus on Hölderlin? Why single out Novalis from the other Jena Romantics? From the above introductory remarks, one can surmise that Hölderlin and Novalis are representative of a larger shift in an episteme of time—to vary the use of Foucault's term. In the discussion that follows, I want to suggest that this surmise is true. On the other hand, Hölderlin and Novalis are not only representative but also exemplary of a new way of narrating future time. They systematically keep ends and endings in abeyance. This fantasy of the end seemed to exercise a lure upon the most critical philosophic and literary minds of the epoch. It attracted without yielding. But the very same lure, which Hölderlin and Novalis documented while escaping, has entrapped many literary critics in their stead. Hence the second main reason for investigating the work of Hölderlin and Novalis in particular: widespread views by the most renowned critics on the secularized triadic structure of Novalis's and Hölderlin's works border on serious misreading. Until very recently such critics have determined both the American and the German reception of these two major authors.

The Secularization Debate

> Wehe, wenn das Land-Heimweh dich befällt, als ob dort mehr
> *Freiheit* gewesen wäre – und es gibt kein Land mehr.
>
> —Nietzsche, *Die fröhliche Wissenschaft*

Although many scholars have noted that chiliastic imagery pervades works written at the close of the eighteenth century, few have described the markedly different treatment of this imagery in comparison with previous periods (e.g., the preceding generation that witnessed the rise of what Kant called "philosophic chiliasm" [GS 6:34; 8:27]). As we are beginning to glean, whenever the post-Enlightenment poet heralds the golden age, millennium, or ultimate, concluding revolution as imminent, he recognizes at the same time that this hope is only the fabrication of his imagination and thus risks serious betrayal. Remembering recent cataclysmic events (Schlegel's universal earthquake), writers constantly expect, yet delay, the apocalypse. Endings and teleological motivation accordingly become problematic. A number of critics would disagree: from Walter Benjamin on the Romantics' messianism to Hans-Joachim Mähl on Novalis, Wolfgang Binder on Hölderlin, or Meyer Abrams on the entire European generation.[13]

Let us first turn to this last author, the one most known in America. In a *Diacritics* article, J. Hillis Miller disputes Abrams's claims on secularization in the latter's 1971 book entitled *Natural Supernaturalism*. Miller does so largely by looking to Nietzsche as his spokesman on the duplicity inherent in metaphor. He quotes Nietzsche: "The same text authorizes innumerable interpretations (*Auslegungen*), there is no 'correct' interpretation."[14] Miller could, however, have cited Novalis: "Es giebt kein *allgemeingeltendes Lesen*. . . . Lesen ist eine freye Operation" [There is no such thing as a generally valid reading; reading is a free operation] (N 2:399, no. 398). In other words, according to Novalis, Nietzsche, J. Hillis Miller, or to the latter's heroes, Derrida, Deleuze, and De Man, secularization threatens to overlook alternative readings. It is precisely this different, even distorting reading that a writer like Novalis wishes to give Christianity. He and Schlegel agreed it was the negativity in the Christian religion that informed their undertaking (N 2:711, no. 1095). Compare this recognition of antithetical influence then with one passage from Abrams that Miller cites: "Despite their displacement from a supernatural to a natural frame of reference, . . . the ancient problems, terminology, and ways of thinking about human nature and history survived."[15] In what could also have been a warning to Mähl, who has written an influential tome on the golden age in Novalis, Friedrich Schlegel observes that this term has been sorely misappropriated (KA 1:268). His brother, August Wilhelm, polemicizes against the phantom of a past golden age which can never be past or coming but is instead processual (*ewig fortgehend* [KA 2:206, no. 243]). In other words, there can be no return to a Rousseauistic originary natural state. Novalis likewise states that the goal of mankind is not the golden age (N 2:180, no. 565).[16] He also waxes virulent against the polar coordinate of any ending, namely, a beginning: "Wozu überhaupt ein *Anfang*? Dieser unphil[osophische] – oder halbphil[osophische] Zweck führt zu allen Irrthümern" [Why a beginning? This unphilosophic or pseudophilosophic goal leads to all errors] (N 2:622). Without an archē or telos, one wonders how Abrams's circuitous journey could have been undertaken.

The urgency with which the Jena Romantics tell us of the

innovation and categorical distinction of their venture undermines the platform on which the advocates of secularization stand. Along with the author of the manifesto-like Romantic essay "Das sogenannte 'Älteste Systemprogramm'"—Schelling, Hegel, and Hölderlin have been the authors put forward—the Romantics repeatedly refer to a "new mythology" (KA 2:313).[17] Indeed, Novalis places himself not *inside* universal history but rather at the outbreak of a new world history (N 2:729). In the preface to the *Phänomenologie*, Hegel writes that his period is one of birth and transition to a different age (GW 9:14). Hölderlin as well announces the beginning of a new world history (StA 3:63). When these turn-of-the-nineteenth-century authors, masters in the art of self-reflection, characterize their work, they consider it neither a continuation/modification nor a culmination, but a radical breach. Hence Novalis writes to Friedrich Schlegel of how time and space have been misapprehended until now (N 1:684). In their conviction that they were ushering in the *novum,* the Romantics testify to sheer discontinuity much more than assert themselves to be the pinnacle of a linear progression. Nor do they see their novelty residing in an accomplished leap to a higher, tertiary stage. They project this development onto the future. Novalis writes: "Wir sind jezt nur im Anfang der SchriftstellerKunst" [We are now only in the incipient stages of the art of writing] (N 2:194).

The studies of an Abrams, Binder, or Mähl of course find their precedent in works by historians and philosophers of history. The major proponents of the secularization thesis—Jakob Taubes, Karl Löwith, Hermann Lübbe, and Wolfhart Pannenberg—apply the structure of salvation history (in particular, the triadic scheme of the twelfth-century Benedictine Joachim of Flora) to narratives of *Geschichtsphilosophie* from the seventeenth-century universal historian Bossuet to the present. In general, these critics state much more about similarities in the structure and periodization of time than, say, about the retention of religious vocabulary in a secular context. Rather, they have observed the mere retention of eschatological terminology in order to come to conclusions about what Löwith calls "meaning in history." The latter writes: "History is more than a history of civilizations. It is also, and even primarily a history of religion."[18] In other words, Löwith tends to transform philosophical constructs into secularized religious statements. The same, of course, can and has been done for literature. In narrative studies the work that perhaps comes closest in tone to Löwith is Frank Kermode's *The Sense of an Ending,* written in 1966. Though cautiously not referring to the secularization debate, Kermode similarly wants to uncover in modern, seemingly ateleological works the desire to create the fiction of an end. The theory of historical continuity is seductive.

Gerhard Kaiser, Wolfgang Binder, August Langen, Hans-Joachim Mähl, and Dorothee Sölle—the major European critics— soon adopted the secularization thesis for their study of the literary texts of German Idealism. Their efforts were easily documented by the Swabian Pietistic family ties of an author like Hölderlin or by either the Moravian or the Quietistic educations of a Lessing, Klopstock, Moritz, Novalis, or Schleiermacher. Kaiser, for instance, demonstrates how religious values and expressions remain present and alive in the consciousness of late eighteenth-century writers.[19] Undeniably the vocabulary of this generation often reflects a Pietist upbringing. But it is precisely the surface, lexical evidence which has led to conclusions on too broad a scale—conclusions which this study wants throughout both to contest and to offset.

The proponents of secularization in both the philosophic and literary disciplines share a belief in historical legacy and an unbroken chain of cultural inheritance. Its scholars uncover motivic and structural similarities in otherwise very disparate world views. However, as we just saw, the Romantics disavowed this type of historiographical approach and therewith precluded their critics. Secularization, they would have contended, threatens to override not only minor temporal variation but, as Hans Blumenberg has most vocally objected, also major paradigm shifts. Blumenberg remarks: "So simple is it, apparently, to identify the substance in its metamorphoses, and to line up the metastases relative to their one origin, once one has found the formula."[20] The upshot of such criticism is to see only derivativeness and to presume to know what substance really is. The theory of secularization, Blumenberg claims, encourages a lukewarm sort of criticism which fails to value the struggle of its authors. And indeed Odo Marquard, who in response to Blumenberg restitutes the thesis of continuity, well exemplifies the resulting despondency. Marquard despairs at the failure of the secular author to institute change: philosophy of history proves the failure of the new age.[21]

But what if we see in the Romantics, or specifically in the 1798 essay by Schelling, a strong critique of the philosophy of history? The debate on secularization was indeed taking place already around 1800. Blumenberg, Marquard, Löwith, and Abrams, as well as the other critics mentioned, need to be read with and against Hölderlin and the Jena Romantics. Indeed, to speak on behalf of Blumenberg, he writes as if he had modelled himself on the authors of that time. They share a keen sense of the uniqueness and the inquisitiveness of the modern age. As historians, they are attentive to shifting strata and, as we shall see more specifically in reference to Novalis, to the serialization of data. Moreover, they would maintain that secularization or, in other words, the belief in uninterrupted transmissibility risks underestimating the responsiveness of the "secular," modern writer to radical, indeed ongoing change—to the open-endedness of all investigation.

Futurus and *Adventus*

> And ye shall hear of wars and rumours of wars: see that ye be not troubled: for all these things must come to pass, but the end is not yet.
> —Matthew 24:6

What exactly are the previous historical paradigms to which we have been alluding and which make critics like Abrams and Mähl—to concentrate now on secularization in literary expression—seem very misleading when applied to Romanticism? What authors fall into which paradigm? I want to suggest that the reader has to guard against finding duplicated in Novalis or Hölderlin two specific ways of structuring the future which can be called *adventus* and *futurus*.[22] For however much the aporiae these models entailed were reflected in writings around 1800, the models themselves were very consistently contested. Let us first examine the latter structure, *futurus*, against which the Romantics had most directly to contend.

Futurus is the future participle of the verb *esse* and thus signifies an extrapolation from the present infinitive "to be." *Futurus* is the extension and development of the present into the future: what was, is, and shall be. It presupposes that time is cinematographic and capable of being mathematically regulated. If we were to visualize *futurus*, we would imagine a vector running from the present indefinitely into the future; the former leads to the latter. The present contains the germ of perfectibility within it. Indeed, if the vector is foreshortened, the present can be seen as capable of realizing the more beatific future immediately. *Futurus* is thus distinct from a cyclical notion of time or, to suggest another model, the Parmenidean notion, whereby the present is identical with any past or future moment. In other words, despite the proximity of the tenses in *futurus*, they are still qualitatively distinct. The future marks an advancement over both the present and a less-enlightened past.

Kant, Lessing, Herder, Hemsterhuis, and Condorcet can be said to represent this mode of temporal thinking. They not only profess an implicit faith in their present abilities to determine their future but also claim to conjure it up accurately in the imagination. Kant refers to the rational expectation of the future as the capacity to render present an often very distant point in time (GS 8:113). *Ratio* was for Kant the faculty by which the beatific future could be presaged and even attained. In other words, reason itself is the means by which one reaches the rational goal.[23] Kant can therefore predict the continuous, progressive development of humanity "zum höchsten auf Erden möglichen Guten" [towards the greatest possible good on earth] (GS 6:136) and "in welchem alle Keime . . . völlig können entwickelt und ihre [der Menschengattung] Bestimmung hier auf Erden kann erfüllt werden" [where latencies can be fully developed and mankind's vocation fulfilled here on earth] (GS 8:30).[24] Kant indeed suggests that we should regard ourselves as citizens of a divine, i.e., ethical state (GS 6:136); this Kingdom of God is to be taken not as a messianic but as a moralistic one (6:136). The present thus assumes eschatological qualities, preempting the final state: "Man kann aber mit Grunde sagen: 'daß das Reich Gottes zu uns gekommen sei'" [One can reasonably say that the Kingdom of God has come to us] (GS 6:122).

This strategy of projecting the present into the future or of pulling the future into the present is repeated in several authors of the Enlightenment. *Futurus* indeed could be termed the temporal episteme of the period. Herder, for instance, had written similarly to Kant that the human sphere embodied the true city of God on earth. And in the essay "Palingenesie: Vom Wiederkommen menschlicher Seelen" he concludes that rebirth must occur in the here and now and not in the afterlife (Suphan 16:352). The present determines the future, indeed engenders it (16:372). In his *Aussichten in die Ewigkeit* influenced by the *Palingénésie philosophique* of the Swiss naturalist Charles Bonnet, Johann Christian Lavater likewise writes that we can only imagine future life as a direct sequel to the present one (Aus 1:103). Lavater describes eternity as growing with the perfection of our capacity to perceive and register present sense impressions: "Die Ewigkeit wird uns immer wachsen, weil wir immer fähiger seyn werden, in jedem Augenblicke mehrere Lebensjahrhunderte zusammen[zu]drängen" [eternity shall grow upon us, the more capable we are of compressing several centuries into one moment] (Aus 1:295). Eternity, in other words, becomes relative to the present. In *Alexis oder von dem goldenen Weltalter,* François Hemsterhuis writes that mankind's goal is to bind what is to what shall be: the eternal nature of existence will thereby be recognized.[25]

The notion of *futurus* also gave rise to Herder's hermeneutic exegeses of Scripture.[26] According to Herder, St. John borrowed his apocalyptic imagery from the writings of the Prophets as well as from his memory of the destruction of Jerusalem. Revelation is a historical document which neither invites conjectural deciphering nor even claims to reveal the future. To interpret Revelation means imaginatively to place ourselves into the first century (Suphan

9:105). Addressing himself to the exegetes of John's esotery, Herder explains that they can envisage an obscure future only by couching it in images familiar to them from the present (Suphan 9:32). So too with John. The central scriptural text of German Pietism thus loses all eschatological import. Herder explicates Revelation with reference to the context in which it was written. Subsequent exegetes followed his suit, most notably Johann Gottfried Eichhorn in his *Commentarius in Apocalypsin Johannis* (1791).

Moreover, the notion of *futurus* allows Klopstock transparently to narrate the Second Coming in his epic poem, *Der Messias*. He confidently sets his poetic persona within the apocalyptic scenario: "O tiefer Genuß, wenn auch ich nun, / . . . / Drüben steh', und schaue" [O deep satisfaction, when I too now stand there and behold] (HKA Abt. 2, 4:178). Moreover, the narrated time of the epic switches incessantly between past, present, and future. By virtue of his genial imagination, the narrator holds sway over all former events and those to come. At the conclusion the narrator is indeed ecstatically transported to the end of time whence he looks back at his poetic achievement: "Ich bin an dem Ziel" [I have arrived at my goal] (HKA Abt. 2, 4:300).

Precisely how the present and future corresponded was disputed. This very divergence leads us further to mistrust oversimplifications introduced by the secularization thesis. Here I can offer only a sampling of responses. Hemsterhuis, for instance, differs from Kant in that he substitutes the sense of beauty or totality (*organe morale*) for *ratio* as the redemptive faculty. This quality is best exemplified in poetry—as Novalis, commenting on Hemsterhuis writes: "Durch *die Poësie* wird die höchste Sympathie und Coactivitaet – die innigste, herrlichste Gemeinschaft wircklich" [Through poetry the highest sympathy and coactivity, the most intimate, splendid communion is realized] (N 2:215). The Hölderlin of *Hyperion* similarly writes of aesthetic reconciliation, using millennial vocabulary to describe the new kingdom awaiting us, where beauty shall be sovereign (StA 3:237; also 3:52−53). In his essay, "Von der heiligen Poesie," Klopstock likewise suggests that poetry presents the vehicle in which to emulate prophetic vision. And Jean Paul, to offer a different example, criticizes rational prognosis in favor of a purely emotive response: he senses the presence of the coming Deity already in his most interior, yet temporal being (SW 14:45).

Yet despite the various means they employ to link present and future, what allows the above authors to posit at least the approximation of a chiliastic end state is not, as would be expected, a Christian notion of time. We will speak more of *adventus* shortly. The roots of what Kant called "philosophic chiliasm" lie rather with Empiricism and the works of Locke, Hume, Condillac, and Diderot. In Locke, for instance, our sense of time is based on perceived duration, with the result that "we have no idea of infinite space or positive infinity but only of infinity as an extension of what we already know." "By being able to repeat those measures of time . . . as often as we will, we can come to imagine *duration where nothing does really endure or exist.*"[27] In other words, it is our present perception of duration which leads us to conceive of a future. The future, according to Locke, then, would be structured after our model of *futurus*: "by being able to repeat any such idea of any length of time . . . and add them one to another, without ever coming to the end of such addition, any nearer than we can to the end of number, to which we can always add, we come by the idea of *eternity.*"[28] Condillac similarly states that we can imagine the future by extrapolating on our knowledge of the past. Memory guarantees that something will occur in the future. Condillac asks his reader to imagine how a statue would progressively acquire human life and its attributes:

> Le passage d'une odeur à une autre ne donne à notre statue que l'idée du passé. Pour en avoir une de l'avenir, il faut qu'elle ait eu à plusieurs reprises la même suite de sensations, et qu'elle se soit fait une habitude de juger qu'après une modification une autre doit suivre.[29]

> [The transition from one smell to the next gives the statue a notion of the past. In order for it to have one of the future, it needs to be exposed repeatedly to a series of sensations and to get used to ascertaining that after one modification another follows.]

It follows then from Locke and Condillac that time is perceived purely subjectively, as well as being the medium in which we record the succession of "objective," empirical data. Kant indeed characterizes time and space as two eternal and unending irrealities that nonetheless hold all reality in their bonds (GS 4:41). Man then *imagines* time as a linear succession that stretches indefinitely into the future. Kant observes that, because our inner intuition of time and space has no form (*Gestalt*), we compensate for this lack by envisaging the passage of time as an unending line (GS 4:37). And since we must record impressions successively, Diderot will go so far as to say that our perception of, say, the soul is never instantaneous and complete but is caught up in the flux of temporality: he compares the soul to a moving picture difficult to render with fidelity and one that we must constantly be painting.[30] Rousseau's Savoyard vicar similarly concludes that his identity is constituted in and through time: there is no identity of the self except by virtue of memory. Hence "tout ce qu'on appelle infini m'échappe" [everything one calls infinity escapes me].[31] The faculty which for Condillac supported our assumptions about the future, i.e., memory, blocks for Rousseau the gateway to infinity.

Empiricism thus saw the rise of man's structuring time solely according to the way he perceived things changing. Conceivably in his imagination he could link past and future events to the present, although he had, of course, no immediate perception of either the past or the future. For Kant and Diderot, temporal flow then in turn determined perception, for things were only perceived in succession. This last step, though, potentially undermines the thesis of a temporal continuum and hence prognosis as well as progressivity. Such radical temporality implies discontinuity and the induction of the unpredictable. As Rousseau suggests, we can never know what lies outside ourselves, i.e., what the future will hold. Another model of future time, however,—what I would like to call *adventus*—had already systematized the notion of the unforeseeable. It then follows that, as an antidote to *futurus*, vestiges of *adventus* resurface to inform turn-of-the-nineteenth-century thought, though they are now drastically modified by being shorn of their Christian associations. And, as we have initially suggested, *adventus* also becomes an iterative concept.

The Christian model *adventus* derives from the Latin word for "arrival." The Greek equivalent, *parousia*, meaning "the visible presence or appearance of someone," is used in the New Testament to refer to the Second Coming or Second Advent of Christ.[32] Indeed, *parousia* or literally "Ankunft Christi" [Christ's arrival] is translated by Luther as the "Zukunft Christi" [Christ's future] (1 Thess. 5:23).[33] In other words, *adventus* is, in a play on words that the German language permits, "die Zeit, die auf uns zukommt." St. John the Divine, in his initial salutation to the seven churches in Asia Minor, twice calls Christ "the Lord, which is, and which was, and *which is to come* (ἐρχόμενος)" (Rev. 1:4, 8). Here then is the crux of the distinction from *futurus*: instead of conceiving the future as a continuation of past and present, John foresees a moment which will break in upon human consciousness from beyond time, from eternity. Again at the close of Revelation he defines Christ as the *coming* Deity: "He which testifieth these things saith, Surely I come quickly. Amen. Even so, come, Lord Jesus" (Rev. 22:20).

Of the two categories, *futurus* and *adventus*, the latter poses problems of a more complex and challenging nature for the writer, for *adventus* eludes representation. *Futurus* is founded on the combined notions of repetition and advancement. The poet can accordingly depict the future by imaginatively extending his present. The present is an effective sign of the future. *Adventus*, on the other hand, implies discontinuity and change.[34] Instead of the present's determining the future, the future structures the present by rendering it temporary and finite. History can then become periodized, divided into successive, interim durations—the most common periodization after Joachim of Flora, of course, being triadic. According to the model of *adventus*, the present is provisory, awaiting completion at a later stage in human development. Yet however much *adventus* allows us to categorize past and present time into epochs, we still cannot foresee the ultimate end itself. Christ's Second Coming promises to thwart accurate prediction: "But of that day and hour knoweth no man, no, not the angels of heaven, but my Father only" (Matt. 24:36). For the writer, this means that the *novum* cannot be represented mimetically. It even threatens to discredit typological prefigurations of the end. As the voluminous eighteenth-century commentaries on Revelation (such as those by Johann Wilhelm Petersen, Johann Albrecht Bengel, Emanuel Swedenborg, Friedrich Christoph Oetinger, and Jung-Stilling) suggest, the apocalyptist dreads the threat of error. These works were invariably preceded by an apologetics of interpretation and were interspersed with lengthy commentaries on the nature of language. Indeed *adventus* calls into question the efficacy of language. John even staves off deviant interpretation with the words: "If any man shall add unto these things, God shall add unto him the plagues that are written in this book" (Rev. 22:18). The token of assurance and familiarity that *futurus* offers us disappears before the turned face of *adventus*.

Adventus signifies sheer difference. It thereby elicits an "apocalyptic" dread of the unexpected that cannot even be mitigated by the numerous recountings and elaborations of the end throughout the ages. Although forever prophesied and interpreted, the apocalypse remains cloaked in mystery. The traditional, intricate sequence of events between the present and the New Jerusalem—i.e., the interpolated motifs of the Last Emperor, the Antichrist, the millennium, and the Last Judgment—does in no way bring *adventus* closer to the present.[35] These motifs function rather as pure ornaments of a divine, essentially unknowable eschaton.

Yet perhaps to mitigate fear of *adventus*, a corollary belief arose: through divine revelation man was to partake of God's omnipresence and stand at the end of time. The tradition of a strict sequence of apocalyptic events was created in the writings of the Tiburtine Sibyl (late fourth century), Tyconius (303–390), Jerome (347–420), Pseudo-Methodius (660–668), and Adso of Montier-en-Der (circa 950) and then rehearsed in Antichrist plays or in such encyclopedic manuscript collections as the *Vorauer* and *Milstätter Handschriften* (1180 and 1170). The eschatological countdown staged for the medieval mind a preordained sequence of events. Once locked within the preestablished plot of fall and redemption, the future became as knowable as the past. All human histories participated in salvation history and could be interpreted as leading up to and culminating in a divine telos which was indubitably given. When a person looked back from this telos, all events in human time could be read anagogically or as prefigurations of what occurs beyond time, i.e., at its end.[36]

The term *prefiguration*, though, does not imply that what shall occur in the future is preexistent in the present; here *adventus* differs again from *futurus*. The prefiguration never shakes off its teleological referent to become independent, or to annex the latter's superior nature to itself. Prefigurations never replace or re-present that of which they remain the "figure" or shadowy outline. In particular the medieval writer, following Tyconius, placed the Antichrist into two categories: the *figurae Antichristi*, embodied in actual historical figures or *antichristi mystici* or *membra*, and the *Antichristus verus, literalis et proprius*. The former appeared in time, the latter at a special time to come.[37] The Christian thus avoids bringing the atemporal into the present and confusing anagogical with tropological or allegorical readings—thereby keeping a potentially fearsome *adventus* at a safe distance.

Because of the barrier it erects between the figural and the literal, prefiguration cannot thus be reconciled with the *futurus* model of time wherein the present sign integrally points to the future it in fact guarantees. In other words, how we envisage time progressing then determines how we speak about language—if we agree with Kant that time is the a priori basis for all perception. *Futurus* and *adventus* then, as two distinct vectors of human time running in opposite directions, operate two different signifying systems. What they do have in common, however, is a telos either towards which the one is heading or from which the other is going. And in both cases this telos, or increasingly enlightened future, promises to recuperate any loss of meaning by incomplete or improper signification. The importance of this similarity is the following: *adventus* and *futurus* both differ from the examples of Romantic discontinuous, ateleological, and thus essentially nonnarrative time with which we opened our discussion. In our treatment of Hölderlin and Novalis we shall see what the ensuing repercussions for the act of signification would be.

To return to our initial discussion in this section, it becomes clear that the concept of secularization would threaten to override the distinction between *adventus* and *futurus* or between the Christian and Enlightenment ways of construing future time. Kant's and Lessing's philosophic chiliasm, in other words, is progressive and hence not indebted to Christian revolutionary chiliasm. It is indeed opposed to it. The notion of secularization misleads us on these grounds; also, as already suggested, when it is applied to writings around 1800, the different structuring of time these works exhibit threatens to go unheeded.

Thus when we apply the foregoing considerations to Romantic texts commenting on Enlightenment chiliasm, a pronounced difference arises where we would otherwise have found an avowal of agreement. One of the best examples of this difference would be readings of Lessing's *Erziehung des Menschengeschlechts*. Friedrich Schlegel, for instance, looked upon Lessing's prophecy that the time of fulfillment would most certainly come (W 8:508) as its author's most important statement. In a sonnet extolling Lessing, Schlegel writes:

> Und dennoch, was der Teure vorgenommen
>   Im Denken, Forschen, Streiten, Ernst und Spotte,
>   Ist nicht so teuer wie die wen'gen Worte.
>
> (KA 2:397)

> [Yet whatever the cherished man undertook in thought, investigation, argument, earnesty, and ridicule, nothing is so special as these few words.]

But Schlegel then continues by commenting in retrospective bitterness on how these lines were received: "the rabble" could not perceive that Lessing had opened the gate to redemption for mankind. The Enlightenment had failed. Although admiring Lessing for his faith in a telos, Schlegel nonetheless sees a break in time and irreparable difference separating him from his forebear. Heine too refers to Lessing's prophecy and indeed imitates the latter's command of Christian rhetoric: "In allen seinen Werken lebt dieselbe große soziale Idee, dieselbe fortschreitende Humanität, dieselbe Vernunftreligion, deren Johannes er war und deren Messias wir noch erwarten" [in all his works lives the same grand social ideal, the same progressive humanity and religion of reason, whose John the Baptist he was and whose Messiah we yet await] (SS 3:371). The parousia envisioned by Lessing was delayed. Consequently, in an irony that is nonetheless sympathetic, Heine recalls that Lessing preached in the desert; because he did not command the art of turning stones into bread, he spent his life in hunger and poverty. Heine could have been describing his own life. His own attempts to conjure up the messianic kingdom, symbol of social justice, were as fruitless as Lessing's; perhaps, however, as Heine's use of the Barbarossa or Last Emperor legend suggests, they were undertaken with more overt self-criticism (SS 4:119, 608–17). Thus, just as Lessing's chiliasm differs radically from the Christian model it supposedly imitates, so too do Heine and Schlegel part ways with Lessing in their views of temporal progression.

Heine's deflation of Lessing's messianic enthusiasm leads us to ponder the extent to which Enlightenment optimism was blind to social or political reality. A significant historiographer of crises, Reinhart Koselleck, has criticized this very belief in the progress of history as "eine ausstehende politische Entscheidung," "Zuflucht in der Utopie," or "Krise verdeckt durch die Fortschritts-philosophie" [suppressed political decisiveness, flight into utopia, crisis hidden by the philosophy of progress].[38] Recalling then Schlegel's review of Condorcet, we must ask the question: to what extent do the Romantics—these most avid readers of Kant, Lessing, Hemsterhuis, and Herder—react to, if not resolve, this crisis now brought to light in the wake of the French Revolution? Furthermore, what do they carry over and then modify from the Enlightenment past they inherited? Let us now investigate the aporiae that *futurus* entailed. We will later do the same for *adventus*.

Temporalization versus Temporality

Die Zeit der Geschichte ist unendlich in jeder Richtung und
unerfüllt in jedem Augenblick.
—Benjamin, *Metaphysisch-geschichtsphilosophische Studien*

Narratives at the turn of the nineteenth century begin system-
atically to evade endings and to avoid strong teleological plot moti-
vation. As a consequence, the fragment becomes the Romantic
contribution to genre. Indeed throughout his theoretical frag-
ments, Novalis sustainedly warns his readers against expecting
endings. In the early Fichte studies, for instance, he writes that we
can never reach the ideal, for upon doing so it would destroy itself
(N 2:170, no. 508). Later in *Das Allgemeine Brouillon* he po-
lemicizes against the notion of closure: "Ein abs[oluter] Trieb nach
Vollendung und Vollst[ändigkeit] ist Kranckheit, sobald er sich
zerstörend und abgeneigt gegen das *Unvollendete*, unvollst[ändige]
zeigt" [An absolute drive towards completion and totality is a sick-
ness, as soon as it becomes destructive and disinclined towards
what is unfinished, incomplete] (N 2:623, no. 638). But this same
suspicion of endings can already be detected in Kant. The notion
that change and, with it, time could cease insults the imagination;
all of nature would petrify (GS 8:334). Kant observes that the
imagination, which thrives on continual variation, disclaims the
notion of a sterile eternity. The major difference, though, between
Kant and Novalis is that the latter mistrusts endings because he
advocates radical temporality, whereas the former dispenses with
"Das Ende aller Dinge" [the end of all things] because he sets faith
in unending temporalization.[39]

If our own discourse will permit us to speak of continuity,
what are the interim stages in the history of ideas between these
two theories of open-endedness—between Kant's statements and
those of Novalis? The Romantic delay of the parousia can be seen as
an outgrowth of Enlightenment *futurus*, both its extension and its
undermining. The Enlightenment eroded the belief in a telos first
by shifting it into the present and then by casting into doubt this
faith that the present could attain a beatific end state. In other

words, once the present was said to generate the future, then the eschaton was pushed further and further from man's present horizons. He would never arrive there. Kant consequently regarded as fundamentally specious or immaterial the question of whether the telos can be attained or merely approximated. The notion of the Kingdom of God became a regulatory ideal which functions prescriptively and makes no performative demands: "Vollendung . . . ist eine bloße, aber in aller Absicht sehr nützliche Idee von dem Ziele, worauf wir . . . unsere Bestrebungen zu richten haben" [Perfection is a mere, but in all intent very helpful, idea of the goal towards which we have to steer our aspirations] (GS 8:65). The eschaton now displays merely symbolic significance (GS 6:136).

The notion of a regulatory ideal, whereby any specific moment in the future becomes on reflection provisional and negotiable, is found repeatedly in various authors of the period. The telos is pushed ever further into the distance. Herder, with his idea of recurring maximal states of cultural growth, is our best example. He writes that the ideal state would only be a fictional utopia (Suphan 16:355); eternal peace can never be sealed in a secular time span but can only be at the end of time, at the Last Judgment (Suphan 18:274). In commenting on Hemsterhuis's letters, Herder further speculates that, although we may approach perfection, we will never be eternally perfect (Suphan 15:326). His words were echoed later by Schleiermacher, who feared the parousia lay outside human time (StW 435). Indeed, Schleiermacher's writings show a noticeable absence of an eschatology and instead evince a theology of immanence.

What prompts Herder to put perfection out of reach is the fear that the naïve belief in its coming will lead to wanton daydreaming. In the essay "Vom Wissen und Nichtwissen der Zukunft," he deploys the New Testament image of Christianity as a building being erected throughout the ages. Whoever takes active part in the moral construction has more to do than dream about the prospects of eternity (Suphan 16:381). The open-ended, asymptotic development of mankind must not, according to Herder, lead to the neglect of present social engagement.[40] Herder thus preempts

Hegel's critique of a "Schlechtunendliches," a vague hereafter which excludes the finite and is infinitely distant from the present.[41] In response to the speculative ending of Lessing's *Erziehung des Menschengeschlechts,* Herder writes:

> Werde sie also unter Schwärmern Mode; nur unter guten Schwärmern. Baue die Vorsehung durch wiederkommende oder durch neu ankommende Seelen ihr großes Gebäude, wenn beiderlei Arbeiter nur rüstig und gut arbeiten. . . . Güte und Wahrheit ist nur Eine; diese bleibt und kommt immer wieder. (Suphan 16:359)

> [May Providence be fashionable among fantasts, as long as they are good people. Providence, like a great building, may be erected by reincarnated souls or by new souls to come, as long as both groups work vigorously and well. Goodness and truth are one, ever extant and ever coming again.]

Herder here combines his two major views on the possibility of the future perfection of mankind. First, the "great structure of Providence" may be constructed by individuals working in the present. Second, and attenuating this progressive theory, Herder conceives truth and goodness as atemporal qualities whose appearance is repetitive and/or cyclical.

Despite what Herder's—or for that matter Schlegel's and Heine's—reading might lead us to assume, Lessing's *Erziehung des Menschengeschlechts* is not without its irony and complications. Like Herder and Kant, Lessing too mistrusts the "sense of an ending" (to use Frank Kermode's term). The *Erziehung* demonstrates precisely how the progressive development of mankind does not lead, however gradually, to a culminating point. As the concluding paragraphs imply, the path to the new, eternal gospel (W 8:508) becomes plagued by detours, and development becomes never-ending: "Du hast auf deinem ewigen Wege so viel mitzunehmen! so viel Seitenschritte zu tun!" [You have so much to carry along with you on the eternal road—so many sideroads to take] (W 8:509). Unlike Kant, who posited the homogeneous development of mankind despite the often asymptotic path taken by the individual,

Lessing maintained that only the successful completion of individual destinies could assure the eschatological fulfillment of mankind: "Eben die Bahn, auf welcher das Geschlecht zu seiner Vollkommenheit gelangt, muß jeder einzelne Mensch . . . erst durchlaufen haben" [Every individual must have completed exactly the same path taken by the human race to reach its perfection] (W 8:509).[42] The metaphor of the parallel path allowed Lessing to adopt the other closely related metaphor of the education of the individual to apply to the human race. But Lessing's argument becomes circular—from the individual to the collective and back. The signified (the race) is subservient to and even invites subversion by the signifier (education of the individual). Human history will be completed only on the unrealizable condition that all individuals sooner or later achieve perfection.[43]

Indeed, Lessing closes his text with a series of self-contradictory questions about the future. Because he refuses to deduce and then delineate a possible future, he ends the *Erziehung* on a note of pure conjecture. After toying with the idea of soul transmigration, Lessing rejects the desire for omniscient memory which would verify the theory not only of palingenesis but, more broadly, of temporal continuity. The present is divorced from the past, and the future can be circumscribed only in the rhetorically hesitant interrogative mode: "Ist nicht die ganze Ewigkeit mein?" [Does not eternity in its entirety belong to me?] (W 8:510). Indeed, in his famous *Duplik*, Lessing admits that, if given the opportunity to possess the truth, he would decline it in favor of the drive towards it, even though he might eternally err (W 8:33).

Friedrich Schlegel documented his admiration for the author of the *Erziehung* not only in the sonnet cited above but also in an essay on Lessing. Here he called his predecessor a writer of fragments whose intention was not always to complete masterpieces (KA 2:106). Indeed, Lessing left his work on utopic discourse—the dialogues on freemasonry between Ernst and Falk—as a fragment. He deferentially declined to write a concluding sixth discussion, as this would seem too confidently to define and concretize the meaning of freemasonry debated in the preceding dialogues. Moreover, any ending would preempt continued further discussion. The narrator says instead that the encounter between Ernst and Falk was not to be reconstructed.

But numerous other writers tried to write Lessing's sixth discussion. Fichte and Friedrich Schlegel, in particular, thematized the notion of insufficiency in masonry. Fichte negatively defines *freemasonry* as a substitute for a perfect political constitution. It functions as a temporary or preparatory measure; yet, since democracy will always be imperfect, masonry shall always exist: "Freue dich, daß noch nicht alles ist, wie es sein sollte, daß du Arbeit findest und zu etwas nütze sein kannst" [Be glad that everything is not as it should be, that you find work to do and can be of service].[44] Similarly, Schlegel posits the continuing existence of masonry but in the guise of Philosophic Idealism, which never finds that for which it ever searches (KA 3:99). Like Lessing at the end of *Ernst und Falk,* Schlegel opens up his text by promising its continuation at a later date. Prompted by the inconclusive ending of the *Erziehung,* Novalis likewise speaks in his last fragments of extending Lessing's work (N 2:830, 836).

We can thus trace back to the Enlightenment a conceptual source for the Romantic open-ended or unending text. After first positing an ideal towards which we move, the advocates of *futurus* turned this ideal into a regulatory, always approximative goal and hence a fictional, elusive and illusive construct of the imagination. Since such a structure of future time is still progressive, however, it is yet far removed from the structure of the open-ended (because radically discontinuous) narrative advocated by Schlegel, Schelling, and Novalis. Even though Herder and Kant were writing contemporaneously with the others in the 1790s, in the aftermath of the French Revolution this older generation still upheld *futurus.* Herder writes at this time that he would continue to choose a constant, natural, and rational evolution of things over revolution (Suphan 18:332). Compare the late Herder, then, with Schelling in the *System des transzendentalen Idealismus* of 1800. Schelling states not only that the eschaton is always receding from us but also that this fact prevents us from making any claims about the unending perfectibility of mankind (Schröter 2:592). Hölderlin, as early as 1795 in his essayistic fragment "Hermokrates an Cephalus," criticizes the belief that we have or even could reach perfection, because either form of the belief would ignore the facticity of limits:

> [I]ch nannte die Meinung, als ob die Wissenschaft in einer bestimmten Zeit vollendet werden könnte, oder vollendet wäre, einen scientivischen Quietismus, der Irrtum wäre, in jedem Falle, er mochte . . . die Gränze überhaupt verläugnen, wo sie doch war, aber nicht seyn sollte. (StA 4:213)

> [I termed the opinion that science could be or has been perfected within a given time span scientific quietism. This would be a mistake, in any case, if it would deny existing limitation where it was but should not be.]

In respect to this distinction between generations, Schiller and Fichte seem closer to the spirit of the Enlightenment. Whether it be the idyll of *Ueber naive und sentimentalische Dichtung* or the "play-drive" and "aesthetic State" of *Ueber die ästhetische Erziehung,* Schiller repeatedly projects the realization of his ideal into the ever-distant future. In the sixteenth letter on the aesthetic education of man, for instance, Schiller writes that harmony and equilibrium are only ideas that will never become realities (NA 20:360). Like Kant, Schiller sees man as always approximating this goal; indeed the essence of the idea of mankind includes the limitation that he can only approximate what is infinite without ever attaining it (NA 20:352–53). In *Ueber naive und sentimentalische Dichtung,* Schiller likewise writes that civilized man can never be perfect because the ideal is unending and unattainable (NA 20:438). This "Annäherung zu einer unendlichen Größe" [approximation of an infinite entity] thus distinguishes the moderns from the Greeks, who believed in "absolute Erreichung einer endlichen [Größe]" [absolute attainment of a finite entity] (NA 20:438). The goal now possesses empirical status only as mere semblance—as an aesthetic construct: "In wie weit darf Schein in der moralischen Welt seyn? . . . In so weit es ästhetischer Schein ist" [to what extent may semblance exist in a moral universe? To the extent that it is aesthetic semblance] (NA 20:403). And thus, even if Schiller specifically does not attest to actual attainment of a goal, nonetheless (like Kant) he sees his epoch striving and progressing towards it with constant vigilance (NA 20:289).

In Fichte too striving becomes an unending process, which, however, is still teleological. In *Über die Bestimmung des Gelehrten*, for example, he writes that the true human vocation is infinitely to approximate the goal (Fichte Abt. 1, 3:32). And in the *Versuch einer neuen Darstellung der Wissenschaftslehre*, he concludes that every consciousness (*Bewußtseyn*) needs to posit another, new consciousness and so on into infinity (Fichte Abt. 1, 4:275). Commenting on the *Bestimmung des Gelehrten* in the *Athenäum*, Schleiermacher defines the unending as the truly real, as the sole possible ground of communication and exchange.[45] Thus for Schleiermacher the process of reaching the goal is unending because the goal itself is.

But to point to the pervasiveness of model of the never-realized third stage as exemplified by the *Über die Bestimmung des Gelehrten* and *Ueber die ästhetische Erziehung* or to the lack of an ending to this ideal as in Schleiermacher is not to say much beyond what has already been documented by many well-known critics. Lovejoy, for instance, attributes this open-endedness to the temporalization of the great chain of being in the eighteenth century. Romanticism then accepts the idea of the temporal unfolding of creation and contributes to it the appreciation of plenitude through diversity. Peter Szondi likewise investigates the overriding significance of the concept of temporalization for the period—in the move from a poetics of the norm to a speculative, deductive poetics wedded to the philosophy of history or, in other words, to the theory of progressivity. Szondi painstakingly and voluminously argues his case, so that any brief rendition of it here must regrettably appear oversimplified. In the lectures "Von der normativen zur spekulativen Gattungspoetik" and "Antike und Moderne in der Ästhetik der Goethezeit," he traces how the task of Idealist philosophy or, in Schelling's terms, the philosophy of art was to explain historical differences between the Greeks and the moderns. The latter could not imitate the former. Present artistic consciousness was articulated in contradistinction to the ancients and yet possessed full validity in its own right. Philosophy thus appraised the role of aesthetics as the future would in turn confirm it. The poet of the present partakes of the fulfillment promised by the progressive model of the philosophy of history he is writing.

In reference to Romantic teleology and temporalization, another major critic needs to be cited: Marshall Brown. Brown's widely circulating *Shape of German Romanticism* comes to theoretically similar conclusions about closure. He summarizes: "Everywhere the romantics see teleology and everywhere they look for circular organization around a center, the symbol of teleology."[46] Whether Brown sees one or two centers informing and structuring German Idealist thought, he in both cases speaks of the Romantic drive towards completion—even though one of the two centers may remain anchored outside the human sphere of activity. Romantic dualism thus, according to Brown, becomes chronic and indeed enacts itself through temporal succession but always with the aim to completion and balance.

In Brown's scheme, as in Abrams's and Mähl's, poetry becomes the vehicle which can best juxtapose and bring together polar coordinates. In Szondi's study too, the final stage in the triadic or, more precisely, dialectic progression is seen as realized solely in the realm of the imagination or in the aesthetic phenomenon—as Schiller's above-cited passage on aesthetic semblance intimated. Poetry becomes the vehicle for reconciliation; or, stated in more sober terms, ultimate reconciliation occurs only in a fictive environment. In trying to overcome the Kantian division between subject and object or between spirit and nature, the "aesthetic Idealists" only came back to Kant's conclusion in the third *Critique* that art could acquire neither empirical nor transcendent status, rather than both. Novalis, for instance, calls his work a mere play of words (2:438). The ironic implications of the Romantics' works, though, are surprisingly overlooked in Szondi's study, as in the studies of those who write on secularization. Instead, Schiller, Schelling, Hölderlin, Novalis, Jean Paul, and the Schlegels are heralded as the most prominent spokesmen at the turn of the nineteenth century of an unambiguous, albeit variously expressed, aesthetic solution—what Gerhard Kurz in reference to Hölderlin has recently called "Mittelbarkeit und Vereinigung" [Mediation and Union.][47]

Novalis, however, had written that one cannot hold poetry in low enough esteem (N 1:384). This ironic voice, as we shall see, surfaces frequently in Novalis's work, as if he anticipated the type of literary criticism his work would induce and he then endeavored to preclude. A writer like Novalis undermines certain of *his own* conclusions and thereby preempts potential criticism through this self-reflexive act. The late Hölderlin is likewise the self-critical poet *par excellence*—to the point of his trying to forget and obliterate the ever-erring self in insanity. Balanced scholarship regarding the Romantics would point to their strategy of persistent undercutting or (in view of the difference between temporalization and temporality) to the enactment of radical discontinuity. Such scholarship would pay special heed to the scepticism voiced in Friedrich Schlegel's clause: "obwohl diese höhere Stufe . . . mir noch fern zu stehen scheint und erst in der Zukunft sichtbar wird" [albeit this higher stage seems to me to lie afar off and will only come into view in the future] (KA 2:316).

In other words, in no way do I want to suggest that the readings of, say, Szondi or Brown are wrong. Undoubtedly the notions of temporality as well as temporalization pervade Idealist texts. Their authors often envisaged themselves caught up within the unfolding of a universal history they then tried to write and thereby to manipulate. But it is another matter to see them accomplishing this writing or admitting that it ever could be accomplished, or that they even wanted to accomplish it. The desire for an ending or, in Brown's terms, for a second center is still an act of closure, only projected onto a future moment. If we ourselves can speak in teleological terms, then the goal of Hölderlin and the Romantics would be to undercut the necessity of even a regulatory ideal and to trip themselves up along the path of the education of mankind or the formation of the individual. Jean Paul hence speaks of the "Entfernung des Ziels" [distance/removal of the goal] (SW 3:387). The issue the Romantics broached is whether the fixed, static telos, once converted to a dynamic, ever-moving, or ever-receding one, can serve a regulatory purpose. The latter's function as a goal is dissolved in its elusiveness, which gives rise to discontinuity and a never-alleviated sense of intermittence. The oft-cited, supposedly Romantic metaphors of organicism—cycles and embryonic development—must consequently be challenged.

Thus we can see the Romantics mistrusting the schematization offered by a philosophy of history, a teleology, or the myth of organicism, even though the vigilance of their mistrust almost approaches a systemization in itself. Friedrich Schlegel, for instance, writes of "künstlich geordnete Verwirrung" [artistically staged disorder] and furthermore states that the highest order is that of chaos (KA 2:318 and 313). Irony is the duty, he writes, of all philosophy that has not yet become historicized or systematized (KA 18:86, no. 678). Thus, the Romantics' prescribing of chaotic form and irony corrects and adumbrates the readings of, say, a Marshall Brown or a Frank Kermode. However admirable their breadth of command of literary, philosophic, and historic texts, the problem with Brown's and Szondi's studies lies precisely within their overriding schematization. The scope of the conclusions of Szondi, Brown, Lovejoy, Abrams, Löwith, and Kermode thus becomes both a virtue and a vice. Were it not for the Romantics' own suspicion of this kind of criticism, we would risk being trite in venturing to correct such informative scholars. But language, according to Novalis as well as Nietzsche and J. Hillis Miller, "scheint kein höherer Schlüssel werden zu wollen" [does not seem to want to become the key to something higher] (N 1:201). It is precisely this ironic awareness of nonclosure in language that gives rise to pluralized, intermittent teloi—as we shall see in the next section—both in Romantic texts and in the tradition to which they indirectly connect, German Pietism.

In summary then, the notion of an indefinitely progressing *futurus* invited criticism by the post-revolutionary generation. Radical temporality (*Zeitlichkeit*) was thus opposed to the theory of temporalization (*Verzeitlichung*). The aftermath of the French Revolution spurred such a switch in the way time was seen to progress and the future would unfold. Endings now became iterative. In other words, significant turnabouts, terminations, crises, and even catastrophes were expected to follow upon one another at irregular intervals. The ultimate ending had been deferred. How then could a person write about the parousia? What forms could expression about the now-outstanding debt of the future assume?

Diverging/Deferred Apocalypses: German Romanticism and German Pietism

> En attendant, essayons de converser sans nous exalter, puisque nous sommes incapables de nous taire.
> —Beckett, *En attendant Godot*

In his marginal glosses to Friedrich Schlegel's *Ideen*, Novalis, after initiating a discussion on the French Revolution, continues by calling this revolution a holy one where the Messiah has appeared "im Pluralis" (N 2:729). Likewise in the *Europa* essay, he speaks of the intimate conception of a new Messiah everywhere at once (N 2:745). Just as Novalis envisages the advent of more than one redeemer, he also refers to revelation in the plural—"neue entzückendere Offenbarungen" [new, more rapturing revelations] (N 1:377; 2:664). And with the same effect of making the apocalypse an ongoing process, Novalis uses the present participle in nominalized form: "sich *Offenbarendes*" [that which is revealing itself] and "das zu *Offenbarende*" [that which is to be revealed] (N 2:416, 840). Jean Paul describes a vision of Last Judgments in the "Traum über das All" (SW 15:115). Karoline von Günderrode likewise refers to the many apocalypses of former and recent times (Gü 105). In a phrase very reminiscent of Novalis, she writes that infinite nature intends constantly to reveal itself anew in the infinity of time (Gü 114). And we, of course, recall Fichte's and Friedrich Schlegel's pluralizing the French Revolution. In the wake of the French Revolution the apocalypse became iterative, and it assumed a variety of guises in the writings around 1800. Novalis, Hölderlin, and Günderrode could in fact have been describing the contemporary literary output on the theme of the apocalypse.

Before turning to the more general problem of teleological narration and its relation to philosophy of history in Hölderlin and

Novalis, and in order to set their contribution in a historical context, it would help to look precisely at various other depictions of this one specific thematic ending—the apocalypse. We shall first examine apocalypses in German writings around 1800 and, after uncovering their shared motivic concerns, see how they are prefigured in Pietist writings until Jung-Stilling's *Heimweh,* which is contemporaneous with the Romantic texts. As we shall see, at the turn of the century the symbol of absolute termination becomes fictive, posed, and—most paradoxically of all—unending. To illustrate the lack of an eschaton, narrated apocalypses are often abruptly curtailed, left as intended fragments, and cast as deluded dreams. They are set into splintered, discontinuous, or unending narratives that reflect on their reasons for being so. The following works by Günderrode, Jean Paul, Tieck, Bonaventura, and Kleist explain why their apocalypses are now fragmented.

One of the most characteristic examples of the incomplete apocalypse is a work by a lesser-known artist of the period, Karoline von Günderrode, that is tellingly entitled "Ein apokaliptisches Fragment" (published in 1804 in her *Gedichte und Phantasien*). Despite her relatively restricted position in life as an instructress in a private girls' school, Karoline von Günderrode by no means stood apart from Germany's intellectual scene at the turn of the nineteenth century. She was courted by two great writers of the age—Clemens Brentano and Friedrich Creuzer—and is recorded as having read, among other seminal works of the period, Herder's *Ideen zur Philosophie der Geschichte der Menschheit,* Jean Paul's *Siebenkäs,* and Schelling's *Naturphilosophie.* She was, moreover, an ardent admirer of both Hölderlin and Hardenberg. Indeed, a posthumously published sonnet entitled "Novalis II" refers directly to the Klingsohr tale.

As her phrase on the "many apocalypses" might suggest, the notion of epiphanic momentariness and the transitoriness of each revelation preoccupied Günderrode: "[der Sinn für Wahrsagerkunst] offenbahrt sich oft nur wie ein schneller Blitz der dann von dunkler Nacht wieder begraben wird" [the prophetic sense comes upon one often only as a flash of lightning that then the dark of night again buries] (Gü 106). This passage from *Die Manen,* subtitled "Ein

Fragment," suggests either that each successive vision is merely
fleeting or, more seriously, that the revealed insight is only relatively
valid. In other words, divine truth not only is perceived darkly but
also is temporal and illusive. Using the same image of the lightning
bolt, for which Hölderlin also had a predilection, Novalis mourns:
"es blizt nur hindurch. Das Ausgezeichnete bringt die Welt weiter,
aber es muß auch bald fort" [It only flashes in passing. That which is
illuminated carries the world onward but must disappear again] (N
2:223). Elsewhere Günderrode more painfully expresses the peri-
odicity of revelation and the sense of dearth and self-division with
which it leaves us. Our life, she writes, is out of joint; only part of us
lives for something higher, which, when awakened in us, consumes
us with longing (Gü 51). Indeed the very title of her prose poem,
"Ein apokaliptisches Fragment," expresses a contradiction in
terms—what the true parousia never would be.

Written in fifteen scriptural-like verses, Günderrode's piece ex-
plores the problem of limitlessness and fragmentariness. The nar-
rator mourns for the undefined object of her desire. Whatever she
finds is not what she looked for; she wanders about longingly in an
infinite universe (Gü 108, v. 11). Günderrode's apocalypse not sur-
prisingly lacks an eschatology: "denn ich hatte von keinem Ende
gewußt" [for I knew of no end] (v. 12). Indeed, the speaker per-
ceives time as variously and uncontrollably paced: "und die Zeit in
mir gieng den gewohnten Gang, indes sie ausser mir, sich nach
neuem Gesetz bewegte" [and time continued its normal pace in
me, while outside of me it proceeded according to a new law] (v.
3). The absence of either spatial or temporal boundaries disorients
her: nothing indicates the time or triggers her memory (v. 8). The
persona is likewise surrounded by a boundless sea (v. 5). Stricken
and driven (v. 7), she repeatedly faints as if in order to halt, at least
temporarily, the dizzying, endless succession of impressions. These
moments of lost consciousness and vertigo (vv. 2, 7) interrupt the
perceptual continuum, so that each verse appears as a disjointed
fragment in an unconnected, nonteleological series. Indeed, exten-
sive indetermination and absence of meaning caused by the sense-
less seaming of opposites can induce dizziness. Narratively speak-
ing, the author of this apocalypse contiguously aligns the speaker's

sensations, so that each moment of forgetfulness erases the previous segment of the vision. Günderrode's text presents us not so much with an apocalyptic fragment as with apocalyptic fragments. By juxtaposing disparate scenes in a paratactic narrative structure, Günderrode elicits a sense of an inclusive sublime. And by reposing the entire vision in the eyes of the persona, she creates an apocalypse which is the conscious fiction of the observer; the text is indeed punctuated by references to the act of seeing, beholding, and perceiving. Thus the totality she evokes is an illusion of the self. As if to atone for this fiction, the persona expresses the unfulfillable desire to destroy the source of fabricated unreality—the self: "ich wollte mich hinstürzen" [I wanted to hurl myself down] (v. 4). The apocalypse of the perceiving subject, though, cannot occur. Although the speaker claims to be redeemed from the constricting limits of her being (v. 14), the vision is essentially still self-induced and self-centered: "ich fühlte mich in allem, und genos alles in mir" [I sensed myself in everything and enjoyed everything in me] (v. 14). In his Fichte studies, Novalis similarly concluded that the self, which cannot annihilate itself, prohibits the attainment of any end: "Streben nach Ruhe – aber eben darum ein unendliches Streben, so lange Subject nicht reines Ich wird – welches wol nicht geschieht, so lange Ich Ich ist" [The striving for repose—but an unending striving, as long as the subject is not a pure self, which shall probably never happen, as long as the self is itself] (N 2:39).

Indeed, for Novalis and Günderrode, it is temporality which creates the self, albeit a disjointed, impure self. Kant had established the a priori nature of time as a pure form of the sensibility that lies at the basis of all perception; it is subjective. Subjective time is discontinuous, both following and delineating the spacings of the self. Thus, although during this period in intellectual history the notion of a temporal continuum is rejected (as one sees in Günderrode's poem), punctuated temporal extensions, intervals, and sporadic durations are not. These discontinuous spacings of time create the self—the disjointed self who marks the break between an estranged past and an enigmatic future. According to Novalis and Günderrode, the facticity of this self, with all its incompleteness and loss of direction, cannot be obliterated. Likewise, radical temporality cannot be overcome.

Günderrode and Novalis exemplify a preoccupation with the problem raised by Fichte's *Wissenschaftslehre*: self-centricity. The question resurfaces in a similar thematic complex in a famous text of the period, the "Rede des todten Christus vom Weltgebäude herab, daß kein Gott sei" by Jean Paul Richter. This black apocalypse indeed shares many themes with Günderrode's piece: the paradoxical lack of an eschatology in a work on the apocalypse; a seemingly exhaustive yet reductive sublime; and the desire to obliterate the destabilized, lonely self which creates the fiction. In the frame of a nightmarish vision, Jean Paul depicts Christ's returning at the end of time only to announce to an expectant humanity that there is no God. The topos was not unfamiliar to the period. Hölderlin, as we shall see, was possessed by the thought of the absconded deity. And indeed the very need for a "new mythology" implies that the old tenets of faith had died.

Inserted into *Siebenkäs,* a 1796 novel in part about an involuntary atheist by the name of Leibgeber, Jean Paul's short text presents a sustained inversion of the Second Coming (cf. especially Rev. 21:3–4). The community of saints surrounding the lamb's altar becomes the confraternity of orphans. The signs of the sixth seal—earthquake, blackened sun, falling stars—all reappear in Jean Paul's apocalypse, with the difference that they betoken not the wrath of God and his approaching arrival but rather his absence. The threshold to eternity opens onto an immense void, into the crypt of all creation. The passing away of heaven and earth (Rev. 21:1) is succeeded not by the descent of the Heavenly Jerusalem but by eternal night.

Although Jean Paul incorporates the teleologically oriented quest theme into the dream, he omits the final stage of the journey: "ich ging durch die Welten, ich stieg in die Sonnen und flog mit den Milchstraßen durch die Wüsten des Himmels; aber es ist kein Gott" [I passed through various worlds, I climbed to the suns and flew with the starry ways through the heavenly deserts; but there is no God] (SW 6:250). Jean Paul sketches the vacant, open interval between now and eternity, which includes neither God nor time

(SW 2, Abt. 3, 164). An earlier version reads that the present is
the caesura between a protracted yesterday and tomorrow (SW 2,
Abt. 3, 401). Instead of depicting an absolute end, the text reads
like an extended apocalypse. Jean Paul toys with our "sense of an
ending," to use again Frank Kermode's term, by postponing all
expected resolution. Images of circularity—the wheel of time and
the snake—thus appear to signify this lack of temporal limits.
Since the speaker-Christ can envisage neither an end to time nor
boundaries to the universe, he cannot find an origin. The prime
mover is absent: "Und als ich aufblickte zur unermeßlichen Welt
nach dem göttlichen *Auge,* starrte sie mich mit einer leeren
bodenlosen *Augenhöle* an" [And when I glanced up into the immea-
surable world for the divine *eye,* it stared back at me with an emp-
ty, bottomless *eyesocket*] (SW 6:250).

As in "Ein apokaliptisches Fragment," the absence of a true
Other betokens the solitude of the self. Indeed, the subject can
only generate its own image—the Fichtean problem Jean Paul ad-
dressed most prominently in the figure of Leibgeber/Schoppe who
appears in *Titan, Clavis Fichtiana seu Leibgeberiana,* as well as in
Siebenkäs. The end of the *Clavis,* for instance, reads: "Ich so ganz
allein, nirgends ein Pulsschlag, kein Leben, Nichts um mich und
ohne mich Nichts als Nichts" [I, so very alone, nowhere a throb of
the pulse, no life, nothing around me, and without me nothing
but nothing] (SW 9:501). Compare Fichte's litotic definition of the
self: one posits the self and inasmuch as not everything else, one
posits the not nonself (see Fichte Abt. 4, 2:55 ff.). Jean Paul ex-
poses the danger of Fichtean solipisism in the preface to his
"Rede": the spiritual universe is destroyed by atheism and dis-
solved into a plurality of isolated selves. No one is so alone, Jean
Paul claims, as he who denies God. In the dream that follows,
meaningless self-referentiality is thematized in the image of the
illegible sundial which displays no ciphers but instead points only
to itself. To escape such circularity, the self longs for the true apoc-
alypse—its own death. After realizing that his only neighbor is
himself, Christ desperately queries why the self, if it is its own
progenitor, cannot also be its own angel of destruction. But in
trying to narrate an apocalyptic end which would include the self,

the writing subject is confronted with the aporia of its endeavor: it cannot participate in the apocalypse it writes. Instead Jean Paul's dream breaks off before its culmination: "und ein unermeßlich ausgedehnter Glockenhammer sollte die letzte Stunde der Zeit schlagen und das Weltgebäude zersplittern . . . als ich erwachte" [and an immeasurable extensive clapper was to strike the last hour of time and to shatter the world . . . when I awoke] (SW 6:252). Because his theme is essentially unnarratable, Jean Paul cuts short the apocalyptic end.

Another dream-depiction of the apocalypse also has an unexpected dénouement—Tieck's satire on the Enlightenment entitled *Das jüngste Gericht. Eine Vision* (1800). The ending is so striking because Tieck accomplishes what no other author of the time could when writing about the Last Judgment: he has the narrated time, the future, coincide with the time of narration. The dream concludes in a self-reflexive turn pointing to its own witty fiction. The Godhead complains that if he were to pardon the writer/persona Tieck, the latter could not deny that he had already depicted ahead of time this Last Judgment. By doing so he has made it ridiculous.[48] As the vision breaks off after this quip from the Lord, we again see the narrating self treating its apocalypse ironically by curtailing its story before this self is judged or obliterated.

Curtailed too, or rather miscarried, is the apocalypse the narrator tries to stage in Bonaventura's *Nachtwachen* (1804), an episodic, pseudonymous novel that both embodies and satirizes Romantic themes. In a mock Day of Reckoning at the turn of the century the watchman/narrator Kreuzgang calls out eternity instead of the hour, an action which frightens members of the various ruling classes and prompts their sudden attempts to right the wrongs they committed. However, the hoax is soon revealed, the fake Last Judgment backfires, and Kreuzgang is robbed of his position as town watchman.

What makes this last parody of the apocalypse especially important for the purposes of our study are the self-reflexive references in the sixth vigil to the delayed parousia: "das Zögern der himmlischen Kriminaljustiz" [the hesitation of divine criminal justice] (Reclam 50), "die feierliche Handlung zögert noch immer" [the solemn event was still being delayed], and "Die Gerichtsanstalten ziehen sich noch in die Länge" [the tribunal measures were still being protracted] (53). Such passages thematize the implications of the title of their work—that the human condition is in a constant state of transition and apprehensive expectation. The night is an extended vigil between the no longer and the not yet. In another passage Bonaventura indeed speaks of sculptured stone saints and knights waiting motionless in vain for a new era to befall (30).

For Bonaventura's narrator, eternity is a poetic convention and a poor one at that (*ein uneigentlicher Ausdruck* [54]). He thus places among the insane in the ninth vigil a believer in eschatology, a mathematics teacher who wants to find the last number (84). Ends and beginnings are invalid conceptual categories. The narrator harangues his audience for inattention on this fake Day of Judgment: what would they begin to do, if time were to come to its close (54)? Bonaventura therewith satirically comments upon the naïve, uncritical belief in the likelihood of future revelatory change. It is thus not surprising to find that the sixth vigil contains allusions to the French Revolution and its egalitarian hopes. Kreuzgang compares the pending egalitarianism of the scene below him to that of the French national assembly (49, 51).

Bonaventura strings Kreuzgang's aborted apocalypse alongside other suddenly abbreviated episodes; its abrupt ending is symptomatic of the rest of its text. Indeed, this novel, "verwirrt und toll genug geschrieben" [written confusedly and crazily enough] (25), often points out its discontinuity to the reader. Kreuzgang, for instance, will state that he does not want to continue with his explanations (26) or will pretend to be ignorant of the subsequent course of events (24). At yet another abrupt narrative transition Bonaventura writes that, because of the numerous examples he had to cite, he has lost his train of thought. Rather than take up the narrative thread again, he would rather break it off (78). The cloaked stranger calls the tale he tells sublimely unmotivated (38) and begins with the comment that it is very boring to tell a cohesive story (33). Indeed, the episode of the mock Last Judgment begins by reflecting on the impossibility of logical, sequential narration: what, the narrator exclaims, would he not give to be able to narrate coherently and straight off the cuff (48).[49]

True to the form of its narrative then, the final vigil stages another interrupted apocalypse. The narrator dreams of a poet who tries unsuccessfully to compose a poem on immortality. The latter prepares unsuccessfully to write of the Last Judgment; as he is about to wake the dead, something invisible restrains his hand (134). Unable to raise the deceased, the despondent poet poses the question Jean Paul did in the "Rede": " 'Wie, ist denn kein Gott!' . . . und das Echo gab ihm das Wort 'Gott!' laut und vernehmlich zurück" ['What, is there no God!' . . . and the word 'God!' echoed loudly and unmistakably back to him] (134). A dream citing another dream, this passage from *Die Nachtwachen* reduplicates the act of echoing another voice; it continues the empty mirroring and unending self-reflection of Jean Paul's text. Here too the apocalypse resists narration.

Of course the apocalypse, as the ultimate unreality, cannot be mimetically recounted. It must thus remain fictitious—a fragment of meaning without a teleological or transcendent referent. To imagine the fiction to perform otherwise invites madness. In the *Nachtwachen* the so-called creator of the world, a parody of Fichte, is critical of teleologians (82) but does not see himself as one; he is placed in the asylum alongside the math teacher for his plans to hold a Last Judgment. In a work by a somewhat later writer, Heinrich von Kleist, Michael Kohlhaas naïvely reifies a metaphor by taking it upon himself to embody the avenging archangel of Revelation (Kleist 2:32, 41). Kleist elsewhere creates ironically misguided readings of what appear to be apocalyptic signs. *Das Erdbeben in Chili* narrates what seem to be stations in the eschatological story of Judgment and paradisiacal return (2:149)—stages only to be reversed and repeated later in the novella. In other words, Kleist's apocalypse is a deceptive one: "als ob das Firmament einstürzte" [as if the firmament were falling] (2:145). But perhaps in his description of the effects of an earthquake, Kleist can be seen as ironically preempting and exceeding the horrors of a world end yet to come. The church elder's statement, that the Last Judgment could not prove to be more terrifying, seems

too true: Kleist's universe *is* apocalyptic (2:155). As Kleist's re-
peated and aborted apocalypses suggest, by 1810 there could be no
genuine recovery of Enlightenment optimism or of the new "para-
dise of knowledge" toward which Schiller saw man progressing
(NA 17:399). In Kleist's image of fraudulent return from the *Ma-
rionettentheater*, we would have to partake again of the tree of knowl-
edge to regain innocence—an implication that this action could
reverse the effect of the original deed. Only by virtue of such an
irony then would we ever arrive at "das letzte Kapitel von der
Geschichte der Welt" [the last chapter in world history] (2:345).

In a letter to Wilhelmine von Zenge, Kleist voiced the di-
lemma of our reliance upon an uncertain, ever-receding future for
the confirmation of our fictions. We cannot decide, Kleist writes,
whether what we call truth is indeed the truth or is only our per-
ception of it. If the latter is the case, then truth does not exist after
our demise (Kleist 2:634). Hölderlin writes of the necessity of a
veiled truth and of its constantly postponed revelation: "Das
Heilige muß Geheimniß seyn, und wer es offenbaret, er tödtet es"
[What is holy must remain a secret; whoever reveals it, kills it]
(StA 3:277). When holiness is always veiled, what, Hölderlin
would ask, is the role of poetry to be? The questioning of our
ability to know about absolutes or endings entails speculation on
language and the reliability (or even possibility) of a referential or
communicational system. The theme of the apocalypse invites self-
reflection. And here Jean Paul, Bonaventura, Kleist, Hölderlin,
and the Jena Romantics tie into another tradition besides the open-
endedness introduced by the Enlightenment—namely, the Pietist
debate on the spirit and the letter. They inherited, if not the cer-
tainty of belief in a coming millennium, then the tradition of its
constant postponement and the deferral of meaning. Like *futurus*,
adventus also presented writers around 1800 with unsolvable
consequences.

In the Pietist circles of the 1700s the authority each new scrip-
tural commentary exercised was habitually contested or, rather,
new exegetes claimed prerogative by uncovering the shortcomings
and misreadings of previous interpreters and by swerving away
from all their predecessors at some essential point. Caught between

the authority of Holy Writ and the *ordo novus* which the actual apocalypse promised to bring, each exegete had to justify himself as well as try to preempt future criticism. Pietist self-deprecation therewith prefigured the sustained deviation from an eschaton and the pattern of repeated apocalyptic expectation and dismay we saw typical of the postrevolutionary generation of 1800.[50]

But Pietism here connected to an older tradition of apocalyptic writing; indeed history gave the Romantics a plurality of apocalypses, at least in ink. In his polemical response to the sociological study of Norman Cohn, Bernhard McGinn proposes that apocalypticism in the Middle Ages was primarily a scribal phenomenon.[51] New renditions of the eschaton usually glossed other written sources. Since Hippolytus's *Commentary on Daniel* (circa 200), most apocalyptic literature has taken the form of a "Commentary on . . . " Thus, while the apocalyptist was reacting to changes in the religious, political, social, or economic scene, he was in addition always struggling with the authority of another written word, usually scriptural or vatic, which threatened to weaken his own belated contribution. The fact that his own *Schrift* had to be justified gave rise to extreme diachronic variation.

Indeed the problem of revision dates back to the rise of apocalypticism. We initially but incorrectly assume that the apocalyptist exercises authority of voice, directly transmitting divine messages. Instead, biblical apocalypticism actually nurtures revisionist, antioral, and even heretic tendencies. For instance, with the exception of Daniel and Revelation, all the books that have been classified as apocalyptic by Old and New Testament scholars are apocryphal (excluded from the canon). Just as Revelation's canonical status was hotly disputed in the early church, especially by the School of Antioch, so did the Book of Daniel enter the Torah only at a late date.

In the case of the Old Testament, apocalyptic writing appeared during the time of exile as a provocative alternative to the rabbinical tradition of oral interpretation. Furthermore, it was distinct from the writings of the prophets, who *verbally* exhorted their contemporaries to repent. Apocalyptists, on the other hand, were mere scribes. They wrote pseudonymously, cloaking their texts with the mysterious air of past revelation. Such was obviously the case with the apocryphal books of Enoch, which claimed origin in the antediluvian age. Belated writers, the apocalyptists longed either for the past, where one once enjoyed the immediacy of celestial presence, or, of course, for the future parousia. In other words, they lacked the prophets' authority of presence and voice.

In view of both McGinn's conclusions and the history of biblical apocalypticism, then, it is not surprising to encounter Protestant scriptural exegetes worried about voice and the threat of benightedness. They discuss how present philological tools can uncover the hidden, enigmatic scriptural text, and how writing can attain the quality of what we earlier termed *adventus*. Can error in interpretation be excused?

In his *Religion und Philosophie in Deutschland,* Heine observed that, after Luther freed us from traditional religious customs and turned the Bible into the sole source of Christian doctrine, literal exegesis ruled as tyrannically as tradition did before it. We worshipped the dead letter (SS 3:589). Following Luther's denunciation of the chiliastically inspired politics of Thomas Müntzer in 1525, the young Protestant church—keen on establishing rather than losing its authority—mistrusted chiliasm. Only as late as 1694 in the *Edikt über die Pietisterei* are discussions about prophecy, chiliasm, and Boehme introduced for the first time into the official mouthpiece of the Reformed Church. Luther was thus far from instrumental in the rise of Protestant adventism. But as Heine's remark suggests, Luther's legacy to subsequent generations who were to muse on the Second Coming was his biblical translation. It both spurred a renewed preoccupation with the meaning of the Divine Word and elicited an often-critical response. Such is the case with August Hermann Francke's *Observationes biblicae* (1695) and Johann Reinhard Hedinger's 1704 edition of the New Testament. Once Luther proclaimed a common and universal priesthood, scriptural exegesis was no longer the exclusive domain of theologians. The Pietists saw themselves as direct successors to Luther in their belief in the validity of personal religious experience and the layman's right to understand and interpret the Bible. In his *Pia Desideria,* for instance, Philipp Jakob Spener placed the reading of the Bible in the fore of Christian life. If Luther pushed deviant chiliasm out the front door, it entered through the back with various new exegeses of John's Revelation. But unlike for Luther, Scripture no longer spoke directly to its reader; it required careful exegesis. In other words, beginning with Johann Arndt's *Vom wahren Christenthum* (1606), a distinction was made between the letter and the spirit. What interpretation precisely entailed became a subject of discussion.

Within the Swabian school of biblical exegesis, Johann Albrecht Bengel (1697–1752) represents the extreme limit to which faith in the hermeneutic endeavor could lead. According to the Denkendorf prelate, the Bible, despite its awesome sublime, could be made clear (*vor Augen geleget*) by methodical, philological study.[52] If the exegete were to read attentively enough, he would be able to foresee fully—down to the actual datings of all eschatological events—God's universal plan of redemption, or *oeconomia divina*. But as could be expected, Bengel's system was subject to criticism and correction, even within his own circle of students and followers. And yet the prelate commanded authority with his claim to hermeneutic precision. How then could his error and the believer's own exegetic uncertainty be excused?

Friedrich Christoph Oetinger (1702–1782) gave one response with regard to Swedenborg: even though his prophecies may not have come true, we must not despise them and fail to see their positive message.[53] The Swabian pastor tried to mediate between respect for past exegesis and his belief in a constant, ever-increasing measure of divine afflatus. As Gerhard Kaiser has observed, the branch of Pietism to which Oetinger belonged saw itself as both the inheritor and the superseder of Reformation spirituality: the radical Pietists saw their prophets as instruments of God who had been granted more far-reaching revelations than the prophets of earlier days.[54] Indeed, according to Oetinger, when authors such as Boehme correct themselves, their writing testifies to progressive revelation.[55] Belief in the revolutionary quality of a person's own message was bolstered, furthermore, by the biblical prophecy that in the latter times God "will pour out [his] spirit upon all flesh; and your sons and your daughters shall prophesy" (Joel 2:28).

Johann Heinrich Jung-Stilling (1740–1817), like Oetinger a follower of Bengel, also felt at liberty to correct his predecessor. The apocalyptic sequence narrated in Jung-Stilling's *Siegesgeschichte der christlichen Religion in einer gemeinnützigen Erklärung der Offenbarung Johannis* was, according to its dedication, discovered by the prelate Bengel yet confirmed and expanded upon by the author.[56] Nonetheless, in acknowledging his source, Stilling by no means thereby recognizes Bengel's seniority or anterior privilege. He denies epigonality and even adjacency to his predecessor, whose "buchstäbliche Aengstlichkeit" [literal timidity] he criticizes.[57] Bengel, Jung-Stilling writes, was not always right.

Revelation thus managed to guard its mystery from exegetical voyeurism and false pretenses to disclosure—but at the cost of spiritual ardor. By 1800 the generations of the eighteenth century had been well schooled in chiliastic delay, and Pietism had by then lost its religious impetus. Its vestiges had indeed all but disappeared from the seminary in Tübingen when Hölderlin, Hegel, and Schelling visited it in the first few years of the 1790s. Biblical exegetes following Bengel had been forced to preempt but could not forestall future critique—as the late Oetinger illustrates. He well typifies the way in which apocalypticism leads to a sceptic analysis of language when the millennium is delayed.

Despite his theory that the order of the signifier and of the signified totally overlapped, Oetinger still had to project full comprehension of the transparent sign onto the future. He admitted that the *signatura rerum* was at present sought for in vain; only in the future would the exterior sign match (*anschauend darstellen*) its spiritual referent.[58] Increasing pessimism in his later years forced Oetinger to leave unfinished his *Biblisches und Emblematisches Wörterbuch* in which he hoped systematically to decipher and catalogue the traces left by *Gottes extensio intelligibilis*. Oetinger's advocation of patient, chiliastic expectation indeed almost approaches passivity. Better, he says, that we wait until the latter days when all shall be revealed.[59] The so-called "Magus of the South" is indeed perhaps best known for his words, "Menschenhände thun nichts dabei" [Human hands have nothing to do with it].

Despite his faith in transparent analogies between the present and future, Lavater also had to admit that much of the detail in his depiction of the millennium was arbitrary (Aus 2:xxx). And Jung-Stilling offered an approach to Scripture radically undermining Bengel's belief in the unambiguous text: "Da es aber auch bei Weissagungen nothwendig ist, daß sie bis auf einen gewissen Grad dunkel bleiben, . . . so wurde auch jeder Schlüssel gleichsam ins Ganze versteckt" [Because it is necessary that prophecies remain to a certain extent obscure, every key was hidden (embedded), as it were, in the whole].[60]

Jung-Stilling indeed figures prominently in a lineage of scriptural exegetes from Luther through the Swabian Pietists to the Romantics, who were equally preoccupied with the Word and its interpretation. Novalis, for instance, had written to Friedrich Schlegel: "Die Theorie der Bibel, entwickelt, giebt die Theorie d[er] Schriftstellerey oder der Wortbildnerey überhaupt" [the theory of the Bible, developed, gives the theory of writing, indeed, of word formation] (N 1:673). This lineage traces an ever-increasing need to read more precisely: as the exegete becomes more self-critical, his writing becomes increasingly self-reflexive. Hölderlin, for example, warns: "doch auch bedarf es / Eines, die heiligen auszulegen" [yet also One is necessary to interpret the holy ones] (StA 2:53). In other words, both the sacred and the secular writer become conscious of the always preliminary and figural, if not to say fictive, nature of their readings. We can briefly characterize the poetics of the Jena Romantics, with their emphasis on irony, in such terms. Indeed Novalis had read Jung-Stilling's *Heimweh* (N 2:764), a lengthy novel written in 1794 on the theme of the constant postponement of the parousia.

In the appendix of 1797 to *Das Heimweh*, Jung-Stilling again takes up the image of the key he used in the *Siegesgeschichte*. Here, however, he reverses its usage. Jung-Stilling pretends to offer his readers the key to an allegorical interpretation: the city Solyma, towards which the pilgrims travel, represents the Heavenly Jerusalem. Unfortunately, the key does not fit, because Solyma never becomes the paradisiacal locus for its inhabitants. When the immediate goal of the protagonists is attained (their pilgrimage to the city ends), their homesickness has not ultimately been stilled. Instead, the eschaton is projected further into the distant future.[61]

For the novelist and biblical exegete, Jung-Stilling, the delay of the parousia has both narrative and hermeneutic implications. The ineffable must be delayed in its coming. Solyma is only an approximative, figural expression that accuses every attempt to read it as also being limited. Both the trope and its reading are insufficient. The true key to literary interpretation is lost, and Stilling's substitute does not fit. Nor is the key to scriptural exegesis to be found. By suggesting that Revelation could be fully understood, Bengel raised false expectations. Jung-Stilling, on the other hand, like Oetinger and Lavater, claimed that the interpretation of John's text will not be revealed until the end of time. Stilling, then, cannot cease to offer supplemental commentary on various biblical passages in his extensive addendum to the 700-page *Siegesgeschichte*. He also resists allaying the perennial yearnings of the characters in *Das Heimweh*.

Coming from the Pietist fear of improperly forecasting the parousia, Jung-Stilling's ever-absent apocalypse is nonetheless as much a token of its time as Jean Paul's absconded Deity. Hegel, for instance, wrote that the religion of the day was based on a feeling that God himself was dead (GW 4:414).[62] Schiller had also written of the gods' departure in "Die Götter Griechenlands" and Hölderlin of their delayed return: "Zu lang, zu lang schon ist / Die Ehre der Himmlischen unsichtbar" [too long, too long now, the honor of the heavenly ones has been invisible] (StA 2:171). The dismay at the failure of the French Revolution is not dissimilar—especially in the poetry of the Swabian, Hölderlin—to the mourning of a Pietistic fervor which dissipated as the parousia was repeatedly deferred. In other words, the delayed parousia could represent the absence of many things, if not sustained deferral itself. Herder thus wrote of both chiliastic sects and modern philosophy:

> Wie nahe der Erfüllung hat man sich bei manchen Systemen geglaubt, und wie schrecklich ward man betrogen! Die glänzende Höhe, die man dicht vor sich sah, rückte weiter und

weiter. Da giebt der Getäuschte dann alle Hoffnung auf und
läßt die Hände sinken. (Suphan 18:275)

[In so many systems how near to fulfillment one felt, and how
terribly one was deceived! The gleaming heights, that one saw
immediately before one, backed further and further away.
Whoever was deluded then gives up all hope and lets his hands
fall slack.]

As the narrating personae in the apocalyptic dreams of Gün-
derrode, Jean Paul, and Bonaventura suggest, the absence Herder
described is filled only by the spurious presence of the merely self-
referential *Ich* or, in other words, by Fichte's *nicht Nicht-Ich*. Bona-
ventura ominously describes this apocalyptic absence:

[E]s war die ausschlagende Zeit, und die Ewigkeit trat jetzt
ein. Ich hatte jetzt aufgehört alles andere zu denken, und
dachte nur mich selbst! Kein Gegenstand war ringsum aufzu-
finden, als das große schreckliche Ich, das an sich selbst zehrte,
und im Verschlingen stets sich wiedergebar. . . . Außer mir,
versuchte ich mich zu vernichten. (Reclam 122)

[Time tolled its final hours, and eternity now stepped in. I had
ceased to think of everything else and thought only of myself.
No surrounding object was to be found except for the great,
frightening self, that devoured itself and in devouring gave
birth to itself once again. Beside myself, I tried to destroy
myself.]

The writing and, in the case of Jung-Stilling, interpreting self
cannot stage its own apocalypse. The narration of the apocalypse
would cease with the poetic persona, and yet, paradoxically, the
apocalypse would never truly take place until this self—the source
of potential error—were obliterated or sublated. As this never oc-
curs, the apocalypse becomes pluralized and at the same time is
never really there. As each depiction of the eschaton differs from
the preceding one, the eschaton is deferred. Language defaults.

In respect to this last point, it is precisely the absent apoc-
alypse—and thus the failure of the imagination—which is truly

sublime. Kant defines the sublime as man's sense of the inadequacy (*Unangemessenheit*) of his imagination for the idea of the whole. The human mind becomes aware of its limitations (GS 5:252). The Kantian sublime is the feeling of the unattainability of the idea through the imagination (GS 5:268). A rhetoric enabling the evocation of what is essentially unportrayable—and hence of an eschaton—must therefore be negatively structured. Kleist, for instance, in comparing Caspar David Friedrich's "Mönch am Meer" with the apocalypse, refers to the "Einförmigkeit und Uferlosigkeit" [uniformity and boundlessness] of the painting (Kleist 2:327). The imagination fails to comprehend the meaning of the two or three mysterious objects depicted on the canvas and the nothingness that stretches between them. Jean Paul's narrator of "Traum über das All" oscillates between calling eternity "lebendige Unermeßlichkeit" [living immensity] and "gränzenloser Nachtkerker der Schöpfung" [limitless nocturnal prison of creation] (SW 15:116, 115). Günderrode's landscape is likewise featureless and horizonless (Gü 108, v. 5). And Friedrich Schlegel says that the sublime is composed of a dual opposition: "*unendlicher Mangel*" and "*unendliche Disharmonie*" [unending lack and unending disharmony] (KA 1:313).[63] To narrate the sublime of the apocalypse then, the author no longer describes (as a Pietist would) how he always anticipates glory. Instead he tells us of the interminable vacancy left by the "not yet" of the ever-absent parousia.

The Future Perfect

> The future is not a single path. So we must renounce the linear.
> —Braudel, *On History*

> Time is the non-definitiveness of the definitive, an ever-recommencing alterity of the accomplished—the "ever of this recommencement."
> —Lévinas, *Totality and Infinity*

We began by suggesting a possible historical explanation for the lack of an ending in writings around 1800. We then traced attitudes and problems Pietist and Enlightenment generations encountered in writing about the future. Before continuing to investigate Hölderlin and Novalis, I would like to pause to consider how today, conditioned by the age of relativism, we might speak of the future. If we reject *futurus* and *adventus* as belying a sense of temporal discontinuity and of rapid, incessant change and as forcibly trying to rectify our estrangement from the future, how can future time be envisaged as actually transpiring? In what words can we couch uncertainties and anticipate error, while still formulating probable prognostications? A third term is conceivable, however, without being necessarily synthetic or dialectic. The following is a theoretical excursus with reference to Jacques Lacan and Jacques Derrida. It will offer a conceptual framework with which to approach the question of the future in Novalis and Hölderlin.

If an imaginary line called *futurus* were to be extended from the present into the future and another line called *adventus* were to extend from eternity towards the present, the two lines would presumably either never meet or go past each other. However, if they were to come close, what structure would this approximation assume? How do the aporiae of *adventus* and *futurus* conjoin?

The future perfect or future anterior is normally used to align sequentially two future events, as in the following sentence: Once the patient approaches the final stages of analysis, he will have been able to cope with past traumatic experiences. I choose an example from psychoanalysis, for it is the Freudian interpreter Jacques Lacan who utilizes the future perfect to speak about the destabilized self. This is the tense, according to Lacan, by which the self anticipates what it is in the process of becoming. Lacan claims that we are continually in search of the Subject of the Unconscious, the Subject that we cannot say has always been, because it is currently not reconstructable. But we can speculate that, at some point in time, it will have been. The "will" of the "have been" delays the Subject from ever completely understanding itself and its past. The Subject is disjointedly constituted by these two nonintersecting planes of past and future. The prolonged use of the future perfect thus dispels the myth of a return to normalcy; it staves off what would be an imagined regaining of an integral self. All the while, however, the future perfect permits patient and analyst to postulate conditions for what the subject currently is not and yet desires to be. The future perfect anticipates supplementarity.

This anticipation can be illustrated by reference to the previous example sentence. The coming to terms with trauma (expressed in the future anterior) precedes the patient's recovery. In other words, a temporal interval separates the "always still" (*futurus*) of the ongoing treatment from the "not yet" (*adventus*) of the cured person. Suppose, wanting to close the gap, the analyst postulated that, at the very instant the patient regains a full consciousness of his self, he will have been reintegrated with his past. Despite the phrase "at the very instant," the use of the future anterior tells us that the alleged simultaneity, indeed the recovery, is spurious. The one event must be completed before the next event can occur. In a sense then, the future perfect as used in the main clause delays the actualization of the statement proposed in the subordinate clause: the successful cure will only occur on the condition that repression ceases. The future anterior not only presupposes that an event will follow it; it also lays down preconditions for the future—preconditions that, Lacan would maintain, are unfulfillable, or at least that lead to more stipulations. These push the terminal horizon into the distance.

If we were to relate the temporal gap illustrated by the future anterior to writing about the apocalypse, we would see that non-closure stands between any empirical event in time and the actual apocalypse. Restoration, reckoning, and revelation do not occur. "Any empirical event," of course, includes any speculative statement about parousia. The writer can never predict "this will happen"; at the most he can say, responding to his own place in time, "this probably will have happened."[64] He may hypothesize a future condition based on present insight (extrapolation being characteristic of *futurus*). Yet he simultaneously leaves a margin for error, anticipating correction to come in the future (future as *adventus*). The future perfect thus juxtaposes these two opposing structures of logical continuity and unpredictable difference.

The preceding considerations create problems in any writing that claims to depict the future. Writing purely in the future would require an omniscient mind whose narration and content would be simultaneous and transparent to itself. In religious terminology this is called *apocatastasis*—the reestablishment or recovery of the past at the end of time. But as an analysis of the future perfect suggests, the moment never arrives in which the narration of the future can become part of the future itself or be integrated into its history. In the psychoanalytic context, we would say that the subject cannot assimilate the act of remembering into the events remembered. The moment also, as we have seen, never comes when the writer can annihilate himself in order to narrate the apocalypse transparently. Narratively speaking, the end of a story that purports to depict ultimate, divine revelation never arrives. Apocatastasis is perennially delayed, because the final correction or addition to the sum—Kleist's "kommende Gegenwart" [approaching present]—is always imminent.

In an essay entitled "D'un ton apocalyptique adopté naguère en philosophie," Jacques Derrida sees in the Johannine apocalypse precisely this deferral. The vision is imparted via angelic messengers and is passed on to the reader by a scribe, John, who does not relay his own voice. Derrida suggestively writes that if messengers always refer to other messengers, then the source is un-ascertainable, the destination yet to come. The reader does not know who speaks and who writes. This angelic, Johannine structure is also that of the scene of writing ("toute scène d'écriture en général").[65] According to Derrida, then, the apocalypse belies the finality with which it is purportedly concerned. It partakes of the deferment that characterizes the future perfect.

At the turn of the nineteenth century, writers who attempt to narrate the apocalypse similarly engender nonresolution. Every narrative approximation is trapped in the bonds of temporality, because, once uttered, every statement about the future is forever banished to an irretrievable past. The future too lies temporally estranged. The writing subject can only situate himself in the future perfect, in a splintered mode of time that is neither past nor future. Yet in spite of the perennial renewal of disappointed chiliastic expectations, the writer repeatedly tries again. In retrospect, each attempt appears insufficient and seems to be one in a series of apocalypses—and so on *ad infinitum*. The lesson of experience can never silence either the persistent modal "should be" or the conjectural subjunctive "could be."[66]

Novalis and Hölderlin raised these and other issues in reflecting upon the relationship of their language to an unknowable future. They thereby worked with the temporal model that we have called the future perfect. Their speculations complicated, in retrospect, the rectilinear structures of *adventus* and *futurus*. On the other hand, we have seen that, while operating within the frameworks of faith of *adventus* and *futurus*, both Christian and Enlightenment writers discovered the very non sequiturs that then radically pervade the work of certain writers around 1800—the constant self-correcting, temporal nature of any apocalyptic utterance and its incorporation into an unending, fragmented text. In different ways, Hölderlin and Novalis now, as we shall see, *sustainedly* delay the parousia. They turn their historical inheritance of apocalyptic aporiae into the very logic which drives their writing.

2 Friedrich von Hardenberg (Novalis)

The Fragment and Its Supplements; or, Nonclosure and the Critics

> La ligne simple, continue, monotone d'un langage livré à lui-même, d'un langage qui est voué à être infini parce qu'il ne peut plus s'appuyer sur la parole de l'infini. Mais il trouve en soi la possibilité de se dédoubler, de se répéter, de faire naître le systeme vertical des miroirs, des images de langage qui ne répète nulle parole, nulle Promesse mais recule indéfiniment la mort en ouvrant sans cesse un espace où il est toujours l'analogon de lui-même.
>
> —Foucault, "Le langage à l'infini"

We began by characterizing perhaps the major theoretical interest of scholars of German Romanticism in the last twenty-five years: the phenomenon of secularization. Its thesis offered results on a linguistic, thematic, as well as structural scale of approach. The advocates of secularization, though, tended to overlook an opposing strain in writings around 1800—namely, the Romantics' furtherance of radical temporality. This latter notion was seen to be in contrast to the temporalization fostered primarily by the Enlightenment. But what in Romanticism has given rise to such oversights, if not misreadings, especially given the diversity of instances to the contrary? Here Novalis is exemplary not only in his seduction but also in his sharp correction of his reader. In other words, Novalis makes his critics want to see in him a strong desire for closure, whether it be in the form of a teleology, in the images of organicism, or in the secular application of a sacred symbol. But he equally challenges their findings. He is our Romantic metacritic of secularization.

Secularization is, of course, a way of looking for referential equivalents. It is, as such, a type of closure. Thus, the question at hand is not if and how secularization occurred but whether Novalis would have found its notion of transference viable. In recent years secularization has undergone its own "secularization" or, to speak more to the point, its politicization. Novalis, first claimed as a conservative inheritor or guardian of Christian tradition, is now the spokesman for its opposite. As a socially engaged liberal with utopic aspirations, Novalis exercises *Ideologiekritik*. However, this difference, as we shall see more closely, is deceptive precisely because of the closure effected by both approaches. The hint of millennial imagery in Novalis's writings grounds both readings. Their only claim to distinction is that in each case the referent for this imagery points elsewhere.

Thus, if I begin by reviewing trends in Novalis scholarship, I trust I am not giving a research report potentially uninteresting to the non-Novalis expert. Details necessary for the specialist will be relegated to the notes. Instead I hope to alert my reader to a more overreaching critical concern, whether he/she be a Novalis scholar or someone generally but keenly interested in Romanticism and the rise of Modernism. The case of Novalis scholarship indicates why it is advisable to guard against seeking closure in a text—a move prompted by our desire for referentiality. In one of his fragments, Novalis warns that age-old error and superstition have come from mistaking the symbol for what it symbolizes (N 2:637, no. 685). Indeed, Novalis responds to our yearning for referential closure—if it can be considered a response at all—by prolonging our desire.

Novalis's most sophisticated theorization on deviation and ateleology appears in his statements on the relationship between the reader and author via the ever-dilating text. Hardenberg's own scriptural readings exemplify unending, constantly mutating extrapolation from the object of commentary. Before getting to this point in our study, though, I want to examine both the strategies that Novalis devises in his fragmentary speculations for evading

endings and semantic closure and the means by which he puts
these devices to work in his famous novel *Heinrich von Ofterdingen.*
But first, how and why has Novalis so successfully generated at-
tempts at closure? What, in other words, has experience taught us
to guard against in reading him?

Frequent use of such adjectives as *apocalyptic* and *utopic* charac-
terizes both recent and older criticism on Novalis. Any student
initially approaching secondary material on the Romantic poet en-
counters such titles as Rudolf Meyer's *Novalis: Das Christus-erlebnis
und die neue Geistesoffenbarung* (1954), Hans Wolfgang Kuhn's *Der
Apokalyptiker und die Politik* (1961), Hans-Joachim Mähl's *Die Idee
des goldenen Zeitalters im Werk des Novalis* (1965), Karl Grob's
Ursprung und Utopie (1976), or Richard Faber's essay "Apokalyp-
tische Mythologie: Zur Religionsdichtung des Novalis" (1979).
Likewise Eckhard Heftrich, in his monograph *Novalis: Vom Logos
der Poesie* (1969), gives his chapters headings which include the
words *parousia* and *apocalyptic mythology.* As confirmed in part by my
own contribution, such captions are symptomatic of the inde-
fatigable fascination of critics with the utopic element in Novalis's
oeuvre.

Surprisingly, though, considering their abundant use in crit-
icism, the nouns *apocalypse, chiliasm, utopia, parousia,* and their cog-
nates do not appear in the critical Novalis edition. Instead, Har-
denberg prefers the term *the golden age* (1:209; 396; 397; 2:180,
no. 565; 745). He will also occasionally use *the Thousand-year Reign*
(2:192, no. 623; 203, no. 651; 447) and *the New Jerusalem* (1:236;
2:750). These terms occur infrequently, and their usage is elliptic
if not enigmatic. For instance, Novalis once uses *the Thousand-year
Kingdom* as a synonym for the Last Judgment: "Der jüngste Tag
wird kein einzelner Tag, sondern nichts, als diejenige Periode seyn
– die man auch das *tausendjährige* Reich nennt" {The Last Judg-
ment will not be a single day but the entire period we also call the
Thousand-year Reign} (2:447).

When Novalis thus conflates the Day of Reckoning with the
millennium, he is not necessarily using these designations loosely
or imprecisely, nor is he proposing an unorthodox sequence of es-
chatological events. Instead, both terms act as reciprocal ciphers or

absolute metaphors that escape exact definition and temporal speci-
fication. Their referentiality is opaque. Other occurrences of these
words tell us little more about the nature of the perfect future state
Novalis might envisage. For instance, he sets the two other uses of
the Thousand-year Kingdom in either the interrogative or the sub-
junctive mode: "Die Menschheit wäre nicht Menschheit – wenn
nicht ein tausendjähriges Reich kommen müßte" [humanity would
not be humanity, were it not imperative that the millennium
come] (2:203, no. 651) and "Träume der Zukunft – ist ein tau-
sendjähriges Reich möglich – werden einst alle Laster exuliren?"
[dreams of the future; is the millennium possible, will all vices
once be banned?] (2:192, no. 623). Thus, in light of the infre-
quency and cipher-like nature of these chiliastic allusions, together
with the hesitancy with which they are voiced, we wonder if the
numerous *concrete* references to the apocalpyse in Novalis criticism
are warranted.

   If Novalis uses various ciphers interchangeably to designate
the perfect state, then his critics, encouraged by this ambiguity,
take even greater licence in wielding and predicating these various
words. Wilfried Malsch, for instance, invents the pairs so-
cial/eschatological and existential/eschatological.[1] For Kuhn,
apocalyptic existence is exemplary.[2] Faber, in turn, writes that for
Novalis apocalypticism turns revolutionary.[3] Heftrich refers to the
poet as the Messiah of the golden age.[4] The exact distinction be-
tween these variations does not have to be painstakingly clarified.
What each critic precisely means by "apocalyptic" or "utopic" is
probably not so important as the reason for the various differences.
Two factors determine the gamut of opinion—one extrinsic and
the other intrinsic to Novalis's work.

   First, the return to a theologically cast critical discourse on
Novalis, which is largely foreign to his own vocabulary, shows that
the scholar in question is articulating a preconceived notion of
secularization. The critic desires to find in Novalis a substitute for or
a translation of Christian salvation history. Novalis is interpreted *sub
specie aeternitatis*. His secular transformations of sacred themes are
decoded back into their original language. Here reader inten-
tionality overshadows textual evidence. To be sure, in the wake of

Kant's division between the phenomenal and the noumenal, the Romantics searched for a vehicle of reconciliation. To the extent that Novalis, Friedrich Schlegel, or the author of "Das sogenannte 'Älteste Systemprogramm'" returned to the Joachite model to write a new mythology, critics are correct in introducing chiliastic vocabulary into their own discourse.[5] They are in error, though, if the Romantics' concept of time shows only surface analogy to Joachim's triadic structure. Scholars should not camouflage Novalis's distinctiveness by retaining strongly emotive chiliastic terminology in their own writing. A just balance between exegetical purpose and textual evidence needs to be found. However, it is doubtful whether most of Novalis's critics have achieved the hermeneutic balance.

Scholars have interpreted Novalis's transformation of Christian salvation history in basically two ways. According to the first group, poetry realizes or objectifies the messianic kingdom.[6] Novalis here dons his priestly robes to transsubstantiate the word into flesh. The poet himself, either Novalis or his spokesman Heinrich, is ascribed messianic qualities. Critics advocating these and similar viewpoints superimpose transcendent values onto fictive constructs. As a result, their writings are marked by the conjunction of such opposites as "past-new," "invisible-visible," and "absent-present." Such glorification of poetry invites comparison with Novalis's own sober statement we cited earlier: "Man kann die Poesie nicht gering genug schätzen" [One cannot hold poetry in low enough esteem] (1:384).

Other scholars maintain that Novalis *anticipates* the culmination of salvation history. The parousia is projected onto a distant future. A recent scholar, Richard Faber, sees Novalis criticizing the ideologies of his day in his expectation of utopia: "Bevor diese 'absolute Gegenwart' Wirklichkeit geworden ist, wird sie vom Dichter repräsentiert, der antizipierten Poesie. – Seine Werke setzen sie gegenwärtig und helfen dadurch, sie auch realiter heraufzuführen" [Before this "absolute present" becomes reality, it is represented by the poet, anticipatory poetry. His works posit it as present and thereby aid in actually bringing it to pass].[7] Scholars like Faber uncover utopic intentionality in Hardenberg's writing but are blind to any scepticism that Novalis voices about the building of heaven on earth. This kind of criticism is misleading in another way: it makes no distinction between descriptive and pre-scriptive, or constative and performative discourse, or more pre-cisely, between the poetological and the ethical import of Novalis's texts. Indeed, Faber shares with those who approach Novalis from the perspective of intellectual history a pronounced moral, even religious zeal.[8]

In both types of Novalis criticism, the word *real* (or *reality*) frequently comes to the fore. The result is a Novalis made palatable to a readership that attends to social concerns and can thus pride itself either on recognizing what is *wirklich* or on actually fulfilling Novalis's "prophecy" of a new kingdom. Such an approach propa-gates the fiction of direct inheritance or of an unbroken continuum between the century in which Novalis wrote and the reader's pres-ent. Does such a notion of uninterrupted transmissibility even ap-pear in Novalis's writing? He seems to imply the opposite with the phrase: "Ich und d[ie] andern Menschen etc. sind im verän-derlichen Zustande" [I and other people, etc. are in a state of flux] (2:655, no. 759).

The possibility of discontinuity or the interruption of triadic progression leads us to consider the second, intrinsic cause of crit-ical interest in Novalis's utopic thought. Soliciting interpretation, Novalis's writing often assumes a certain elliptical, prophetic, and oracular tone: language is delphic (2:495, no. 122). The bulk of Novalis's compositions are fragmentary—recorded thoughts invit-ing further execution or elucidation. Whereas numerous studies from 1796 to 1800 were conceived as fragments, other works such as the *Lehrlinge zu Sais* and *Heinrich von Ofterdingen* remained in-complete at the time of Hardenberg's death. In the latter case, the degree to which Novalis intended to execute his plans fully is purely conjectural. Scholars, though, are tempted to complete the fragmentary statement. In other words, they pad it with explana-tory paraphrase. Novalis's ciphers for the ideal future state are es-pecially susceptible to ideological closure by critics who operate with predetermined teleological notions. The possibility of inten-tional delay or complete absence of a telos is rarely considered. Novalis, though, tends to resist the lure of a definitive ending.

The Jena Romantics reflected on the necessary incompleteness of the fragment.[9] They thereby obviated their readers' efforts to explicate in full their writings. For example, Hardenberg published a collection of fragments in Schlegel's *Athenäum* under the title of *Blüthenstaub* [Pollen], pointing thereby to the purposefully incomplete and embryonic nature of the work. Elsewhere he writes of "Erzählungen, ohne Zusammenhang, jedoch mit Association, wie *Träume* . . . aber auch ohne allen Sinn und Zusammenhang – höchstens einzelne Strofen verständlich – sie müssen, wie lauter Bruchstücke aus den verschiedenartigsten Dingen [seyn]" [Stories, incoherent though associative, like *dreams*—but also meaningless and disconnected—at the most a few strophes are comprehensible—like sheer fragments they must be composed from the most diverse things] (2:769, no. 113). The fragment intentionally lacks context or *Zusammenhang*. According to Friedrich Schlegel, it is separated from the surrounding world (KA 2:197, no. 206).[10] Thus, it is not a fraction of or excerpt from a temporal continuum that must be archeologically reconstructed. Instead, the fragment resembles surface, extraneous, or marginal detail—"Randglossen zu dem Text des Zeitalters" [marginalia to the text of the age] (KA 2:209, no. 259). The fragment signifies present deficiency or incompletion that categorically rejects future closure.[11]

Because the fragment cannot adequately represent ultimacies, Schlegel calls it mystical: "alle Künstler und Weise sind darin einverstanden, daß das Höchste unaussprechlich ist, d. h. mit andern Worten: alle Philosophie ist notwendigerweise mystisch" [All artists and sages agree that the highest is ineffable, i.e., all philosophy is necessarily mystical] (KA 3:99). The enigmatic utterance thus alludes (*hindeuten*) to a possible future state, while resisting definitive interpretation (*Deutung*): "Die Sprache ist *Delphi*." Indeed, the entire oeuvre of both Novalis and Friedrich Schlegel can be conceived as glossing the famous pre-Socratic fragment: "The master to whom the oracle of Delphi belongs, does not speak, does not hide, he makes signs."[12]

Disputing both the immanent and imminent interpretations of Novalis's messianism, a third, new group of critics investigates the implications of fragmentary form. These critics focus on the self-reflexive rather than on the metaphysical import of Romantic poetics. Jochen Hörisch, for instance, suggests that the absence of transcendent salvation in early Romantic texts signals poetic self-reflexivity: "Mit dem ihr immanenten Verzicht auf die Kategorie transrealer Erlösung betreibt poetische Reflexion die Stillstellung einer Geschichte, die sich als teleologisch sanktionierte traditionell mißverstand" [With the immanent renunciation of transempirical salvation peculiar to it, poetic reflection causes history, which traditionally mistook itself as being teleologically sanctioned, to stand still]. [13] Recent work carried on by Hörisch, Hannelore Link, Karl Grob, Manfred Frank, Philippe Lacoue-Labarthe and Jean-Luc Nancy alerts us to the fictive or u-topic quality of Novalis's texts. [14]

Situated in an imaginary archē or telos, the ideal realm cannot possibly be found in actuality. Its locus is always elsewhere, constantly eluding the writer's grasp. The French critic Louis Marin states that utopic and imaginary discourse inhabit the same realm: the utopic is enveloped in fiction and affabulation. [15] Novalis, in turn, writes: "Das oberste Princip muß schlechterdings Nichts Gegebenes, sondern ein Frey Gemachtes, ein *Erdichtetes, Erdachtes,* seyn" [The foremost principle must not be given but freely created, something fantasized, invented] (2:184). Hence, the golden age and its related ciphers are not just one theme among many to depict. Instead, they form a collective symbol for imaginative, poetic expression. In other words, whenever Novalis borrows from the network of golden-age imagery, he points to the fictive quality of his utterance. He thereby asserts that the closed, self-reflexive realm of poetry is conscious of its illusory characteristics.

The discussion here initiated by Link, Grob, and Frank needs to be developed in specific reference to fictive *eschatological,* in contradistinction to *utopic,* constructs. What is the precise relationship of Novalis's poetics to his oblique references to the future? Does the eschaton elude him or does he deliberately delay it? How does he set the fragment into play against the drive towards an ending? How, in other words, does Novalis circumvent closure?

Novalis read Lessing (the *Erziehung des Menschengeschlechts*), Condorcet, Hemsterhuis and, although not documented, most likely the minor *geschichtsphilosophische* essays of Kant and Herder.

In addition he was familiar with Lavater (2:785, no. 226), possibly with Oetinger, and had himself an upbringing among the Herrn-hüter, whose songs so often evoke eschatological glory. Novalis thus inherited from his eighteenth-century predecessors the theme of (philosophic) chiliasm.[16] Indeed, perhaps the influx of *both* strains, the religious and the philosophical, will help to explain some of the seemingly opposing voices in Novalis's oeuvre. Novalis had to confront the problem of how to cast a previously theological and philosophical postulate in poetic form. How was he to depict a theme which escapes all mimetic description, since it is totally unprecedented empirically? The eschatological aporiae in Novalis mirror the problems we encountered in Jung-Stilling, Oetinger, and Lavater. Novalis likewise reflects upon the insufficiency of language to express the future. Furthermore, in the search for a proper vehicle, he was forced constantly to transform his inherited theme. For Novalis this rewriting of the apocalypse constituted its delay. The heuristic category of the future perfect—as opposed to that of either *futurus* or *adventus*—will help us plot Novalis's stance with respect to his forerunners and to the future he endeavored to avoid.

Writing in the Interim

> Es ist wie ein Zauberrhythmus im Leben der Organismen; die eine Triebgruppe stürmt nach vorwärts, um das Endziel des Lebens möglichst bald zu erreichen, die andere schnellt an einer gewissen Stelle dieses Weges zurück, um ihn von einem bestimmten Punkt an nochmals zu machen und so die Dauer des Weges zu verlängern.
>
> —Freud, *Jenseits des Lustprinzips*

In his studies on Fichte, Novalis writes:

> Inwiefern erreichen wir das Ideal nie? Insofern es sich selbst vernichten würde. . . . [F]olglich kann das Ich in gewisser Rücksicht nie absolut erhoben seyn – denn sonst würde seine Wircksamkeit, Sein Genuß, i. e. sein Sieg – kurz das Ich selbst würde aufhören. (2:170, no. 508)

[To what extent do we never reach the ideal? To the extent that it would destroy itself. Therefore the self can never be elevated to an absolute position, for then its effectiveness, its pleasure, i.e., its victory, in short the self would cease to exist.]

Hardenberg does not consider attainment of the ideal as a desideratum, not even, as with Kant, Lessing, Herder, Schiller, or Fichte,[17] as a prescriptive or regulatory idea. Instead, the telos is charged with negative connotations of cessation and annihilation. The difference is significant, placing Novalis's concept of parousia in a radically new context—one peculiar not only to Novalis but to other writers of this post-revolutionary period as well. Because the main trend in Novalis criticism until recently has been to ignore this Novalis who defers the synthetic, third stage, I want to present in the following sections ample material to the contrary from the fragments and then from *Heinrich von Ofterdingen,* even at the risk of being repetitive.

In his Fichte studies, Novalis juxtaposes *das Ideal* with the concept of the self as a mutable and mutating entity. Yet, lest we substitute the ego as a surrogate telos, Novalis elsewhere defines it in desultory terms: the self can only be negatively realized because action (*Handeln*) permits us solely to discover that what we search for is unattainable (2:181). Since the ego can only be recognized by default, it must therefore always be a negative entity, ever impure and ever striving (2:39, no. 44). For the Romantics, every such absolute resists our cognitive forays. Friedrich Schlegel, for instance, maintains that whatever is absolutely negative cannot be imagined:

> [E]in *höchstes Häßliches* [ist] offenbar so wenig möglich wie ein höchstes Schönes. Ein unbedingtes *Maximum der Negation,* oder das *absolute Nichts* kann so wenig wie ein unbedingtes Maximum der Position in irgendeiner Vorstellung gegeben werden. (KA 1:313)

> [The totally ugly is obviously just as impossible as the totally beautiful. An unrestricted maximum of negation, or absolute nothingness is just as incapable of being posited as the unrestricted maximum of any thought.]

For Novalis the ideal itself becomes deviatory, obeying a higher law of the circuitous (2:653, no. 748).

Novalis thus categorically rejects teleological beliefs and breaks up linear progression to trace out digressions instead. He speaks of the crooked line, the victory of unencumbered nature over regulation (2:167, no. 485). Novalis furthermore cautions us against believing that a point in time could arrive when time would be no more, that the ideals of philosophic discourse could be anything more than virtual (2:180, no. 564). In place of an absolute ending, then, Novalis substitutes an absence or extended lacuna. This postulated void at the end of time serves to incite change and to prolong stimulation and incentive (*Wircksamkeit* or *Reitz*). Hardenberg writes of an eternal *Reitz* which would cease to be if attained. [18]

Friedrich Schlegel is likewise less interested in defining an ontology than in discussing man's calling and therefore what makes him open to future change: "Es war nicht zu erwarten eine Theorie des innern Menschen, sondern eine Beantwortung der Frage von der Bestimmung des Menschen" [Expected is not a theory of human interiority but rather a response to the question of the vocation of man] (KA 12:49). Paradoxically, the future influences us the more it is distanced from us—the more the interim allows room for imaginative play: "Daher wirckt auch das Vergangne und Zukünftige so wunderbar auf uns, weil je unabhängiger ein Obj[ect] von unsrer Wircksamkeit ist – desto freyer unsre Wircksamkeit spielt" [Therefore the past and future exert such a wonderful effect on us, because the more independent an object is from our agency the more freely we play with it] (2:207, no. 662). To circumvent the loss of self or the resulting silencing of the imaginative voice, Novalis constantly projects the realization of the ideal onto the future: "die gänzliche Vereinigung [bleibt] immer künftig" [total union always remains yet to come]. [19]

Reversing teleological expectations, Novalis answers the question of where we are going: always homeward (1:373). Indeed, progressive movement towards a telos is deceptive; only seemingly (*scheinbar*) do we move forward (2:60, no. 129). But the child's famous response in the second, unfinished part of *Heinrich von*

Ofterdingen not only undermines teleological direction but also perpetuates the inversion: the emphasis in the reply should be placed on the adverb *always*—"Immer nach Hause."

In Novalis's vocabulary the words *eternal, always,* and *unending* often modify values which could rarely be construed as transcendent—concepts such as incitant, lack, history, and time. As the phrase "ewiger Mangel" [eternal lack] (2:181) suggests, Novalis tends to protract deficiency. Elsewhere he writes that *Reitz* will never cease to be without our likewise ceasing to exist; nor will world history ever come to an end (2:212, no. 1). The term *unending* thus does not characterize, as in the Enlightenment, the drive towards perfection. Indeed for Novalis such a desire is dangerously one-sided: "Ein abs[oluter] Trieb nach Vollendung und Voll[ständigkeit] ist Kranckheit, sobald er sich zerstörend, und abgeneigt gegen das *Unvollendete,* unvollst[ändige] zeigt" [An absolute drive towards completion and perfection becomes a sickness, as soon as it destructively turns itself against the incomplete and imperfect] (2:623, no. 638).

Novalis warns against interrupting, once and for all, the unending chain of affiliations between ideas. To prevent both the realization of perfection and referential closure, he instigates a *series* of interruptions and displacements: "Im Unterbrechen liegt der Begriff des Fortsetzens, der Thätigkeit"; "Denn jede Reflexion sezt die andre voraus – Es ist Eine Handlung des Brechens" [In interruption resides the concept of continuation, activity. For every reflection presupposes another; it is an act of rupturing] (2:112; 122, no. 300).[20] Thus, the interminable relationship between entities is stigmatized with caesuras, recapitulations, and breaks. These insure the perpetuation of mutual conditioning. Affiliations are contiguous and unpredictable, not predetermined, codifiable, and continuous. Links in the chain are forged by chance. Novalis observes that all life's chance occurrences provide us with the material to do what we like with them; they can form the beginning of an unending sequence, of an unending novel (2:252, no. 65). Indeed Novalis later characterizes poetic production as this discontinuous, chance concatenation of ideas: "Der Poët braucht die Dinge und Worte, wie *Tasten* und die ganze Poësie beruht auf thätiger Idéenassociation – auf selbstthätiger, absichtlicher, idealischer *Zufall-produktion* – (zufällige – freye *Catenation*)" [The poet requires things and words as the keys one touches on a piano; all poetry rests on the active association of ideas, on the independent, intentional, ideal production of chance (chance, free catenation)] (2:692, no. 953).

As the phrase "every reflection presupposes another" implies, no reflection can be originary: "[E]ine Mittelanschauung [muß] vorhergehn, welche selbst wieder durch ein vorhergehendes Gefühl und eine vorhergehende Reflexion, die aber nicht ins Bewußtseyn kommen kann, hervorgebracht wird" [An intermediary intuition must precede, that is itself again brought forth by a prior reflection that, however, cannot surface to consciousness] (2:19, no. 17). The most antecedent reflection escapes our perception. Thus, akin to the arbitrarily posited telos is the myth of a beginning: Novalis calls it a pseudophilosophic means leading to all error (2:622). Every apparent beginning is in actuality derivative, secondary, or relative (*ein 2ter Moment* [2:380, no. 284]). When every action and state thus posit a previous one, the search for the originary becomes folly (*Unsinn* [2:164, no. 472]). Any attempt to trace back to the originary source is met with an unending string of antecedent moments: "Alle Wirckung ist verkehrt etc. Jede Ursach erweckt Ursachen – die Caussa prima ist nur das erste Glied der ursächlichen Reihe – diese Reihe ist aber vorwärts und rückwärts unendlich" [All influence is inverse. Every cause awakens causes; the prime origin is only the first link in the causal sequence. This sequence, however, is infinite forwards and backwards] (2:614, no. 615). Therefore, Novalis states that the notion of a beginning is in itself belated to what it describes. In other words, no beginning can be aware of itself as being so. Reflection is always subsequent: "Der Anfang ist schon ein späterer Begr[iff]. Der Anfang entsteht später, als das Ich, darum kann das Ich nicht angefangen haben" [The beginning is already a belated concept. It arises later than the self; the self can thus not have begun] (2:485, no. 76). Every possible origin is dissolved in plurality and extended contingency: every object presupposes something else, which it posits in advance (*sezt voraus* [2:107, no. 282]).[21] When Novalis does speak of an origin, as in the *Lehrlinge zu Sais,* it is incidental or chance (1:206).

Just as Novalis posits an absence for the telos, so too does he equate origin with a moment of deprivation. For example, he states that the novel arises from the lack of history (2:829). If there is an originary moment, then it marks a point of separation. Following Fichte, Novalis defines the ego only in its relationship to the non-ego. Fichte writes that the self can only be intuited through its contact with the nonself. Therefore the self *an sich,* without relation to the nonself, is nonexistent, is purely imaginary (*bloße IDEE* [Fichte Abt. 4, 2:55]). But by turning to its other for its definition, the self forever forfeits self-contained, integral being. Novalis echoes Fichte: the self is only conceivable through the nonself. It only is itself, inasmuch as it is a nonself (2:179, no. 562). Given the elision of initial oneness of being, no return can be postulated to a predisjunctive state.[22]

Desire for what is not the self occasions intermediary, subsidiary, and supplementary objects which in turn elude our grasp:

> Das Ich glaubt ein fremdes Wesen zu sehn – durch Approximation desselben entsteht ein andres *Mittelwesen* – das Produkt – was dem Ich zugehört, und was zugl[eich] dem Ich nicht zuzugehören scheint – Die Mittelresultate des Processes sind die Hauptsache – das zufällig gewordene – oder gemachte Ding – ist das Verkehrt Beabsichtigte. (2:610, no. 601)

> [The self believes it sees an exterior being. By approximating it, another intermediary being arises—the product—that both belongs to the self and seems not to. The intermediary results of the process are primary; what is arbitrarily made is the opposite of what is intended.]

The dialectic process here described occurs over a stretch of time, whereby Novalis values the interim but deemphasizes its terminal points. As we have observed, though, these points can in turn be dislocated, so that any moment in the interim can designate another relative or arbitrary beginning.

Illusion is the force behind this relative, sequential movement. The above section is preceded by the statement: "Alle Synth[ese] – alle Progression – oder Übergang fängt mit *Illusion* an . . . Glauben ist die Operation des *Illudirens* – die Basis der Illusion – Alles Wissen in d[er] Entfernung ist Glauben" {All synthesis and progression or transition starts with illusion. Faith is the operation of deception, the basis of illusion. All knowledge kept at a distance is faith} (2:610). Origin and eschaton are thus figments of a belief whose limits are extensible. To be aware of beginnings and ends is to be cognizant of their fictional, nonempirical grounding. Yet this insight does not stop us from pushing back the boundaries, from searching for origins or imaginary endings.

We have already encountered the term *transition* in item 601 of *Das Allgemeine Brouillon*. Number 634, which questions the purpose of beginnings, concludes by speculating about a theory of transition and transsubstantiation. Between the imaginary and elusive archē and telos stretches an unending *Übergang*—a fundamental concept in Novalis's work and one which has yet to be investigated convincingly. To give an example to the contrary: Johannes Mahr has written on the subject of metastasis, borrowing a famous phrase from Novalis's letter to Caroline Schlegel to entitle his study *Übergang zum Endlichen: Der Weg des Dichters in Novalis' "Heinrich von Ofterdingen."* Hardenberg's letter reads: "Das Wort *Lehrjahre* ist falsch – es drückt ein bestimmtes *Wohin* aus. Bey mir soll es aber nichts, als – *Übergangs Jahre* vom Unendlichen zum Endlichen bedeuten" {The term *years of apprenticeship* is wrong; it expresses a certain direction. In my case it ought to mean nothing more than transitional years from the infinite to the finite] (1:691). Mahr reads this passage as a reference to the poet Heinrich's coming to maturity. Heinrich, he claims, objectively and concretely depicts an inner infinity by means of poetry.[23] Mahr thereby postulates an end to the "years of changeover."

But Novalis warns against teleological readings or, in his words, "ein bestimmtes *Wohin*." He does not want his novel to be like Goethe's, where the Society of the Tower ultimately presents

Wilhelm with a nobleman's diploma (1:733). In *Heinrich von Ofterdingen*, on the other hand, Novalis depicts the *interim* period of Heinrich's life instead of its possible beginning or end. Indeed, in the novel, Novalis frequently voices the notion of constant, erratic change: "Wie veränderlich ist die Natur," "der Zufall der ewigen romantischen Zusammenkunft, des unendlich veränderlichen Gesamtlebens," "In ewigen Verwandlungen" [How mutable is nature; the accident of the eternal romantic coincidence, of the infinitely changing entirety of life; in eternal metamorphoses] (1:327, 379–80, 239).

According to Novalis, then, transition signals pure change and transformation: "Der Transitus macht die Verwandlung" (2:105). Change, accident, arbitrariness, and transition obey their own statutes (2:665, no. 793).[24] *Übergang* signifies neither causal nor teleological movement, for it is determined by the laws of chance. Likewise, its significance is not retrospectively specified. It is neither the outcome of a past event nor the prerequisite for the future. Instead, the transition itself arbitrarily brings forth transient or relative ideals: they are the product, according to Novalis, of a transitory moment (2:654, no. 753). Prolonged transition puts any postulated goal into question: it erases the future before it comes. Likewise any past episode eludes eidetic recall. Indeed, as an inseparable verb, *übergehen* means "to omit, to neglect, and to pass over."

Übergang thus expresses an exemplary notion of constant transformation found throughout Novalis's writings in multiple guises, for "[m]ehrere Namen sind einer Idee vortheilhaft" [many epitaphs are advantageous to an idea] (2:242, no. 36). For instance, Novalis relates *Übergang* to *Kraft*: "Alle K[raft] Äußerung ist instantant – vorüberschwindend. . . . Alle Kraft erscheint nur im *Übergehn*" [All expression of force is instantaneous, transitory. All force appears only in passing] (2:343, no. 123).[25] Here the process of transition is arbitrary, noncontinuous, and hence always incomplete. Fulfillment of desire or a surrogate response to unending questioning would curtail all transformation: "Aller . . . Trieb oder Reitz läßt sich nur durch eine unendl[iche] *Reihe* bestimmter Handlungen befriedigen. . . . Er ist die ewige Triebfeder unendlicher terminirter Veränderungen" [All drive or incentive can only be satiated by means of an infinite series of fixed actions. It is the eternal driving force of infinite, limited changes] (2:543, no. 378). [26]

For Novalis, then, the medium in which transformations and alternations occur, in fact the prerequisite for them, is time itself. [27] It is the stipulation for all synthesis (2:60, no. 117). It creates, destroys, joins, and divides everything (2:492, no. 100). According to Novalis, we only perceive time through change, and hence we can simulate elapsed time by establishing succession or context:

> [D]enn die Zeit ist ja Bedingung des denkenden Wesens – die Zeit hört nur mit dem Denken auf. Denken außer der Zeit ist ein Unding. (2:180, no. 564)

> Zeit – Basis alles Veränderlichen. . . . (Allem Moment muß ich einen Vor- und Nachmoment hinzudenken). (2:668, no. 809)

> [For time is the stipulation for all thinking being. Time only ceases with thought. Thought outside of time is an absurdity.] [Time, the basis of all that changes. To every moment I must add a preceding and subsequent one.]

Novalis perceives time as constant motion towards an unattainable goal. Indeed, the question Novalis ultimately poses is not how to attain the goal but how to depict this prolongation, how to construct a *Perpetuum mobile* (2:530, no. 314). [28] Novalis never suspends succession. Indeed he defines *synthesis,* which is usually understood as the final cessation of time, as successive or iterative: "Die Synthesis wird in der Zeit realisirt, wenn ich ihren Begriff *succesive* zu realisiren suche" [Synthesis is achieved in time, when I try to realize its concept successively] (2:611, no. 603). [29] Time is endless (*unendlich*) because it never reaches or coincides with eternity. As time is unending, so too is human striving and, hence, human freedom (2:53, no. 87). Indeed, for Novalis, the eternal prolongation of difference betokens freedom: "Das Universalsystem der Filosofie muß, wie die Zeit seyn, Ein Faden, an dem man durch unendliche Bestimmungen laufen kann – Es muß . . . Compass der Freyheit seyn" [The universal system of philosophy must be like time: a thread along which can run infinite modifications. It must be a compass marking freedom] (2:201, no. 649). A compass, of course, serves to orient and direct, is ever vibrant, and marks tension. The freedom which it gages dispenses with end purposes. This instrument for measuring spatial direction is used here to relate to ateleology and temporality.

Novalis therefore conceives time as neither *futurus* nor *adventus*. Chronologies consequently become both arbitrary and cumbersome. For instance, at the time he was composing *Heinrich von Ofterdingen*, Novalis speculated that its individual chapters must be independent of one another. A chronologically progressive narrative is irksome (2:806, no. 316). As there exists no integral relationship between perception at one moment and at the next—as there was, we remember, for Locke and Condillac—duration cannot be established, let alone be forecast. The linear thrust and stretch of both time and narrative become irregularly and infinitely parcelled.

The telos thus being unapproachable, Novalis inverts the traditional meaning of eternity and indeed writes to Friedrich Schlegel that time and space had previously been misunderstood (1:684). The Romantics' novelty resides in the fact that they no longer define eternity in terms of sacred time. Indeed the opposite is true: eternity is the sign of spiritless, dull (*geistloses*) being (2:677, no. 869). Eternity, for Novalis, now means unending diachronicity; it is the sum of time (2:59, no. 110):

> Was nur durch Handeln erkannt werden kann und was sich durch ewigen Mangel realisirt. / So wird Ewigkeit d[urch] Zeit realisirt, ohnerachtet Zeit d[er] Ewigkeit widerspricht.
>
> (2:181, no. 566)

> [What can be recognized only through action and what can only be realized through eternal deficiency. Thus eternity is realized through time, although time contradicts eternity.]

In the switch, Novalis endows time with eternal qualities. Time cannot cease; it cannot be imagined away (*Wegdenken* [2:180, no. 564]). If eternity exists, it can only be apprehended in time: "Unendlich und Ewigkeit – blos Zeitvorstellungen" [Infinite and eternity—merely temporal conceptions] (2:60, no. 124). This is not to say, though, that the present intimates or prefigures the future, for what resides outside of time can only be active or perceived in time (2:202, no. 650). Indeed it is a contradiction that something occurring in time should alleviate (*aufhebt*) time once and for all (2:180, no. 564).

Once removed from its teleological position, eternity can be imagined as originating at any point within time. Any moment can generate the *illusion* of eternity by instigating an involuted, unending chain of resemblances, which, however, do not function prefiguratively.[30] In the fourth Dialogue, for instance, while claiming that eternity can be perceived fully in the here and now, Novalis also maintains that this epiphanic consciousness is illusory: "das Leben [ist] wie eine schöne, genialische Täuschung, wie ein herrliches Schauspiel zu betrachten. [Wir können] schon hier im Geist in absoluter Lust und Ewigkeit seyn" [Life is like a beautiful deception, like a glorious stage play. Spiritually speaking, we can right now experience absolute pleasure and eternity] (2:433). Similarly, in the *Lehrlinge zu Sais,* Novalis calls the moment a dream when diachronic history is perceived as an unending, unfathomable present (1:209).

Novalis not only sets time in opposition to immutable eternity as "spiritless being" but also to its cipher, the golden age: "Ich realisire die goldne Zeit – indem ich die polare Sfäre ausbilde" [I realize the golden age by developing its polar coordinate] (2:622).[31] The golden age is attainable over and over again or therefore only relatively. We can no longer think of it as teleological: "Es können goldne Zeiten erscheinen – aber sie bringen nicht das Ende der Dinge – das Ziel des Menschen ist nicht die goldne Zeit – Er soll ewig existiren" [Golden ages may appear but they do not bring the end of things. The goal of man is not the golden age. He shall eternally exist] (2:180, no. 565). Novalis evidently uses secularized religious terminology still infused with emotive content, like *the golden age,* but these terms now apply to an iterative process. Novalis retains the notion of a telos but puts into play against it the principle of sustained deviation.[32] What role does the future then play for Novalis?

The notion of an imaginary telos is the driving force that instigates change. Indeed Hardenberg writes that educated man lives through and through for the future (2:841, no. 438). By envisaging a teleological resting place, Novalis transforms even the idyllic past and the "spiritual present" (2:282, no. 123) into incomplete hieroglyphs that at most shadow forth a better state. He also asks at the close of the third manuscript collection of the Fichte studies: "Wo muß ich aus, wo muß ich hin und wie muß ich fortschreiten?" [Where do I exit and go, and how must I proceed?] (2:140, no. 372). The deficient present throws the writer into expectation of a future revelation or apocalypse, whose continued deferral in turn detours the writer back to his present aeon. Thus, in their study of the *Athenäum,* Philippe Lacoue-Labarthe and Jean-Luc Nancy paradoxically label this systematic equivocation, this unattainment of infinity, the Romantics' true achievement.[33] Circularity is never broken. Philosophy is an unending activity, because its infinite desire for an absolute cause (*Grund*) can only be relatively stilled (2:180, no. 566).

The prolonged delay of the parousia instigates repeated attempts at approximation. Novalis's *Approximationsprincip* (2:482, no. 61; 530, no. 314), however, signifies not ever-increasing proximity to the desideratum but rather sustained or *repeated* efforts at approximation. The Romantics do not want truth itself but a *relatives Proximum* (2:467, no. 57). Friedrich Schlegel likewise speaks of the "Kategorie Beinahe" [almost category] (KA 2:157, no. 80). All resolution thus becomes relative, approximate, or imaginary: "Diese erweiterte Poësie . . . [kann] nur durch Annäherung gelößt werden" [Amplified poetry can only be solved through approximation] (1:657). The poet composes in enigmatic fragments or in an unending chain of extended fragments, which only approximate completion.

But the deferral of the parousia never gives rise to chiliastic disappointment: "Was jetzt nicht die Vollendung erreicht, wird sie

bei einem künftigen Versuch erreichen, oder bei einem aber-
maligen. . . . Aus unzähligen Verwandlungen geht es in immer
reicheren Gestalten erneuet wieder hervor" [Whatever does not
now attain completion will do so upon a future attempt or one yet
after that. After innumerable attempts, it will reissue regenerated
in ever-richer forms] (2:735). Repeated postponement never halts
but incites the *Ergänzungstrieb* (2:134, no. 326) or the drive *towards*
closure: "[D]ie Vorstellungen der Zukunft – treiben uns zum
Beleben – zum Verkörpern, zur assimilirenden Wircksamkeit"
[Notions of the future drive us to enliven, to embody, to assimilat-
ing effectiveness] (2:282, no. 124). Thus the Romantics leave the
future open to unpredictable change, even if this change means
resolution. For instance, for Friedrich Schlegel the Kingdom of
God is *der elastische Punkt,* generating associations that pull time
incessantly forward; only that which stands in relationship to the
infinite has any significance or is of any use (KA 2:256, no. 3).[34]
Irony, then, is a temporary, preliminary mode of thought, which
may turn out to be permanent (though we shall never know).
Irony, according to Schlegel, is the duty of all philosophy that has
not yet become historical or systematic (KA 18:86, no. 678). Even
the notion of unendingness is itself yet unverified: *"Ist* d[ie] Welt
unendlich oder wird sie es nur?" [*Is* the world infinite or is it only
becoming so?] (KA 18:93, no. 765).

For Novalis and Schlegel, then, the notion of the future con-
tains two diametrically opposed moments—the postulated advent
of the *novum* and projected deficiency. These two views are insep-
arable: in present dearth man envisages change, yet any future re-
versal is reliant upon that prior sense of emptiness for its radical
effect. Everything depends on differential positioning. Novalis
therefore says in his Fichte studies that the identity of an object
must be derived from its opposite (2:112), and in *Das Allgemeine
Brouillon* he writes: "Alles *Fixiren* geschieht durch Verknüpfung –
durch eine mehr oder minder individuelle *Beziehung*" [all limita-
tion occurs through connection, through more or less individual
association] (2:665, no. 791). References to prophecy and divina-
tion thus bespeak in Novalis not an irrational, mystic prediction or
preempting of the future but keen attentiveness to shifting, histor-

ical contexts: the visionary sense is explainable from the deep, un-
ending relationships of the entire world (2:794, no. 255).[35]

Novalis exemplifies well the continued deferral of the parousia
and the concomitant hollowing out of the present in the *Hymnen an
die Nacht*. In the third hymn he sets the narrator's visionary dream
of the dead beloved into the past, with the effect that this past
event estranges the speaker from his present and makes him long
for the future: "Noch sind der Spuren unserer Offenbarung wenig"
[As yet the traces of our revelation are few] (1:159).[36] The present
becomes emptied of immediate significance, as centuries pass by
into the distance (1:155). As a result, the world around the speaker
becomes unfathomable and abyssal. To counteract this deficiency
the narrator repeatedly projects himself into the future, while at
the same time pointing out that he still speaks in a voided present:

> Hinüber wall ich,
> Und jede Pein
> Wird einst ein Stachel
> Der Wollust seyn.
> Noch wenig Zeiten,
> So bin ich los.
>
>   (1:159)
> [I travel across, and every agony will once be a thorn of volup-
> tuousness. Yet awhile and I am free.]

What appears to be prophetic in these hymns is constantly only
anticipatory. Desire is always prolonged; in fact, the yearning is
what endows these love-hymns with their Romantic religiosity.
Schleiermacher wrote: "Sehnsucht nach Liebe, immer erfüllte und
immer wieder sich erneuernde, wird ihm zugleich Religion"
[Longing for love, always fulfilled and always again renewing it-
self, becomes religion] (StW 229). Likewise for Friedrich Schlegel
the longing for the infinite must always remain longing (KA 12:8,
11). At one point the speaker in *Hymnen an die Nacht* indeed yearns
not to have his desires fulfilled but to be given reason to anticipate:
"Erklänge doch die Ferne / Von deinem Zuge schon" [Would that

the distance already sounded of your lineament] (1:171). These verses, perhaps better than any other, express what we called the structure of the future perfect—the stationing of ourselves in a future but still preliminary point in time. The speaker then longs for death in the last hymn, not so much because it would bring with it the plenitude of the parousia but rather because it would most thoroughly execute and radicalize this underdetermination and absence. It would render permanent the threshold experience that the third hymn, the center of the cycle, depicts.

Hymnen an die Nacht leads us away from Novalis's theoretical work and to his more literary output. Before turning to *Heinrich von Ofterdingen,* however, we should investigate briefly how Novalis relates the notion of temporality to poetry. For the Romantics, poetic utterance—like time—is caught in a state of constant, unpredictable flux and transition. Friedrich Schlegel, for instance, doubts that modern poetry registers improvement: it always undergoes change, but it can progress backwards as well. It may even distance itself from a given goal (KA 1:255). In a letter to August Wilhelm Schlegel, Novalis too writes that poetry fluctuates, its receptivity to stimulation (*Reitz*) is limitless, and the combinations it sets up are unpredictable (1:656–57).[37]

This passage shows Novalis describing with the concept of *Reitz*—and by extension the concepts of *Kraft, Trieb,* and *Übergang*—the economics of poetry. Letters (*Buchstaben*), he says, are spiritual coinage (2:476, no. 31). The rhetorical laws, such as association and inversion, that govern poetry are not construed along a vertical, synchronic axis of simple substitution but operate instead along a horizontal and diachronic one of transferral, displacement, and environmentally determined exchange. A word forms a nodal point in an unending contextual chain: every individual is the central point of an emanational system (2:274, no. 109). Every separate predicate makes explicit a multiple relationship (2:189, no. 598).[38] Contextuality thereby replaces teleology. The associations thus formed are for Novalis constantly changing into infinitude (1:653) and are therefore always merely fictive (2:698, no. 997).[39] Consequently, Novalis can advocate a pragmatic, flexible use of language that allows for individuality and arbitrariness: "Jedes Wort hat seine eigenthümliche Bedeutung, seine Nebenbedeutungen, seine falschen, und durchaus willkührlichen Bedeutungen. Etymologie ist verschieden – genetische – pragmatische – /wie es gebraucht werden sollte/" [Every word has its peculiar meaning, its secondary meanings, its false and totally arbitrary meanings. Etymology is diverse, genetic, pragmatic, as the need requires it] (2:188, no. 590).

Figuratively speaking, the fragment is not like the tip of an iceberg that hides more than it reveals. Instead, the fragment, like the pollen grain (2:274, no. 104; 270, no. 93; 486, no. 79) wafted by the wind, is received elsewhere than at its place of origin and excites further reflection. This process is unending: "Alles ist Samenkorn" [Everything is spermatic] (2:352, no. 188). For Novalis, the task of the reader is not qualitatively different from his own task as writer; it is the temporal continuation of his work. Meaning cannot be excavated the more the reader probes into the text. On the contrary, the text requires extension and extrapolation: "Der wahre Leser muß der erweiterte Autor seyn" [The true reader must be the extended author] (2:282, no. 125).

The referentiality of any given term is thus linear: it evokes a succession of essentially chance or oblique associations. At each subsequent moment, the context of a word shifts.[40] Affinities become opaque, arbitrary, and unpredictable. Novalis speaks of the unendingly accidental (2:123, no. 303). Words form peculiar combinations (2:811, no. 343). For instance, the teacher in the *Lehrlinge zu Sais* tells of one student to whom at times stars seem like men and at other times men like stars, stones like animals, etc. (1:202). As the construction "at times/at others" implies, metaphors are generated within a discontinuous temporal scheme. Neither the origin nor the end of a string of associations can therefore be located. Indeed, according to the *Lehrlinge,* the process of forming and breaking relationships continues into infinity (1:210, 205, 223).

To assure the repeated breakage of the temporal continuum, Novalis systematically looks out for contradiction: "Wir müssen die Dichotomie überall aufsuchen" [We must be on the lookout everywhere for dichotomy] (2:201). Only inasmuch as something passes (*übergehen*) into another sphere does it exist or arise (2:156, no. 453). Novalis's dialectical logic explains his predilection for litotic constructions, as in the fragment: "Rythmische Kraft. / negative Negation ist in der Positiven Position Eigensch[aft]" [Rhythmic force; negative negation is character in a positive position] (2:139, no. 370). It also accounts for his use of the prefix *Gegen:* "Alle Position ist aber Negation et vice versa – Folglich kann man allein [allem?] das *Gegen* anhängen" [Every position is negation and vice versa. Therefore one can add "anti" to everything] (2:138, no. 363). Indeed, if we can speak of teleological intention in Novalis, it is always to abet this ability to sever and disrupt: "mit fortdauernder Uebung wird auch diese Zerspaltung zunehmen" [with constant practice even this cleavage will increase] (1:205).[41] Schleiermacher likewise sees division as an unending and even divine principle: the Deity has set itself, as an immovable principle, infinitely to disunite (*entzweien*) its creation. Forces are pitted against one another in an eternally continuing play (StW 6). As in Novalis, such fracturing, of course, leads not to linear progression but to its opposite—radical temporality and the relativity of every positive form (2:309, no. 68).

As time never passes over into eternity, so too language cannot escape into the realm of absolutes.[42] The symbol cannot be identified with the thing symbolized. Indeed, one could attribute this nonconcurrence precisely to the delay of the parousia. Hans Blumenberg thus writes: what reality should be compared to, what constitutes it, does not exist for Novalis.[43] Friedrich Schlegel similarly believed that the copy can never become (*übergehen in*) its original (KA 1:289). Sounding like Saussure on the division between signifier and signified, Novalis warns:

> Auf Verwechselung des *Symbols* mit dem Symbolisirten – auf
> ihre Identisirung – auf den Glauben an wahrhafte, vollst[än-
> dige] Repraesentation – und Relation des Bildes und des Ori-
> ginals – der Erscheinung und der Substanz – auf der
> Folgerung von äußerer Aehnlichkeit – auf durchgängige innre
> Übereinstimmung und Zusammenhang – kurz auf Ver-
> wechselungen von Sub[ject] und Obj[ect] beruht der ganze

Aberglaube und Irrthum aller Zeiten, und Völker und Individuen. (2:637, no. 685)

[All superstition and error of every epoch, race, and individual resides in mistaking the symbol for what it symbolizes, in identifying them, in believing in true, complete representation, the relation between the image and the original, the appearance and the substance, in inferring external similarity, in thorough, inner agreement and correlation, in short, in exchanging subject and object.]

Novalis constantly reminds his reader that language is not referential but self-reflexive: an image (*Bild*) for him is neither an allegory nor a symbol of something foreign, but a symbol of itself (2:352, no. 185). In the famous "Monolog," Novalis writes that discourse merely plays with itself. In ludicrous error, people think they speak about things; what no one then realizes is that language is only concerned with itself (2:438). Novalis's polemic against "error" is strong and leads to astonishingly radical statements on language's determining being—for example, the statement that man is a metaphor (2:351, no. 174 and 2:354, no. 197).

On the basis of these fragments, though, it would be incorrect to claim that Novalis contests empiricism. Differential relationships constitute for him the warp and woof of reality, as of language. Reality is thus a text, woven like a discourse. It recognizes itself as reality only by virtue of relationships, form, appearance—in other words, *ex negativo* (2:89). Friedrich Schlegel had similarly written: "alles ist Beziehung und Verwandlung, angebildet und umgebildet" [Everything is relation and metamorphosis, connected and transformed] (KA 2:318). The empirical world stages unending play: "Dieser Satz, *daß die Welt noch unvollendet ist,* ist außerordentlich wichtig für alles. . . . Der Empirie wird dadurch ein unendlicher Spielraum gegeben" [This sentence, that the world is yet incomplete, has extraordinary importance for everything. Empirical existence thereby is granted unending room in which to play] (KA 12:42). The notion of *Beziehung* thus permits Novalis to define empirical being much like Condillac:

> Seyn drückt gar keine absolute Beschaffenheit aus – sondern
> nur eine Relation des Wesens zu einer Eigenschaft überhaupt
> aus – eine Fähigkeit bestimmt zu werden. Es ist eine absolute
> Relation. Nichts in der Welt *ist blos.* (2:156, no. 454)

> [Existence does not express any absolute condition—rather
> solely a relation of being to a quality. The capability of being
> determined. It is (a question of) absolute relation. Nothing in
> the world merely exists.]

As the above passage suggests, Novalis focuses his attention on
relations, exchanges, influences, and conflicts—in other words, on
the movement between two terms, on their interstices, at the
points where their distinctions dissolve. Unconcerned with refer-
entiality, the poet writes both about the strange unending in-
terplay (*Verhältnisspiel*) of things and about pure wordplay (2:438).
For the author of *Die Lehrlinge zu Sais,* language is a script of
ciphers that defies closure "und scheint kein höherer Schlüssel
werden zu wollen" [and seems not to want to become the key to
something higher] (1:201). Instead, the play of language follows
its own peculiar laws—those of rhetoric. Poetry then is a language
of tropes and puzzles (2:290, no. 1).

By focusing on how language functions, Novalis relegates to
virtual insignificance the question of the origin of language. The
search for origins would be, for him, a vain endeavor. Novalis's lack
of interest, however, was not shared by many eighteenth-century
thinkers such as Hamann, Goethe, Mendelssohn, and Süßmilch,
who were heatedly involved in the debate over Herder's prize essay,
Über den Ursprung der Sprache. The question of the origin of human
discourse had also engaged the minds of Vico, Condillac, and
Rousseau. Fichte too had contributed an early essay on the subject
entitled *Von der Sprachfähigkeit und dem Ursprung der Sprache.* For
these various authors, the question of origins always entailed the
concomitant one treated in Plato's *Cratylus*: were signs conven-
tional or natural? With his disregard for the origin of language,
Novalis dismisses the concept of the natural sign; for him all lan-
guage is arbitrary and contextually determined.

Faint suggestions, enigmatic allusions, and understated po-
tentialities are the fugitive moments in time that catch Novalis's
attention. Thus, the word *Schweben* recurs throughout his writing
as a token of this refusal to alight upon one element in an unend-
ing analogy: "Sollte es noch eine höhere Sfäre [als das Nur Seyn
oder Chaos] geben, so wäre es die zwischen Seyn und Nicht-Seyn
– das Schweben zwischen beyden – Ein Unaussprechliches, und
hier haben wir den *Begriff* vom *Leben*" [Should there exist a higher
sphere than mere being or chaos, it would be poised between
being and nonbeing—hovering between the two, ineffable. And
here we have the concept of life] (2:11).[44] Novalis was not alone
in wanting to protract suspense and suspension. In his contribu-
tion to the *Blüthenstaub*, Schlegel also prescribes the alternation
between absolute comprehension and absolute incomprehension
(KA 2:164).[45] Schleiermacher too writes of "ein stetes Hin- und
Herschweben" [a constant hovering to and fro] (StW 110).[46]

To depict this suspension or abeyance—this sustained tem-
poral play between absence and desired recuperation—Novalis
never lets his poetic voice reside in one mode for very long. As we
shall see in *Heinrich von Ofterdingen*, intimations are short and char-
acters are labile. In the preliminary work on his novel Novalis
prescribes the ideal poetic nature as not attached to any object, not
possessed by any true passion, but rather versatile and receptive
(1:385). Already in the Fichte studies, Novalis writes of the in-
stability (*Veränderlichkeit*) of character and indeed of relative char-
acter per se (2:193, no. 626).[47] As a consistent advocate of vari-
ability, Novalis constantly oscillates between desire for and
rejection of the parousia: "Jede immer getäuschte und immer er-
neuerte Erwartung deutet auf ein Capitel in der Zukunftslehre hin"
[Every always-deceived and yet ever-renewed expectation points to
a chapter in futurology] (2:530, no. 314).[48] In like manner,
Friedrich Schlegel called writing the mere intimation of what is
higher and infinite (KA 2:334). A major segment in the unending
Romantic text was, of course, Novalis's unfinished novel, *Heinrich
von Ofterdingen*, to which we now turn.

Heinrich von Ofterdingen

> What would be the narrative of a journey in which it was said
> that one stays somewhere without having arrived, that one
> travels without having departed—in which it was never said
> that, having departed, one arrives or fails to arrive? Such a
> narrative would be a scandal, the extenuation, by hemorrhage,
> of readerliness.
>
> —Barthes, *S/Z*

In my introduction I suggested that eschatological specula-
tions ultimately resist concrete depiction, for any attempt to nar-
rate the apocalypse falls short of its goal. The paradox then
surfaces: although the future ideal state is the most literary—be-
cause most imaginary—of themes, it also most eludes our repre-
sentation. Friedrich Schlegel therefore stipulates that any ex-
pression of the absolute must be in itself paradoxical: "Alle
höchsten Wahrheiten jeder Art sind durchaus trivial . . .
auszudrücken . . . nie eigentlich ganz ausgesprochen werden kön-
nen" [All the highest truths of every kind can only be trivially
expressed . . . are never really able to be uttered] (KA 2:366).

Novalis, aware of these difficulties of expression and of the
necessity of delay, asked in his Fichte studies how true, living phi-
losophy was to be depicted (2:116). Granted that philosophy has
something to say, that it sets out to confirm the existence of an
absolute, is that absolute even educible and representable? Once
posed, this question entails a more fundamental problem: meaning
relies upon the vehicle for its existence. When the absolute eludes
circumscription, its existence becomes questionable. Novalis,
making this extrapolation, asks the more radical question, comple-
menting and correcting the first: How is philosophy possible?
(2:132, no. 320).

Unlike his Enlightenment predecessors who were primarily
philosophers and not poets, Novalis tried imaginatively to portray
the millennium. He did so in the form of the fairy tale. Indeed, in
his later, more literary period, in which he was writing the tales of
Heinrich von Ofterdingen and the *Lehrlinge,* the cipher, the golden

age, comes more frequently to the fore. Just as he had queried how
true philosophy was to be portrayed, Novalis now asks how he can
depict the future. Indeed, he relates the two notions in *Das Allge-
meine Brouillon* of late 1798: the idea of philosophy is a contour
(*Schema*) of the future (2:680, no. 886). Letters from this period
give ample testimony to his concern with vivid description—with
filling out the *Schema* (1:732, 742). Novalis wonders how he can
possibly narrate the ineffable and avoid in the depiction of perfec-
tion the effect of boredom (2:676, no. 862). Yet he also poses the
other question: how is the golden age possible? In other words, the
notion of ineffability carries for Novalis the additional meaning of
the nonexistent and purely fictional.

The above reference from *Das Allgemeine Brouillon,* while call-
ing attention to the forward-looking thrust of philosophy, also im-
plies that the future can *only* be sketched schematically. In the
preceding fragment, Novalis also writes: "Der allg[emeine] in-
nige, harmonische Zusammenhang ist nicht, aber er *soll* seyn.
(Folgerungen auf Magie, Astrologie etc. − es sind Schemata der
Zukunft −)" [Universal, intimate, harmonic interconnectedness
does not exist but should. Implications for magic, astrology, etc.
They are contours of the future]. The divinatory "sciences," al-
though springing from a desire to control the future, never satisfy
this longing and thus remain imprecise. Representations of the
future are always vague and shadowy.

Keeping in mind the conclusions reached in the previous sec-
tions on language and the future, I want now to investigate the
extent to which the fairy tales of *Heinrich von Ofterdingen* function as
"schematic drafts of the future." Are they intended either to be
mere outlines or to preempt the future itself? Do they embody the
golden age equally, and, if not, does Novalis then establish in the
course of the novel a hierarchy among them?

The answer to these questions cannot reside solely in the tales or
in the thematically similar dreams themselves. The context or nar-
rative frame into which they are set is also germane. We need to see
how the tales function in the novel as a whole, aside from the fact
that we are studying a fragment. In some way they presumably

influence or predict Heinrich's future actions. I shall therefore re-
frain from extensive interpretation of the tales themselves, which
have already been the subject of sufficient allegorical speculation,
and will focus on the interpretations of the tales as presented in the
novel.[49] We can approach the novel assuming that the narrative
frame affects the inserts. In the play between the two, Novalis
explores a discourse of delay.

If we want to study endings, we should also look at begin-
nings, especially since Novalis expressly tells us that the goal of his
protagonist lies in his origins. Lacking a conclusion to the novel,
we can turn our attention to its beginnings for signs or prefigura-
tions of its development. Aside from the introductory poem, the
first lines of *Heinrich von Ofterdingen* are its most prosaic: as his
parents sleep, Heinrich lies awake hearing the wind beating
against the shutters and the wall clock ticking out its uniform
rhythm (1:240). Novalis presents us with a picture of mundane,
monotonous reality. These homely, unpretentious origins are most
likely not those to which Heinrich will return. Only with reserva-
tion can we even speak of this beginning as an origin or source.
The novel instead actually commences *in medias res* or, figuratively
speaking, in the fallen state, instead of in prelapsarian paradise:
Heinrich lies restless upon his bed. Instead of setting out to depict
childhood innocence, Novalis opens his novel with a rupture, with
the protagonist's loss of bearings; Heinrich remarks that he has
never felt this way before. He then inquires about origins—those
of the stranger he met that day. This search for an origin, a true
home, propels the narration forward and ironically sets Heinrich
on his circuitous journey *nach Hause*.

In the second half of the novel, Novalis offers a retrospective
interpretation of Heinrich's childhood. Entitled "The Fulfillment,"
this book was intended to respond to the first half, "The Expecta-
tion." The protagonist here claims that he has learned to appreciate
his homeland after having departed from it and seen other regions
(p. 376). Understanding is thus retrospective, belated, and never
contemporaneous with the interpreted act—in other words, not
truly speculative. Indeed the reader is given cause to doubt the
extent of Heinrich's understanding. His backward-turned glance

results in a glorification of a childhood which is tinged with nostalgia: "So ist die Kindheit in der Tiefe zunächst an der Erde, da hingegen die Wolken vielleicht die Erscheinungen der zweyten, höhern Kindheit, des wiedergefundnen Paradieses sind" [Thus in its depths childhood is closest to the earth, whereas the clouds are perhaps the semblance of a second, higher childhood, of paradise regained] (p. 378). Heinrich establishes here a hierarchy of intensity, whereby a future return to innocence ranks higher than the past, and both score better than the impoverished present. Thus the narrated time of the second part of the novel cannot represent a "fulfillment." Indeed Heinrich voices his faith in childhood with a certain degree of hesitancy, attenuating his claim with the word "perhaps." As his interlocutor Sylvester reminds us, clouds can also take the form of dark, serious, and terrible skies (378); Heinrich's metaphor therefore seems weak and ambiguous. Furthermore, according to Sylvester, the child lacks the Kantian sublime sense of man's moral superiority with which to conquer his fear of nature. Presented with these conflicting perspectives, the reader does not know how to value childhood. Heinrich might be wrong in trying to regain this paradise. His interpretation of his past threatens to be misleading.

This very problem of interpreting the past is introduced as a theme at the outset of the novel. Heinrich does not know how to interpret the tales of the stranger, nor can he even verbalize their effect on him: he does not know why he alone has been so moved by the stranger's speech (p. 240). The novel thus begins with an inexplicable, inarticulated, anterior event: "ich hörte einst von alten Zeiten reden" [Once I heard tell of faraway times] (p. 240). Novalis introduces his protagonist as somewhat deficient in verbal dexterity, as hampered in understanding because of an inadequate vocabulary. Heinrich surmises that there must be many words he does not yet know; were he to know more, he would be better able to understand (pp. 240–41). At the end of chapter six, Heinrich has not progressed very far from his starting point. His dream of Mathilde ends with her imparting to him a wonderful, secret word which fills his whole being. He tries to repeat it, but awakens only to have forgotten it (p. 326). Although the word precedes and even awakens consciousness, it cannot be grasped by the conscious mind.

Correct textual interpretation or hermeneutic certainty is all the more important for Heinrich because his knowledge is grounded not in experience but in books. We can trace even the first mention of the blue flower of Heinrich's dream back to the stranger's tales. The dream thereby loses much of its apparent visionary quality. The narrator constantly alludes to Heinrich's bookish learning; indeed the world, the reader is told, was only known to Heinrich through tales (p. 248). He has never visited his mother's homeland, Swabia, but after hearing her accounts and those of various travellers, the country seems to him like an earthly paradise (p. 248). The elder Ofterdingen supports this kind of vicarious *Bildung* by maintaining that old stories and writings are today the only sources from which to glean some knowledge of a transcendent world (p. 243). Heinrich's means of acquiring knowledge changes little throughout "The Expectation." The body of the text is devoted to storytelling or verse recitation, of which Heinrich is the recipient. Instead of diminishing as the novel progresses, the urgent necessity of exegesis only increases.

The use of the subjunctive further imprints the beginning of the novel with interpretive uncertainty. Heinrich says, "es ist, als hätt' ich vorhin geträumt, oder ich wäre in eine andere Welt hinübergeschlummert" [It is as if I had dreamt before, or as if I had slumbered over into another world] (p. 240). Heinrich here compares his childhood past to the unconscious state of sleep. What follows, though, is also a dream. We therefore do not know when Heinrich finally awakens.[50] The narrator continues the subjunctive mood into his description of the dream.[51] At first we believe the narrator to be reporting omnisciently, until he begins to question whether Heinrich himself knows what he is dreaming: the phrase "it seemed to him as if" recurs throughout the dream narrative (pp. 241–42). The effect on the reader is uncanny and estranging. Do people ever dream in the subjunctive? Does Heinrich indeed dream what he is narrated to be dreaming? The episode alerts its reader to its consciously fictive irreality. As the narrator says of part of the dream sequence, it is a "herrliche[s] Schauspiel" [spectacular theatrical play] (p. 241).

At this point in our inquiry into the beginning of Hardenberg's novel, we have to consider the inaugural function of the dream itself. There are three possibilities. The first is proleptic: Heinrich's dream of the face in the blue flower determines the action of the story, inasmuch as it anticipates or prophesies his meeting Mathilde in the last sections of "The Expectation." Heinrich's father, on the other hand, takes a second, different stance towards the interpretation of dreams. He maintains that they can be rationalized in purely psychological terms. Before telling how he once dreamed of Heinrich's mother as a blue flower, he claims that it was the most natural thing for him to have dreamt, once he had met her (p. 245). Mathilde, in whom Heinrich later finds a resemblance to the blue flower, is, of course, the niece of his mother. There is nothing predictive or divinatory in these apparently coincidental resemblances. Our third possibility, though, presents quite the opposite explanation of dreams—that they are opaque and uninterpretable. These three approaches are mutually exclusive, yet all are suggested by the frame.

Heinrich claims the first view: "Gewiß ist der Traum, den ich heute Nacht träumte, kein unwirksamer Zufall in meinem Leben gewesen, denn ich fühle es, daß er in meine Seele wie ein weites Rad hineingreift, und sie in mächtigem Schwunge forttreibt" [Certainly the dream I dreamt tonight was not accidental, without repercussions for my life, for I feel how it reaches into my soul like a vast wheel that is to drive it along in its mighty sweep] (p. 244). I have already suggested, though, that the dream does not so much initiate Heinrich's quest as it is itself instigated by the stranger's tale. As Novalis said in his theoretical writings, every true beginning is secondary (2:380, no. 284). We further suspect that the dream of the cornflower was not revelatory, when we learn that the old Ofterdingen also had a similar dream. We therefore cannot exclude the possibility that Heinrich's father had mentioned the blue flower to him at a moment before the narration began. In other words, we cannot uncover the origin of the flower motif.

Our ignorance of origins is further complicated later in the text when Heinrich chances upon a book written in Provençal. As he glances at its pictures of faces that seem familiar, the story appears to match his own, just as his father's dream also mirrors the one he had. But these three stories of Provençal poet, father, and son are temporally estranged and causally unconnected. We do not know whether one anticipates or prefigures the other. Heinrich's future promises to differ from his father's bourgeois style of life.[52] But how does it differ from the medieval singer's life? Presumably Heinrich's career could reincarnate that of his double but at a higher level of accomplishment, or it could be a mere repetition.[53]

This ambiguity is left unresolved in the novel, largely because Heinrich's viewing of the Provençal book does not induce a change in his development. He is indeed filled with utmost delight and avidly studies the pictures, but he cannot understand the language of the written text. The book resists ultimate interpretation and full comprehension: its final pictures are dark and incomprehensible. Just as this episode sketchily evokes a past that is somehow related to Heinrich's story and even perhaps influences or generates it, so too does it raise questions about Heinrich's future. By not giving the Provençal manuscript an ending, the narrator refuses to prefigure the end of his own narrative. Heinrich's future is left undetermined, open, and mysterious. This passage, classified by Lucien Dällenbach as a "mise-en-abyme,"[54] thus resists closure in two ways. Its relationship to the narration is sketchy, suggestive, and not fully explicit. It also thematizes this hermeneutic incompleteness by lacking both an ending *and* a beginning: the Provençal book has no title.

The novel thus pursues the very problem with which it begins, namely the questioning of and questing for origins. We can interpret Heinrich's dream as this pursuit of an origin or of a significant primordial past. In this search Heinrich proceeds from one enclosure to the next. He enters an opening in a cliff which leads to an interior cave with fountain and pool.[55] Here Heinrich bathes. He then swims down the river leading from the basin into the mountain. At this point, another dream is set into the first:[56] "Eine Art von süßem Schlummer befiel ihn" [Some kind of sweet drowsiness overcame him] (p. 242). Awakening from this second slumber, Henrich finds himself beside yet another fountain. Here, next to the source, is a light blue flower. Its petals form a wide, round collar, from the middle of which a delicate face gazes up at Heinrich (p. 242). This process of encapsulation marks an effort to draw closer to the center or origin of these manifold concentric circles. At each successive encapsulation, the contained becomes the container, the unveiled the veiled, and the inner the outer; the concentric shows itself to be excentric. Thus the progressive enclosings turn out to be a series of reversals instead. In the course of the linear narrative, they appear as displacements of one another. This movement carries on indefinitely, because the center cannot be found.

As we have seen, the blue flower—the apparent telos of the dream—is a false origin because it is derivative. The stranger, whose identity and native land are also unknown,[57] mentions the flower the day before. In addition, the flower does not represent the "source" itself but stands displaced, adjacent to the fountain. We cannot therefore speak of the dream's center.[58] The successive encirclings move diachronically and randomly, so that no point can be said to encompass the whole. In other words, the moments of the series are not perceived together or synchronically by an omnipresent mind,[59] which interprets simultaneously the fantasy being dreamed. Such is especially the case with the vision and its loss depicted at the end of chapter six. Heinrich dreams that Mathilde tells him a magical, secret word, which he forgets upon awakening. A rift opens between the full, sensuous, yet unpredictable and random consciousness of the dream state and an impoverished, yet rational waking state. Heinrich awakens to continue his quest.

Heinrich's surmise that his dream was no mere chance calls for confirmation later in the novel. The narration thus continues after the dream or grows out of it, because the latter needs to be motivated within the text. The reader expects some clarification. The father's dream, also narrated in the first chapter, offers a parallel to Heinrich's but is not an explication of it. Indeed, as the chapter ends abruptly with the father's narration but with no account of

Heinrich's reaction, we feel that the second dream has posed more enigmas than it has solved. Heinrich's father dreams that understanding will be granted to him on the day of St. John: "Wenn du am Tage Johannis gegen Abend wieder hieher kommst, und Gott herzlich um das Verständniß dieses Traumes bittest, so wird dir das höchste irdische Loos zu Theil werden" [If, on the day of St. John, you return here towards evening and entreat God to explain this dream to you, the highest earthly fortune will be imparted to you] (p. 247). But chapter two begins by stating that the day of St. John had passed (p. 248). Thus, symbolically speaking, the opportunity for explication has slipped away, and the rest of the novel begins with the quest for renewed opportunity. The lack of a sufficient interpretation propels the story forward, and the subsequent chapters carry with them the hope for resolution or *Erfüllung*.

The problems posed by Heinrich's dream—its abyssal inner structure and its relationship to the frame as an incomplete outline of the future that wants narrative confirmation and interpretation—prefigure the problems that arise regarding the other inlaid sections of the novel, i.e., the three fairy tales. "Prefigure" is perhaps not the correct word, because it can imply progressive development. Instead, the initial chapter of *Heinrich von Ofterdingen* establishes an *exemplary* structural pattern that is repeated at different intervals throughout the work.[60] It initiates or generates a series of narrative insets, each of which attempts anew the process of encapsulation. The process of embedding is repeatedly broken by the reintroduction of the narrative, just as Heinrich always awakens abruptly from his dreams. The end of a fairy tale or dream signals the sudden reentry of the frame whose ongoing narration stands in opposition to the closed, self-contained, timeless structure of the preceding account. Enclosure becomes nonclosure. Novalis defines this play of teleological satisfaction and doubling-back as follows:

> Der Gang der Approximation ist aus zunehmenden Progressen und Regressen zusammengesezt. Beyde retardiren – Beyde beschleunigen – beyde führen zum Ziel. So scheint sich im Roman der Dichter bald dem Ziel zu nähern, bald wieder zu

entfernen und nie ist es näher, als wenn es am entferntesten zu
seyn scheint. (2:272, no. 98)

[The process of approximation is composed of increasing pro-
gressions and regressions. Both retard, both quicken, both lead
to the goal. So it seems in the novel that the poet now ap-
proaches the goal, now distances himself from it, and is never
closer to it than when he appears to be most distant from it.]

Seen separately and in themselves, the fairy tales function as tokens
of progressivity. However, as digressions halting the narrative,
they act as relapses.[61] Ideally, the narrative would link together the
various inserts. But do the tales indeed stand consecutively and
causally *nacheinander* instead of contiguously *nebeneinander*?[62]

The main obstacle to the integration of the fairy tales is their
obvious antiquarian or antedated interest. This tone of interpreta-
tion is set by Heinrich's father, when he says that the days have
passed when the divine ones appeared to men in dreams (p. 243).
Heinrich himself locates the heights of poetic inspiration in the
past: in former times the art of poetry was more widespread, and
everyone possessed a few of the writer's skills (p. 254). The mer-
chants who narrate two of the novel's three tales, the Arion and the
Atlantis stories, likewise speculate that all of nature must once
have been more meaningful. Traces of it, mementos for the pres-
ent, have remained, but the art of bygone generations and a sen-
sitive feeling for nature have disappeared (pp. 256–57).

The merchants value *Märchen* then not for their meaning,
which is not only antedated but also lost to the reader of the pres-
ent. Instead the fairy tales are a vehicle of entertainment—an ex-
ample of the "free play" to which Novalis imputes such high value
later in the novel and in the fragments: "Das Gemüth sehnt sich
nach Erholung und Abwechslung, und wo sollte es diese auf eine
anständigere und reitzendere Art finden, als in der Beschäftigung
mit den freyen Spielen und Erzeugnissen seiner edelsten Kraft, des
bildenden Tiefsinns" [The mind longs for recreation and change,
and where should it find these in a more decent and pleasing way,
than in the pursuit of free play and in the products of its most

noble faculty, creative reverie] (p. 251). Much like the old king at the beginning of the Atlantis *Märchen*, Heinrich's travelling companions see poetry as one of the precious commodities enhancing life (p. 259).[63] It merely helps pass the time away pleasurably and offers no direct application to the present. Indeed, just as Klingsohr's tale occurs in a mythical, timeless realm, so too the Arion and Atlantis tales take place in an ahistorical, mythical past. The two stories told by the merchants recall an absence. They evoke happy, bygone days in implied contrast to the materialistic present. The *Märchen* thereby become inverted projections of present deficiency. The implication is that Heinrich shall effect a change at some future stage in the novel, an assumption which only emphasizes present dearth and casts the desired utopia elsewhere. Novalis writes of this deferral to Friedrich Schlegel in a letter dated December 10, 1798: "Der *Kaufmann* ist jezt an der Tagesordnung. . . . Das Andre muß warten" [the businessman is now an everyday occurrence. All else must wait] (1:680).

In sharp contrast to the deconstructive implications of the narrative frame, Novalis scholars have often interpreted the *Märchen* as incarnations, embodiments, or emblems of the golden age and as the manifestation of the ubiquitous and glorious imaginative faculty. Since their main protagonists are poets, Novalis's *Märchen* by themselves undoubtedly celebrate the magical powers of verse. At the close of each of the three tales, Arion, the young bard, and Fabel respectively triumph over destructive forces and reinstate social order. But cast in the narrative framework, the tales either substitute for an intended eschatological utopia or tell us that this ideal end state can only be repeatedly approximated or circumscribed in poetical fictions. There never comes a point where the frame and the tales coincide in what they describe. The narrative always reminds its reader that it is a vehicle of radical temporality—that temporal gaps cut one section off from the next. The discontinuous structure suggests therefore not that the end of the novel will see the apotheosis of the poet but that writing fictionalizes the eschaton and in so doing points to its absence. In other words, Novalis's narrative never *is* that which it describes.

His is a narrative that is never present to itself and that constantly postpones such a moment of reconciliation. What the tales are supposed to be telling is projected into the future.

To make clear the above claims about the relationship of frame to insets, I want to focus on the transitional points between them—the gaps where we would expect the interstices to be. The second chapter, for instance, ends with the Arion tale. Its circular structure is a gesture of its self-enclosed nature: with the help of the indebted sea creature, the treasure is returned to its owner (p. 259). Without any commentary on the Arion legend, the third chapter then begins with the narration of the second tale: "Eine andere Geschichte, fuhren die Kaufleute nach einer Pause fort, die freylich nicht so wunderbar und auch aus späteren Zeiten ist, wird euch vielleicht doch gefallen" [Another story, the merchants continued after pausing, will perhaps please you, although it is not so wonderful and comes from more recent times] (p. 259). A *Pause* or break marks the lack of transition from one narration to the next.

The Atlantis tale ends with a reference to its fictional, antiquarian nature. No one knows what happened to the country of Atlantis, but legends tell that it disappeared (*den Augen entzogen*) in mighty floods (p. 275). Belonging to the past, Atlantis escapes present scrutiny. Resuming the narrative frame, chapter four immediately follows upon the above passage with rather mundane reporting. The road was hard and dry; a few days of journeying passed without the slightest interruption (*ohne die mindeste Unterbrechung* [p. 276]). When we consider the break in continuity between the third and fourth chapters—i.e., the deletion of commentary and the absence of interpretation—, the phrase "without the slightest interruption" reads almost ironically. The fifth chapter, in contrast, begins with another reference to disconnections: after some days on the road, the travellers come to a village at the foot of a few pointed hills that are interrupted (*unterbrochen*) by deep ravines (p. 285). Like the described landscape, Novalis's text is marked by figurative chasms, breaks, and suspensions. Each new chapter signals a new beginning, loosely or tangentially connected to the previously narrated string of events.

Before turning to the problem of the interrelationship between the various inlaid *Märchen* and dreams, we need to consider the tie between the tale told by Klingsohr at the close of "The Expectation" and its introductory frame. In chapter nine, Klingsohr narrates his tale in fulfillment of a promise made to Heinrich in the previous chapter. Here Klingsohr first comments that the writing of stories is a difficult task, to which a young poet is rarely equal. He then goes on to say that he does remember a tale he once composed, although it distinctly shows traces of his immaturity (p. 335). Supposedly, although we hear no further critique of the Fabel *Märchen*, Klingsohr has written better poetry, which the reader then never witnesses. Also implied is that a future narration, presumably Heinrich's, will surpass Klingsohr's abstract allegorical tale, a product of the latter's inexperienced youth.[64]

According to Klingsohr, poetry in general is still at an early stage in its development: it is not mature enough to portray a poet who would simultaneously be a hero, a divine emissary (p. 333). The sublime eludes depiction, especially for the apprentice poet. Klingsohr concludes that there are limits to representability. Whenever the poet tries to overstep them, his depictions lose their necessary compactness and form; they become an empty, deceptive absurdity. Young poets especially are susceptible to such extravagances (p. 333). If Klingsohr is correct—the text at this point does not lead us to doubt the authority of his voice—Heinrich, whose experience is grounded in secondhand information, has not yet answered the poetic calling.[65] From two perspectives then, the end of "The Expectation" is indeed intentionally incomplete, anticipatory, or future oriented: we await significant development in Heinrich's career as a poet, and we expect the narration of a tale surpassing Klingsohr's. In other words, Novalis keeps the novel in a constant state of transition.

Just as Klingsohr's story, anticipating another and better tale, projects beyond its opening and closing lines, it also duplicates itself within these boundaries. Like Heinrich's dream of the blue flower, Klingsohr's tale is composed of encapsulated, yet successive, episodes which repeat while recasting the plot of the entire tale.[66] For instance, seeing the constellation of the phoenix (*das*

Sternbild des Phönixes), symbol not merely of palingenesis but also of cyclical repetition, the child heroine Fabel begins to sing:

> Der Morgen ist nicht weit.
> . . . .
> *Ein* Herz wird in euch wallen,
> Von Einem Lebenshauch.
>
> (p. 351)
>
> [Morning is not far. *One* heart shall well up in you, from one breath of life.]

Fabel therewith foretells the outcome of the story in which she is also the prime agent. Her song is in turn preceded by another insert towards the beginning of the tale. Singing "as if in a thousand voices," a lovely bird forecasts the development to come:

> Wenn Fabel erst das alte Recht gewinnt.
> In Freyas Schooß wird sich die Welt entzünden
> Und jede Sehnsucht ihre Sehnsucht finden.
>
> (p. 340)
>
> [Once Fabel wins back ancient privilege, the world shall ignite in Freya's womb and every yearning shall find its match.]

By preempting the ending, Novalis weakens the teleological movement of the tale. A repetitive structure is grafted onto a teleological one. Fabel's song, while predicting, both repeats and substitutes for the entire action.

Parallel to Fabel's realm (poetry) is the realm of the shadows. The court of the moon, this world within a world, in turn contains a treasure chamber where theater plays portray a microcosm of the universe. Here the events of the entire tale are suggestively traced:

> Die Szenen verwandelten sich unaufhörlich, und flossen endlich in eine große geheimnißvolle Vorstellung zusammen. Himmel und Erde waren in vollem Aufruhr. . . . Ein Scheiterhaufen thürmte sich empor. . . . Plötzlich brach aus dem

> dunklen Aschenhaufen ein milchblauer Strom nach allen Seiten
> aus. . . . Bald waren alle Schrecken vertilgt. Himmel und
> Erde flossen in süße Musik zusammen. Eine wunderschöne
> Blume. (p. 348)

> [The scenes were constantly changing and finally flowed to-
> gether in a great, mysterious performance. Heaven and earth
> were in turmoil. A funeral pyre grew skyward. Suddenly from
> the dark pile of ashes a milky blue stream poured forth round
> about. Soon all fears were stilled. Heaven and earth flowed
> together in sweet music. A wonderfully beautiful flower.]

The notions of play or game (*Spiel*) run throughout the tale.
Both symbolize the imitation of external events in an imaginary
form, thereby calling attention to the fictive status of their frame.
At the outset, for instance, the king and his daughter engage in a
fascinating game of stellar constellations drawn on leaves—an en-
chanting image for the hieroglyphs we read on the pages of Har-
denberg's novel. Like the scenes in the moon's treasure chamber,
the leaves continuously form changing configurations. Again at the
end of the novel, the image of the theater play—a world within a
world—appears. With Fabel's aid, the moon promises to delight
the royal couple with theater performances in the kingdom of the
Fates (p. 364). In addition, Perseus brings the king a chessboard,
and Sophie explains that all war has been banished to this game (p.
363). What happens here is the reduction and repetition of the
previous action of the story in miniature. The *Schauspiel* and
Schachspiel mirror and, in an aesthetic form, contain the entire tale.
Novalis comments on this process in the second part of the novel:
"Das Weltall zerfällt in unendliche, immer von größern Welten
wieder befaßte Welten" [The universe breaks down into infinite
worlds, which are always contained by more immense worlds]
(1:379). And earlier in the Fichte studies he writes: "Jedes Ding
steckt im höhern Dinge, oder weitern – extensivern und inten-
sivern Dinge" [Everything is hidden in something greater, or more
expansive, extensive, intense] (2:151, no. 445). Klingsohr's tale,
already embedded in the novel, now encapsulates other imaginary
constructs. The framed becomes frame. In the words of *Die*

Lehrlinge zu Sais, the play becomes iterative, unending, and immeasurable (1:219, 225).

Perseus also carries to the king a distaff with which Fabel will continue to spin her tales: she will eternally delight, spinning out of herself an unbreakable, golden thread (p. 363). Unlike the evil character, the "Schreiber," who merely copies given texts, Fabel generates verse out of herself—from the heart. In other words, poetry is not referential but self-reflexive. It is also eternal; as a token of the open-endedness of the text, the phoenix now descends to sit at Fabel's feet.

This constant retelling and specular revision is actually thematized towards the end of the tale in the symbol of the mirror. The father lies asleep in a bath of molten gold over which Ginnistan bends to see her reflection. The gold then becomes a mirror, "der alles in seiner wahren Gestalt zurückwerfe, jedes Blendwerk vernichte, und ewig das ursprüngliche Bild festhalte" [that reproduces everything in its true form, destroys all optical illusion, and eternally holds to the original image] (pp. 360–61). Just as the framed becomes frame, the specular image becomes the original and the reflection the reflected. The realm of fiction and affabulation becomes unexpectedly real; the *Bild* and the *Spiel* are not imitative but *ursprünglich.*

Yet Heinrich's initial dream and Klingsohr's tale are not the only instances where apparent mirroring actually inverts and displaces. The tale of Atlantis similarly embeds various renditions of its own story. The first inlaid poem describes an encapsulation. The youth enwraps the princess's lost talisman (a carbuncle worn in the middle of her necklace) with a poem. The stone itself is engraved with a mysterious writing, which the youth compares to the image of the unknown beloved in his heart. Playing on the word *heart,* the poem concludes: "Wird dieses [Herz] auch das Herz des Herzens haben?" (p. 265). The complicated analogy, the layered encapsulation, and the dense play on words make it difficult to distinguish the literal meaning of the last line.[67] What contains and what is contained?

The next embedded lyric, the bipartite song that the youth performs at the king's palace recapitulates the action of the tale and serves the function of narrating to the court the events that are already familiar to the reader. Both sections conclude by preempting the end of the tale: the poet becomes son of the king and thus heir to the throne.

Klingsohr's tale shares with the other two inlaid ones the theme of redemption and restoration through poetry. Each new story therefore calls to mind its preceding sister narration. They are structurally interchangeable. Indeed, rather than forecasting a future state, the inserts refer to one another. Yet, even though in each case the tales end on a positive note, their respective endings are not powerful enough to halt or even sublate the entire narration. Instead of embodying the eschaton, the fairy tales displace it. Thus, given the *ongoing* teleological thrust of the entire novel, each new attempt to narrate the entry of the golden age promises to be better than the last. Hardenberg finds each succeeding portrayal insufficient and reformulates it in new guise, while continually projecting the ultimate *Erfüllung* into the future. The expectation of resolution generates new tales; Fabel continues to spin. And indeed, part two opens with a poem containing the line, "Fabel begins to spin" (p. 366).

Referring to the various tales, one Novalis scholar, Gordon Birrell, calls this repetitive structure ritualistic—in particular the insertion of songs which foretell the action:[68] "The underlying structural and thematic similarity of Novalis's works is not the result of an impoverished imagination but of a profoundly religious one, which sought to reiterate the ritual process toward triumph over death on as many levels as possible."[69] But ritual suggests strict observance and undeviating iteration. Novalis's speculative play, however, is not repetitive and probably not religious. Proportion and coherence characterize instead the kingdom of the sculptured flowers of ice and snow with which Klingsohr's tale begins (p. 339). Fire, the element of the phoenix, consumes and transfigures this static and timeless realm. The *Schauspiel*, we remember, changes unpredictably and unceasingly.

As each reformulation differs from the next, we can see each rendition not as a reenactment of a ritual but as one in a series of repeated attempts to circumscribe the ineffable. The writer searches

for a point where speculative vertigo would cease. Yet as long as
Novalis delays the end, and endings are always—however
slightly—varied, we cannot speak of the embodiment of the golden
age in Novalis's novel. The telos is constantly changing, multiply-
ing itself, and shifting its position. Indeed Schleiermacher could
have been characterizing his friend's novel when he claimed that, in
writing, everything requires "einer doppelten und dreifachen
Darstellung . . . , indem das ursprünglich Darstellende wieder
müßte dargestellt werden . . . durch vervielfältigte Reflexion"
[double and triple representation, for what does the original portray-
ing must be portrayed again, through reduplicated reflection] (StW
319–20).

Just as the tales are temporally set apart from and thematically
contrasted with the frame, so too are there moments when the
linear temporal movement of the narrative is diverted and a brief
glance is cast towards an enigmatic past or future. For instance, at
unpredictable stations in the text a character will experience déjà
vu. Responding to the merchants, Heinrich muses that it seems as
if he had somewhere in the depths of his past heard similar views
on poetry (p. 256). As is typical, though, of the systematic eva-
siveness of the novel, Heinrich cannot specify the memory. The
fleetingly introduced character Zulima likewise experiences a pale
déjà vu. Having been abducted to a foreign land and rendered the
victim of a godless present, she pursues an eccentric course. But
she discerns in Heinrich's features odd similarity with someone
from her former, happy life (p. 282). The novel is further spotted
with such instances. It seems to Heinrich, when he hears the
miner's song, that he had heard it somewhere before (p. 297).
Zyane appears to Heinrich like an old acquaintance (p. 372), and
Heinrich believes he sees in Sylvester the miner standing before
him (p. 374). But in all three cases our protagonist does not probe
the latent coincidence further—and the narrative continues. The
past, while seeming to influence the present, escapes closer scru-
tiny. Recollection thereby elicits the presentiment that in the fu-
ture all will cohere.[70] These intimations are unending, however, as
Novalis says in the *Lehrlinge* (1:219).

Heinrich indeed does speak of dark intimations (p. 254), and the hermit, the owner of the Provençal book, refers to presentiments as the angels that accompany us here on earth (p. 313). Thus, while his thoughts, like those of the miner (p. 294), are preoccupied with former times, the hermit yet appears to himself like a dream from the future (p. 308). With his gaze focused on messianic time, he clings to neither the present nor the past. Caught between the no-longer and the not-yet, the present is for him a vale of tribulation (pp. 301, 311). Although the hermit pieces together history out of hope and recollection (p. 305), his ultimate effort falls short of its goal: "Wir kommen nur zu unvollständigen und beschwerlichen Formeln" [We only arrive at incomplete and cumbersome formulas] (p. 305). Does the second part of the novel bring us any closer to an end, to completion or fulfillment?

"Die Erfüllung" begins in a symbolic wilderness landscape. Heinrich finds himself on a narrow path. Noontide has passed, and the pilgrim's glance is cast once again towards the bygone days (p. 368). Our expectations of reversal or clarification are thus disappointed. What underlies the cliché about Romantic yearning—and indeed the novel is replete with references to *Ferne* (pp. 249, 250, 266, 273, 280, 298, 331, 347, 366, 368–69)—is actually a complex network of opaque temporal relationships, a labyrinth of indistinct yet provocative reflections. The self is repeatedly displaced from the present, as the poem beginning "Die Erfüllung" states: "Und was vordem alltäglich war / Scheint jetzo fremd und wunderbar" [what formerly was ordinary, is now strange and wonderful] (p. 366). For example, the narrator in the second part of the novel comments upon Heinrich's new state of mind. Past and future have so intimately conjoined for him that he stands apart from the present (*weit außer der Gegenwart*) [pp. 370–71]). This perception corresponds to the merchant's view that former and future ages arise in us, as from deep caves, in order to tear us away from a familiar present (pp. 255–56). And in his last fragments, Novalis wrote that mankind actually lives within the past or future—least of all in the present (2:844, no. 451).

Throughout his novel Novalis consistently evokes the past and future, avoiding mention of the present while paradoxically always resting within its sway. In other words, he continually keeps both archē and telos in abeyance. In Hardenberg's temporal strategy, past and future overlap. For instance, in the initial poem to the second part, "The Monastery or the Forecourt," whose title alone suggests a prologue to future development,[71] Novalis writes: "Hier Zukunft in der Vergangenheit" [Here future in the past] (p. 366). Later in the same poem he similarly states metaleptically: "Und was man geglaubt, es sey geschehn, / kann man von weiten erst kommen sehn" [What one believed had happened can only be seen coming from afar] (p. 367). Focusing his attention on these temporal horizons, the persona is always estranged from himself: "Nichts war noch nah, ich fand mich nur von weiten, / Ein Anklang alter, so wie künftger Zeiten" [Nothing was still near, I found myself only from afar, an echo of former, as well as future, times] (p. 366). As this verse suggests, Novalis never conjures up the future; he only offers an *Anklang,* a foregoing echo or *Nachhalle.*[72] He thus creates what Schlegel called *"echappées de vue ins Unendliche"* [glimpses into the infinite] (KA 2:403), which evince the immeasurable distance more than sight the eternal. In his Berlin manuscript Hardenberg comments upon this intentional evocation, this focusing on interstices: "Zwischen jedem Capitel spricht die Poësie" [Poetry speaks between each chapter] and "[Das siderische Wesen] spricht nun immer zwischen den Kapiteln" [The stellar being now speaks always between chapters] (1:392).

We recall Novalis's statement that the novel arises from the deficiencies of history (2:829). Friedrich Schlegel had also written: "der Sinn für Fragmente und Projekte sei der transzendentale Bestandteil des historischen Geistes" [the receptivity for fragments and projects forms the transcendental part of the historical spirit] (KA 2:169, no. 22). This originary lack and awareness of the fragmentary prompts the longing for completion and propels the novel forward: it generates the narrative. Indeed in *Heinrich von Ofterdingen,* Novalis perpetuates deficiency by repeatedly pointing to eccentric moments and by disrupting durations. His is "die Kunst, auf eine *angenehme* Art zu *befremden"* [the art of estranging in a pleasant manner] (2:839, no. 431). He reiterates teleological intentions while never fulfilling them. This ongoing, continuous, yet deficient present—Novalis's term is *Zeit* as opposed to *die goldene Zeit*—is janus-faced. It glances both backward and forward in time, simúlating thereby the sensation of a temporal, sublime expanse. But neither past nor future, neither archē nor telos are to be perceived or circumscribed, even furtively in the symbol.[73]

Even in what Tieck defined as the end of the novel (1:413), in "The Marriage of the Seasons," Novalis describes the cessation of time schematically and sequentially:

> Führe man schnell den Wagen herbey, wir holen sie selber
> Erstlich die Zeiten des Jahrs, dann auch des
> [Menschengeschlechts.
> Erst zur Sonne, holen den Tag. Dann zur Nacht. Dann nach
> Norden. Winter. nach Süden. . . . Dann zur Jugend. zum
> Alter Zur Vergangenheit Zur Zukunft.
>
> (p. 404)

> [Quickly drive up the carriage, we will bring them ourselves, first the seasons, then the ages of man; first to the sun, to pick up day, then to the night, then to the north, winter, to the south, to youth, to old age, to the past, the future.]

How does the writer describe the new aeon without retaining successive binary oppositions? In other words, how is apocatastasis, or the return of all things, possible in a linearly conceived narrative? Hardenberg's oeuvre implies that it is not. In *Das Allgemeine Brouillon* he writes: "Die Unendliche Schwierigkeit dieses Problems kann auch nur successive und Stückweise d.h. in unendlichen Raum und in unendlicher Zeit gelößt werden" [the infinite difficulty of this problem can only be solved successively and in pieces, i.e., in infinite space and time] (2:564).[74] Indeed, according to Tieck, Novalis planned to follow *Heinrich von Ofterdingen* with six other novels. By anticipating the arrival of yet another supplementary golden age, Novalis perennially delays the parousia.[75] For Novalis, then, there is never one single universal history but rather a plurality of temporal unfoldings: "Alles Göttliche hat eine Geschichte" [All things divine have a (hi)story] (1:222). As

Schleiermacher suggests, these diverse stories diverge from one another: he speaks of the "Verschiedenheit des Weges" [the differences in the path taken] (StW 306).

If then, we are permitted to use the word *apocalyptic* in Novalis criticism, it should signify this constant *annihilation* of the previously written material under the promise of a new aeon to come. We indeed recall Novalis's using the word *Apocalypse* in its present-participial form "offenbarend" (2:416, no. 457; 840, no. 434). In the last fragments he likewise speaks of "eine fortwährende Erlösung in der Natur" [a constant redemption in nature] (2:826), and in the *Lehrlinge* of the ongoing history of the world (1:206). Schleiermacher wrote of "das große, immer fortgehende Erlösungswerk der ewigen Liebe" [the great, always ongoing work of redemption of eternal love] (StW 240). And in the *System des transzendentalen Idealismus* Schelling, much like Novalis, wrote that God never exists but *reveals* himself constantly (Schröter 2:603). Just as Novalis's *Geschichte* of Heinrich is a never-ending intertwining of multiple tales, so history for Schelling is "eine nie ganze geschehene Offenbarung jenes Absoluten" [a never fully transpired revelation of the Absolute] (2:603).[76] Each new and always partial revelation exposes its preceding versions as fragmentary and temporal. The period of transition, the future perfect, never glides into *adventus*. Schelling observes that we cannot say when the latter will begin, for its arrival would mean that we would cease to exist (*so wären wir nicht* [2:603–4]). As we have seen, Novalis refuses to sustain the notion that writing could ever prefigure an atemporal moment. For him, a writing which would claim to do such a thing would err. The absolute could then command the arrest of the poet's pen.

"Die Unendlichkeit eines guten Gedichts": The Romantic Reader

> Die Theorie der Bibel, entwickelt, giebt die Theorie d[er]
> Schriftstellerey oder der Wortbildnerey überhaupt – die
> zugleich die symbolische, indirecte, Constructionslehre des
> schaffenden Geistes abgiebt.
>
> —Novalis

We have witnessed Novalis's views on the unending process of writing—in the image of Fabel beginning to spin in the poem following Klingsohr's tale and in Novalis's plans to compose sequels. So too does Hardenberg speak of the unending nature of reading and interpretation. In the second part of *Heinrich von Ofterdingen,* Novalis writes: "Ewig wird er lesen und sich nicht satt lesen und täglich neue Bedeutungen . . . gewahr werden" [He will read forever and never read enough; daily he will become aware of new meanings] (1:377). The act of reading is as unending as that of writing precisely because, according to the Jena Romantics, critical response should partake of the nature of its subject. Friedrich Schlegel thus writes that poetry can only be criticized by poetry (KA 2:407, no. 87). He also maintains that a theory of the novel would have to be a novel itself, fantastically reproducing the eternal imagination (KA 2:337). Schlegel does not mean reduplicating through paraphrase but rather extending the fanciful impetus of the so-called original into the critical work. If the review prolongs the original, it follows that the closure which the former evades cannot be performed by the latter: a classical work, Schlegel writes, must never be fully understandable (KA 2:149, no. 20). Similarly, Novalis stipulates that a poem be totally inexhaustible (2:826). When the critic engages in the role of the author, the latter ceases to be the origin of canonical texts.[77] His writing becomes impersonal, anonymous, lacking a signature. Indeed, it is the "classical" work that most invites amplification by the reader. In what sounds like an appeal to the reader, Schlegel closes the *Athenäum* fragments by stating that even the most universal, complete works of poetry and philosophy appear to avoid final synthesis (KA 2:255, no. 451).

Just as the critic plays the role of the author, so does the author act as critic. The impersonal author embodies a multiplicity of readers. For Novalis, writing is a process of constant revision with the result that the writer resembles his reader: "Die meisten Schriftsteller sind zugleich ihre *Leser* – indem sie schreiben – und daher entstehn in den Werken . . . so manches, was dem Leser zukömmt und nicht dem Schriftsteller" [Most authors are at the same time their readers, by the fact that they write. Therefore so much arises in their works that applies to the reader and not to the writer] (2:398–99, no. 79). Indeed Novalis brings critical reception—this necessary appendix to any work—into the text itself. In other words, the work becomes self-reflexive: "Recension ist *Complement des* Buchs. Manche Bücher bedürfen keiner Recension. . . . Sie enthalten schon die Recension mit" [The book review complements the book. Many books do not need to be reviewed, for they contain the interpretation already in themselves] (2:605, no. 581).

This does not mean, though, that even the most perfect work of art can ever be totally present to itself or, in other words, speculative in the Hegelian sense. Its own *raison d'être* always escapes it. Friedrich Schlegel writes, for instance, that even the most complete statue is only a disconnected, incomplete fragment, not a self-contained, perfected whole (KA 1:295). Thus, whenever the author is his own critic, he must avoid the reader's trap: he must curb the desire to complete his work. Schlegel writes:

> Manches Erzeugnis . . . ist . . . kein Werk, sondern nur Bruchstück. . . . So mächtig ist aber der Trieb nach Einheit im Menschen, daß der Urheber selbst, was er durchaus nicht vollenden oder vereinigen kann, oft gleich . . . ergänzt; oft sehr sinnreich und dennoch ganz widernatürlich. (KA 2:159, no. 103)

> [Many products are not works but fragments. However, the human drive towards unity is so powerful that the author himself often supplements what he cannot totally complete or unify—often very ingeniously but still rather unnaturally.]

One of the means to resist closure in writing would be to diversify the intentions of a work—like assimilating reading to the act of writing. Novalis further amplifies the notion of the text. He says that a book can be interesting from various perspectives. The author, the reader, an intent, an action, even its pure individual existence can be the axis around which a book is centered (2:193, no. 632).[78] Such diversity makes reading engaging. A work will be most interesting when it can be understood and loved in several ways, when it has several meanings and motives (*Veranlassungen* [2:399, no. 82]). By bringing the tasks of reviewing and reading into the text, Novalis turns his writing into a compendium of the various kinds of imaginative activities: "Mein Buch muß die kritische Metaphysik d[es] *Recensirens,* des Schriftstellens, des Experimentirens, und Beobachtens, des Lesens, Sprechens etc. enthalten" [My book must contain the analytic metaphysics of reviewing, writing, experimenting, observing, reading, speaking, etc.] (2:598, no. 552).

In so developing and diversifying what could be understood by the notion of a text, Novalis comments on what reading entails. His remarks are neither prescriptive nor descriptive. On the contrary, Novalis states that there is no such thing as a commonly accepted reading. Reading is a free activity; no one can prescribe how and what a person should read (2:399, no. 79). Although autonomous and unconstrained, any reading does not wantonly distort the text. Novalis sees the reader not so much as interpreting or misinterpreting but as in fact originally constructing the book. He arbitrarily emphasizes things, thereby making a book out to be what he wants (2:399, no. 79). Moreover, the text constantly eludes and even antagonizes the reader: "Die höchsten Kunstwercke sind schlechthin *ungefällig* – Es sind Ideale, die uns nur approximando gefallen können – und *sollen* – ästethische Imperative" [The highest works of art are simply unaccommodating. They are ideals that can and should only halfway please us—aesthetic imperatives] (2:652, no. 745).

The unendingness of the Romantic work thus lies not only in its specular nature—the fact that it reflects unendingly on the conditions of its own being. This Benjamin suggested in his dissertation *Der Begriff der Kunstkritik in der deutschen Romantik.* In addition and even in contradistinction to this quality, the Romantic text is open-ended because its significance never resides within itself but is always displaced onto its varying receptions. Each text becomes dissolved and dispersed in a plurality of readings. Lacoue-Labarthe and Nancy observe that this absence of the "work of art" results in "une débauche d'oeuvres qui ne ferait plus oeuvre" [a debauchery of works that would no longer form *a* work].[79] The unending text generates a proliferation of texts.

In his poetics of the extended text, Novalis could have been describing his own reading of the Bible; it was not just another reading of Scripture but rather its written extension: "Wer hat die Bibel für geschlossen erklärt? Sollte die Bibel nicht noch im Wachsen begriffen seyn?" [Who has declared the Bible to be closed? Should not the Bible still be in the process of growing?] (2:766, no. 97). Hardenberg's concept of the future—as the fictive construct of an imagination which both anticipates revolution and yet protracts temporality, which both posits a future and in the same breath denies its realization—can be exemplified by reference not only to *Heinrich von Ofterdingen* but also to his epistolary debate over Schlegel's "Bible project." Here Hardenberg theorizes on how Revelation is both prolonged and yet postponed.

Hardenberg wrote: "Mein Buch soll eine scientifische Bibel werden – ein reales, und ideales Muster – und Keim aller Bücher" [My book wants to become a scientific Bible—a real and ideal model—the seed of all books] (2:599, no. 557). The extent to which Novalis planned to pattern his work on Holy Scripture, to adapt and develop its imagery, can be observed in the last sketches to the *Lehrlinge* which immediately precede his writing of *Heinrich von Ofterdingen* in the early months of 1800. Novalis jots down the words: "Das *Kind* und sein Johannes. Der Messias der Natur. *Neues Testament* – und neue Natur – als *neues Jerusalem*" [The Child and its St. John. The Messiah of nature. New Testament and a new nature as the New Jerusalem] (1:236). References to Christian mythology also appear in the paralipomena to "The Fulfillment" (1:398). And in *Heinrich von Ofterdingen* itself, Novalis writes that the Bible and narrative theory (*Fabellehre*) are constellations in the same orbit (1:381). To what extent did Novalis intend his novel to be not only an innovative exegesis of the Scripture but also in itself a gospel, the absolute text, and the seed of all books?

On November 7, 1798, Novalis responded to Friedrich Schlegel's suggestion of a common Bible project. Novalis admitted that he had also considered composing an ideal Book that would be nothing other than a critique of the notion of a Bible, an essay in the universal method of biblicizing, the introduction to a true encyclopedia (1:672–73). The Bible as canon can thus be seen to prefigure the absolute book which the Romantics tried to write (KA 2:265, no. 95). This ultimate text, according to Hardenberg, would take the form of a compendium or encyclopedia.[80] In his letter to Friedrich, Novalis intimates that he conceived his writing as a preface to this extensive project. However, according to the next letter dated December 10, Hardenberg does not even want to attempt the writing of an introduction. He retracts his vote of solidarity: "Auf Deine Gedancken von Religion und Bibel geh ich jezt nicht ein – kann auch nicht eingehn, weil mir das Meiste davon cimmerisch dunkel ist – einige treffliche Einfälle . . . ausgenommen" [I shall not pursue your ideas on religion and the Bible here—I cannot pursue them, for most of it seems illusively obscure to me, except for a few excellent notions] (1:679). Even though the proposal in its entirety was too amorphous, vague, and auspicious, a few of its ideas were nonetheless seminal. Thus, although the project was for all intents and purposes abandoned abruptly by Novalis, who made no further reference to it, various of its key notions persisted and can be traced throughout his other writings.

In *Christenheit oder Europa,* for example, Novalis speaks of the historical significance of Christianity and its sacred text, plotting thereby both his own place in the tradition as well as his revision of it. He accuses Luther of abolishing Catholic medieval tradition only to institute in its place the tyranny of the letter. The Bible as sole canon restricted and repressed the workings of the spirit:

> Luther . . . führte einen andern Buchstaben und eine andere Religion ein, nemlich die heilige Allgemeingültigkeit der Bibel, und damit wurde leider eine andere höchst fremde ir-

dische Wissenschaft in die Religionsangelegenheit gemischt –
die Philologie – deren auszehrender Einfluß von da an un-
verkennbar wird. (2:737)

[Luther ushered in another letter and another religion, i.e., the
sacred general validity of the Bible. Unfortunately, another
very foreign earthly science was thereby confused with re-
ligious matters—from then on the consuming influence of
philology was unmistakable.]

Novalis aligns himself with the countermovement to which
Boehme and Zinzendorf belonged—a movement in which the
members, by freely interpreting biblical canon, dispensed with its
restricting letter. Indeed we saw how eighteenth-century Pietists,
in the wake of Luther's endorsement of laymanship, insisted upon
their right to interpret the Bible, especially Revelation. The book
whose canonical status since Origen was most hotly disputed gave
rise to the most uncanonical, subjective readings. Thus someone
like Herder stands within Pietist exegetical tradition inasmuch as
he prescribes personal empathy with John in order to understand
him. The Pietists and Herder paved the way for the Romantics'
idiosyncratic reading/writing of the Bible. Indeed, Novalis called
the Protestant church service a continuous apotheosis of the Bible
(2:764, no. 87), because of its emphasis on preaching and hence
interpretation and dissemination of the Holy Word. The sermon
was a fragment of the Bible (2:676, no. 862). Moreover we can see
the late Schleiermacher's lectures on hermeneutics (published in
1838) as an outgrowth of the Jena Romantics' theories on subjec-
tive interpretation.

For the Pietists, Revelation was the main book that solicited
interpretation, because it claimed to predict for its reader the near
future: "Blessed is he that readeth and they that hear the words
of the prophecy, . . . for the time is at hand" (Rev. 1:3). Thus,
anyone undertaking to explain its imagery was bolstered in his
endeavor by the conviction that the time was ripe and the end
imminent. The Johannine text promised full meaning only to the
last generation. What fanned the Pietists' exegetical excitement
equally informed the Romantics' rereading, indeed rewriting, of
Scripture. Both fostered the belief that they were heralding a new

age to supersede the old. According to Novalis, a new era, the sacred age of eternal peace (2:750), was dawning, which in its symbolism resembles the Christian millennium while radically modifying it. Christian tradition thereby serves as a *negative* springboard for future development. In *Christenheit oder Europa*, Novalis calls Christianity "das Zeugungselement der Religion" [religion's reproductive environment]—the same phrase he uses earlier in the essay to characterize "true anarchy" (2:749, 743). And writing to Friedrich Schlegel on January 20, 1799, Hardenberg comments on how the negativity of Christianity appealed to him: "Deine Meynung von der Negativitaet der Xstlichen Religion ist vortrefflich – das Xstenthum wird dadurch zum Rang der *Grundlage* – der *projectirenden Kraft* eines neuen Weltgebäudes und Menschenthums erhoben" [Your opinion regarding the negativity of the Christian religion is superb—Christianity is thereby raised to the status of a foundation, of the projectile force of a new earth and humanity] (1:684).

The Romantics' enthusiasm thus derived from their conviction that they were writing a new gospel. Novalis indeed asked if there could not also be a gospel of the future (2:753, no. 9). And in the Jena lectures of 1800–1801, Friedrich Schlegel called Christianity an open-ended, future-oriented religion, "a religion of the future" (KA 12:79). The Bible, the former text of all texts, suddenly becomes subject to correction and extension—to what Novalis called "biblicizing" (1:673). When succeeded by a new impending canon, the former, closed canon is rendered incomplete and apocryphal or secondary: "In den Evangelien liegen die Grundzüge künftiger und höherer Evangelien" [In the Gospels lie the basic lineaments of future and greater gospels] (2:831). The once-authoritative work with its fixed commencement and conclusion, Genesis and Revelation, now becomes open-ended. Novalis thereby reduces the status of the Bible to that of a fragment or seed. Schlegel too writes of the new Bible as an unending book, a book eternally becoming (KA 2:265, no. 95).

Novalis considered himself to be preeminently engaged in writing this extension of the Bible. In a statement like "Der Heilige Geist ist mehr, als die Bibel. Er soll unser Lehrer des Xstenthums seyn" [The Holy Spirit is more than the Bible. It should be our teacher of Christianity] (2:844, no. 451), Novalis lays claim to divine afflatus: "Wenn der Geist heiligt, so ist jedes ächte Buch Bibel" [When the Spirit sanctifies, every true book is the Bible] (2:274, no. 108). Novalis clearly designates this book as his own: "*Beschreibung der Bibel* ist eigentlich mein Unternehmen . . . (Erhebung eines Buchs zur Bibel)" [The description of the Bible is what my endeavor is about, the elevation of a book to the Bible] (2:602, no. 571). Indeed, Novalis writes of extending Lessing's *Erziehung des Menschengeschlechts* into a second part, with the implication, of course, that Novalis's contribution would be the new, albeit not the ultimate, gospel Lessing predicted (2:830, 393).

But insofar as Novalis's enterprise either claims spiritual invigoration or partakes of scriptual authority, it is subject to imminent erasure as well. His book is also only disseminative. The Bible, whether it be the sacred or secular version, is caught up in the process of change: "Diese erweiterte Poësie ist . . . ein Problem, was nur durch Annäherung gelößt werden kann. . . . Man könnte jene höhere Poësie die *Poësie des Unendlichen* nennen" [This amplified poetry is a problem that can only be solved through approximation. One could call this higher poetry the poetry of the infinite] (1:657). Novalis breaks with preceding poetologies and yet attenuates his radical pose by calling his beginnings weak in comparison with their potential for unending development: "Wir sind jezt nur im Anfang der SchriftstellerKunst" [We are now only in the incipient stages of the art of writing] (2:194).[81] We recall Novalis's saying that his Bible project is only an introduction to true encyclopedistics (1:673). Thus, while inscribing Holy Scripture into his own overarching scheme, Novalis realizes that his endeavor is also inscribed or contained in a wider, ever more integral venture whose full execution is imaginary. Friedrich Schlegel categorically states:

> Aus dem Satz nun: Alle Wahrheit ist relativ, – denn über jede Combinazion wird sich noch eine höhere, und so ins Unendliche, finden lassen – folgt nun unmittelbar der Satz: *Alle Philosophie ist unendlich.* . . . *Absolute Wahrheit kann nicht zugegeben werden.* (KA 12:92–93)

[Now from the proposition 'all truth is relative,' because
for every synthesis one finds a higher one, and so forth into
infinity, follows directly the proposition, 'all philosophy is
unending.' Absolute truth cannot be conceded.][82]

The Romantics thus keep the end in abeyance.

Hardenberg probably dropped the *Bibelprojekt* when he realized
it was destined to be as incomplete as the most exhaustive book,
the Bible itself. In relinquishing this enterprise, though, Novalis
did not stop toying with other orthodox beliefs. Another example
of his radical alteration of Scripture is his doctrine of manifold
incarnations. Novalis envisaged the Messiah, the Holy One of
God, appearing on the earth "im Pluralis" (2:729). In the *Europa*
essay, he writes of "das innige Empfängniß eines neuen Messias in
ihren tausend Gliedern zugleich . . . unter zahllosen Gestalten
den Gläubigen sichtbar" [The intimate conception of a new Mes-
siah everywhere at once, visible to believers in innumerable forms]
(2:745). Man becomes the new Messiah: he proclaims himself and
his new gospel of nature (1:235). Friedrich Schlegel likewise infi-
nitely multiplies and apportions divine attributes:

> Wenn jedes unendliche Individuum Gott ist, so gibts so viele
> Götter als Ideale. . . . Wem dieser innre Gottesdienst Ziel
> und Geschäft des ganzen Lebens ist, der ist Priester, und so
> kann und soll es jeder werden. (KA 2:242, no. 406)
>
> [If every infinite individual is God, then there are as many
> gods as there are ideals. Whoever makes this inner religious
> service his goal and the business of his entire life becomes a
> priest. Everyone can and should become one.]

In the fragments of 1800, Novalis writes that God can appear to
him in every person. We can study eternities in Christianity, ever
higher, more diverse, and more magnificent (2:827, no. 388). Di-
vine inspiration is not the exclusive property of the past. Instead, the
spirit searches continuously for new vehicles: "Geistvoll ist das
worinn sich der Geist unaufhörlich offenbart – wenigstens oft von
neuen, in veränderter Gestalt wieder erscheint – Nicht blos etwa nur

Einmal – so im Anfang – wie bey vielen philosophischen Systemen"
[Spiritual is that within which the spirit unceasingly reveals itself—
or at least often reappears anew in changed form—not just once, say,
in the beginning, as is the case in many philosophic systems]
(2:240, no. 31). Novalis draws this process of duplicating into the
future and corrects his initial thought by rewriting it in the future
tense: "Jedes Menschen Geschichte soll eine Bibel seyn – wird eine
Bibel seyn" [The story of every person should be a Bible—will be a
Bible] (2:556, no. 433).

Thus we can see Novalis carrying this contesting of authority
over into his Romantic poetology. His concept of the author re-
flects this undermining of religious orthodoxy. Novalis extends the
scriptural canon, just as he amplifies the notion of the text. The
sparagmos of the Messiah figure matches the previously observed
shift of emphasis from author to reader. The result of the superses-
sion is in both cases paradoxical: the secondary or posterior figure
borrows from the authority of the first, although the former's sov-
ereign status is put into question. The dividing line between the
activities of exegesis and writing becomes unclear. Novalis both
continues and extends the eighteenth-century tradition of radical
scriptural interpretations, and he innovatively transforms his in-
heritance. In so doing, he prescribes the role his reader should play.

As our concluding example, we can turn again to *Heinrich von
Ofterdingen* and the scene of reading in the cave. We recall how the
episode enacted what Schlegel prescribed as the enigmatic por-
trayal of an enigma (KA 2:334). Heinrich leafs through a book
whose language he does not understand but whose pictures he en-
joys, probably because he recognizes himself in the protagonist.
Other characters look vaguely familiar. The manuscript lacks not
only an ending—like Novalis's own text—but also a beginning. It
has no title. The novel mirrors itself here in miniature *ad infinitum.*
As readers, our questions probably resemble the unuttered ones in
Heinrich's mind: is his life prefigured here, or does he belatedly
reenact a tale told before? Will the illuminated manuscript have
been Heinrich's autobiography? Furthermore, how is this unreada-
ble text related to the parallel dreams of father and son narrated in
the first chapter? Novalis prematurely curtails all these narratives,

with the result that our questions are left unanswered. We are only given intimations that Heinrich's vocation, in the text Novalis did not write, will be that of a poet whose life completes what the hermit's manuscript does not. This episode precludes, though, the very act of closure it invites by virtue of this very unending mirroring not only between the episode and its text but also between Heinrich as reader and ourselves. The novel becomes a fragment,[83] like the Provençal book Heinrich reads. Because both texts lack closure, their reception becomes all important. However, our readings are destined to be unending. We see ourselves as Heinrich, browsing eclectically through the hermit's library "mit unendlicher Lust" [with infinite pleasure], reading "zu wiederholten Malen" [over and over again], all the while wishing nothing more longingly than to be able to read the book and to grasp it completely (1:312).

3 Hölderlin

The Threat of the Fixed Letter

Who shall hold it, and fix it, that it be settled awhile, and
awhile catch the glory of that ever-fixed Eternity, and compare
it with the times which are never fixed, and see that it cannot
be compared.
—Augustine, *Confessions*

. . . darüber
Hab ich zweideutig ein
Gemüth, genau es zu sagen.
—Hölderlin, "Das Unendliche" from *Pindar Fragmente*

In his third version of "Mnemosyne," Hölderlin writes:

Vorwärts aber und rükwärts wollen wir
Nicht sehn. Uns wiegen lassen, wie
Auf schwankem Kahne der See.
(StA 2:197, ll. 15–17).

[Forwards, however, and back we do not want to see. To let
ourselves be cradled, as if on a swaying skiff of the sea.]

The death wish implicit in these lines is clear in a similar passage
from *Hyperion* where the protagonist abandons himself to the rock-
ing of a boat, which he imagines belonging to Charon. He dreams
of drinking from the cup of forgetfulness (3:49). In both cases the
speaker, while trying to escape extremes, falls prey to what
"Mnemosyne" elsewhere terms excessive desire: "Und immer / Ins
Ungebundene gehet eine Sehnsucht" [a longing always seeks the
unbound] (2:197, ll. 12–13). Given Kant's faith in progressivity,

Schiller's or Fichte's moral restlessness, and Novalis's energetic exploration of the temporality of discourse, Hölderlin's willful intention to block out the past and future and to remain in a secure, restrictive present sounds disturbing and aberrant, despite the lulling imagery. To be sure, we have seen how not only Novalis but also Schelling, the Schlegels, Karoline von Günderrode, Jean Paul, and the author of the *Nachtwachen* have focused attention on a prolonged present by either delaying or subverting endings. In these cases, the eschaton is never attained, precisely because it remains the product of a self-conscious imaginative faculty. It is knowingly fictive or u-topic. Despite its delay, the apocalypse constantly entices its writers to articulate ever more elaborate and fantastic renditions. For Hölderlin, though, the imaginative journey is not so playfully or harmlessly undertaken: "Aber bös sind / Die Pfade" [but the paths are evil] (2:197, ll. 8–9). Even the desire to resist taking the road into the future and to remain in a forgetful present is an example of unbounded, misguided longing. Hölderlin knows too well that he cannot stem the advent of crises and of error. To the same degree, neither can he will to delay the parousia. And, above all, he knows that language misleads. Its potential for stating presence awaits to be realized. The following is a study of how closure constitutes, for Hölderlin, exemplary error.

In this chapter I plan to investigate the post-1800 context of the lines, "Vorwärts und rükwärts wollen wir / Nicht sehn." The poetic works that fall into this period are, of course, the hymns, the elegies, the late lyric fragments, and the revisionary work on "Patmos" and "Brod und Wein." To all readers, even those nominally exposed to Hölderlin, the words from "Mnemosyne" seem to contradict a major tendency in his thought, the desire to do just the opposite: to construct a beatific history where human time culminates in the return of the gods. Tokens of such a secular salvation history are readily found at various stages in Hölderlin's poetic development. He brings the chiliastic elements from his early work to their full expression in the late hymns. Indeed, at first it seems to be an anomalous voice in Hölderlin that wishes to stave off parousia.

What characterizes this "conventional" Hölderlin who, qua adventist, espouses closure? The term "Kingdom of God" figures frequently in the correspondence of the Tübingen seminarians Hegel, Schelling, and Hölderlin (6:126). The tone of ecstatic anticipation is then heralded in Hölderlin's Tübingen hymns, beginning with the Klopstock-like "Bücher der Zeiten"—a catalogue of eschatological events. In "An die Vollendung," the persona apostrophizes perfection (1:75, l. 2) but does not yet claim to foresee its attainment. In the "Hymne an die Menschheit," the two "Hymnen an die Freiheit," and "Dem Genius der Kühnheit," however, the persona actually envisages the earthly appearance of the divine after first invoking it. This early Hölderlin, following Rousseau, sees a natural state as the origin and goal of mankind. Then during his Frankfurt period, Hölderlin links chiliastic imagery to the notion of beauty as the agent of reconciliation: "Es ist vorhanden – als Schönheit; es wartet, um mit Hyperion zu reden, ein neues Reich auf uns, wo die Schönheit Königin ist" [It is present as beauty. To speak with Hyperion, a new kingdom awaits us, where beauty reigns as queen] (3:237; 3:52–53). Beauty as parousia is Hölderlin's answer to Kant's split both of the noumenal from the phenomenal world and of duty from desire. He also herewith criticizes the narrowness he felt inherent in Fichte's solipsistic philosophy.

The chiliastic references in Hölderlin become even more pronounced after 1800. In the first version of the ode "Ermunterung," for instance, Hölderlin strongly voices his longing for divine afflatus:

> O Hoffnung! bald, bald singen die Haine nicht
> Der Götter Lob allein, denn es kommt die Zeit,
>   Daß aus der Menschen Munde sich die
>   Seele, die göttliche, neuverkündet.
>
> (2:33, ll. 13–16)

[O hope, soon, soon the groves will not alone sing life's praises, for the time shall come, when from human tongue the divine soul will announce herself anew.]

A mood of chiliastic expectancy then partially informs the closing lines of "Der Archipelagus": "und siehe! des Jahrs Vollendung ist nahe!" [for behold, the year's consummation is nigh] (2:111, l. 274). "Germanien" likewise ends by promising imminent parousia: "Wie anders ists! und rechthin glänzt und spricht / Zukünftiges auch erfreulich aus den Fernen" [How different it is! Distances away there gladdeningly gleams and speaks what is yet to come] (2:152, ll. 101–2). The closing of "Der Rhein" mentions the celebration of a marriage feast between the gods and mankind (2:147, l. 180). The visionary or prophetic voice finally pervades the entire structure of "Friedensfeier."[1] The theme of secularized chiliasm can therefore be quickly identified throughout Hölderlin's writings.

"Der Archipelagus" and "Germanien" not only intimate a future of reconciliation and peace but also reconstruct past human history. Just as Hölderlin on numerous occasions claims to foresee the parousia, so too does he glance "backwards" in time; references to memory and recollection frequently figure in his texts. For instance, following Schiller's model in the philosophic poems entitled "Die Götter Griechenlands" and "Der Spaziergang," Hölderlin traces in "Brod und Wein" the occidental history of man. In "Patmos," the persona flies to the Greek island, which marks a scene of reflection upon Christ's death and Ascension. By reenacting in the poem the story told in Acts and the Gospels, Hölderlin establishes "bestehendes" [what endures]. He locates "der veste Buchstab" [the stable letter]. This link between past and present leads into the future: German song shall further the Christian heritage (2:172, ll. 225–26). In "Der Archipelagus" the parousia contains within itself a commemorative or elegiac moment: the proud triumphal day concludes in quiet remembrance and thanksgiving (2:111, l. 277). The most intense moments are those in which we retain or recall the best of the past, as in "Der Rhein":

> bis in den Tod
> Kann aber ein Mensch auch

Im Gedächtniß doch das Beste behalten,
Und dann erlebt er das Höchste.

(2:148, ll. 199–201)

[even into death a man can retain in memory the best; then he
experiences the highest.]

However, these moments—both of recollection and of intima-
tion—demand closer investigation and shall be examined in greater
detail. If Hölderlin so highly values memory as the guiding or
controlling force that assures both continuity and stability in the
future and thus permits interpretation or hermeneutic confirma-
tion, how is the decease of memory in "Mnemosyne" to be under-
stood?[2] Why, in other words, does mourning—the token of mem-
ory's presence—err: "dem / Gleich fehlet die Trauer" [therefore
sorrow is wrong] (2:198, l. 51)?

I do not want to advocate a recantation or radical shift in Höl-
derlin's thought at the writing of those lines cited from
"Mnemosyne."[3] But I do wish to identify a notable, disturbing
moment in the late Hölderlin which has the potential of alerting us
to a problem that expresses itself in more than one line of his
poetry. The trepidation or even latent anxiety of the lines quoted
from "Mnemosyne" perhaps marks a prevalent tone in significant
opposition to the historical overview. How anomalous are these
verses? Are they perhaps symptomatic of a more cautious approach
to the parousia found at other stations in Hölderlin's writings—a
muting of the strong, perhaps too self-assured poetic voice claim-
ing divine afflatus? Where else does Hölderlin see memory unable
to construct or falsely construing a linear history?

"Mnemosyne" helps its reader return to Hölderlin's earlier and
contemporaneous writings with a new perspective and a keener
view. It exhorts us to read intertextually, or hermeneutically, ap-
plying insights gained from one work to another. Yet these lines
also encourage us to read, where necessary, against the grain of
traditional Hölderlin readings that have identified only those
strong, often concluding moments of happily valorized memory
and vision.[4] Given Hölderlin's principle of "Wechsel der Töne"

[alternation of tones], we can expect his text to be marked by reversals and interruptions, by different poetic voices pitted against one another. Is Hölderlin, though, exploring alternatives, or does he establish a hierarchy to their succession?

We need only return briefly to the poems just mentioned to find self-correcting elements. In "Der Rhein," for example, the celestial marriage is not eschatological but a moment either inscribed within flux (2:147, l. 183) or endangered by the oncoming night (ll. 193–94). "Der Archipelagus" also closes in subdued meditation in the midst of "die reißende Zeit" [devouring time] (2:112, l. 293). Such similar moments of calculated hedging appear, as we shall see, in "Friedensfeier." Indeed, as early as 1795 in the essayistic fragment "Hermokrates an Cephalus," Hölderlin ironically postulates what it would be like if the perfection everyone searches for and no one finds were actually already present (4:213). In general, whenever recollections and intimations of divine presence become too strong, Hölderlin backs away. In "Germanien," for instance, a too-intense recollection of Greece threatens to endanger the present: the persona wishes to refrain from fleeing back to a past (*Zu euch, Vergangene!*) that is too dear to him (2:149, ll. 12–13). In "Patmos," *bestehendes* can also imply restriction and fear of millennial change or of an all-too-searing parousia.

In this last hymn, to which I now want to turn in detail, Hölderlin deftly plots these various conflicting moments. Access, of course, to the late Hölderlin can only be wrested by attending to textual specificities. Although I therefore have to restrict my study primarily to "Patmos," references to other late works will confirm its exemplary nature. In "Patmos" Hölderlin tempers his defense of memory by intimating the danger of its collapse. The hope for divine presence is, in turn, countered by the refusal to speculate about its arrival. But if indeed the poet refuses to look backward or forward, the present, cut off from all referential and delimiting points of comparison, becomes meaningless. The voice of the poet is hollow. "Mnemosyne" again offers a disconsolate commentary: "Ein Zeichen sind wir, deutungslos" [a sign are we, meaningless] (2:195, l. 1). What, then, is the status of the sign, and how does language relate to the theme of the parousia and its delay? In this reflection on nonclosure and the sign, Novalis and Hölderlin move into the same ken.

To define the question at hand, let us start with Hölderlin's conclusion. "Patmos" ends with the lines:

> . . . der Vater aber liebt,
> Der über allen waltet,
> Am meisten, daß gepfleget werde
> Der veste Buchstab, und bestehendes gut
> Gedeutet. Dem folgt deutscher Gesang.
>
> (2:172, ll. 222–26)

[The Father, however, who reigns over all, loves most that the letter is kept fast and that what endures is well interpreted. This German song follows.]

This ending is not only vigorous and pithy but also axiomatic. It opens the end of the poem by prescribing the task of future German verse. As we know from Hölderlin's remarks on his translations of Sophocles and from his letters, modern poetry has a function distinct from that of the Greeks and, according to Hölderlin's binary typology, should follow a peculiarly occidental or Christian thematic. German in opposition to Greek verse, he suggests, should make use of its national traits; its content should be selected according to a Hesperidean worldview.[5] The last lines of "Patmos" reflect upon such an accomplishment, upon the poem's achievement—the reviewing of Scripture or "the fixed/stable letter"—as exemplary.

Yet at the same time that the persona defines the future of "German song," he relates it to a proven tradition, to *bestehendes*. The inheritance, though, it not gratuitous but instead must be cognizantly received and correctly interpreted (*gut / Gedeutet*). Once the poet-exegete performs his task well, he establishes historical continuity and duration. In these concluding lines, the poetic voice posits the retrievability of the past—or, to express their content litotically, as the persona notably refrains from doing, he refutes absence. Indeed, the adverb *gut* can equally function as an adjective: the existing should be interpreted as being intrinsically good.

This injunction originates, however, not with the persona but with God the Father, who reigns supreme (ll. 222–23). The prescriptive conclusion thereby gains considerable authoritative weight and even assumes the quality of an imperative mandate, issued by the divine progenitor who holds creation in control. The voicing of divine preference closes the text: the father-instance has the last word. Thus, our first impression of an open conclusion looking backward and forward in time is corrected by a sense that the persona longs for security, imposed boundaries, and for the assurance that *bestehendes* is good. Our perspective suddenly shifts: is Hölderlin intimating that writing/interpretation both recuperates the past and can be extended into the future, or is he actually more cautiously advocating temporal restriction? The text supports two opposed readings.

Other signs reinforce this additional, second interpretation. Compare, for instance, Hölderlin's "fixed letter" with Friedrich Schlegel's commentary on how the letter, in order to be effective, must be converted into its exact opposite: "Ohne Buchstabe kein Geist; der Buchst[abe] nur dadurch zu überwinden, daß er fließend gemacht wird" [Without the letter there is no spirit; the letter, however, is only to be overcome by being made fluid] (KA 18:344). This opposition of letter and spirit, also much debated by the Pietists, originates, of course, with Paul in his second epistle to the Corinthians: "God . . . hath made us able ministers of the spirit: for the letter killeth, but the spirit giveth life" (2 Cor. 3:6). Exposed during his childhood to Pietist circles, Hölderlin was certainly aware of their concern for inspired scriptural readings.[6] Oetinger, for instance, stated in his *Biblisches Wörterbuch*—a prelude to his last, incomplete work, the *Biblisches und Emblematisches Wörterbuch*, which was to be a compendium and interpretation of all natural and scriptural signs—that God gave us the office of scriptural exegesis in order that we could interpret the Bible spiritually and not literally.[7] The influence of Swabian Pietism resonates in a letter Hölderlin wrote to his mother in 1799 wherein he laments the discrepancy between the living scriptural word and its false exegeses. The scribes and pharisees of our day, Hölderlin writes, have turned God's word into a dead letter and the Godhead himself into an empty graven image (*Gözenbild*) [6:309–10]). Merging with this initial, Pietist influence on Hölderlin is that of the early Hegel and his critique of positive religion in the *Positivität* essay and in *Geist des Christentums*. From various sources, then, Hölderlin was aware of the danger of literal interpretation.

The word *Buchstabe* thus can contain two diametrically opposed meanings: the dead letter and the living letter of Scripture. Does Hölderlin, though, use the word *Buchstabe* in "Patmos" to refer exclusively to the latter? Lawrence Ryan operates the secularization switch and maintains the letter symbolizes the well-founded poetic rather than the interpreted scriptural word.[8] Yet, whether the letter means strictly secular or sacred writing, the implied contrast with spirit still holds and is even enhanced in Hölderlin's hymn by the attribute "stable." According to our alternate reading then, the ending intimates a submissive attachment to the past, even to the degree that it dominates the future.[9] Tradition can potentially suppress or petrify all attempts at innovation.

These conjectures further suggest that the laconic conclusion to "Patmos" may forcibly close its preceding text. The questions raised in the body of the poem would thereby be resolved or possibly even foreclosed by an assertive, authoritative ending, which claims to stabilize (*befestigt*) previously voiced uncertainties. On the other hand, if Ryan is correct in perceiving a self-reflexive statement at the close of "Patmos," does this mean that the end grants its previous lines the status of good, sound exegesis? What is the situation which *bestehendes* purports to remedy?

The last line of "Patmos" raises the question of whether Hölderlin accomplishes in his poem what he claims, at its end, to be the task of the German poet. *Bestehendes* implies that a continuous thread stretches not only through historical time but through the length of the poem as well. In contradistinction to Schelling's position, the writing of a philosophy of history would thus be possible. Hölderlin would divine a *bestehendes* and establish transitions between "the disparate pinnacles of time" (l. 10). How, though, would the sign/the letter permit Hölderlin to do so? In an effort to trace out the *bestehendes* and *der veste Buchstab,* we have to return, as readers on the eccentric path, to the beginning. We shall see whether the letter is indeed, as "Mnemosyne" suggests, uninterpretable and meaningless, preventing access either to the parousia or to the past.

"Patmos"

> Condamnés à . . . ignorer l'avenir et le passé de l'humanité et de la divinité et à y penser toujours.
>
> —Vigny

> Le récit n'est pas la relation de l'événement, mais cet événement même, l'approche de cet événement, le lieu où celui-ci est appelé à se produire, événement encore à venir et par la puissance attirante duquel le récit peut espérer, lui aussi, se réaliser.
>
> —Blanchot, *Le livre à venir*

"Patmos" begins by establishing the two poles between which the text then endeavors to mediate. Here Hölderlin announces the thematics of proximity and distance: "Nah ist / Und schwer zu fassen der Gott" [Near and difficult to grasp is the God]. [10] Divine presence renders interpretation difficult or subject to error. It thereby threatens to overwhelm and even annihilate the perceiving subject. The initially posited proximity is therefore corrected in the next line by the persona's awareness of spatial and qualitative separation. And yet in verse four the persona claims this difference to be the source of salvation (*das Rettende*). Separation insures the uniqueness of both God and man (the purely other and self) and instigates renewed attempts to understand their distinct natures. Hölderlin thus stipulates in a variant to "Der Archipelagus" that the interval separating the speaker from the gods must in fact be enlarged: "Aber weil so nahe sie sind die gegenwärtigen Götter / Muß ich seyn, als wären sie fern" [Yet because they, the present gods, are so near, I must act as if they were distant] (2:646, ll. 22–

23). As we shall see, this mapping and tracing out of the boundaries of divine closeness is the problem of the writer in particular. The speaker of "Der Archipelagus" is the writing self.

Distance and proximity imply temporal categories as well as spatial ones. Thus the first lines of "Patmos" express a certain chiliastic urgency. The parousia is imminent and yet beyond our full grasp. The first stanza describes in spatial terms the problem of temporal disparity:

> Drum, da gehäuft sind rings
> Die Gipfel der Zeit, und die Liebsten
> Nah wohnen, ermattend auf
> Getrenntesten Bergen.
>
> (ll. 9–12)

[Therefore, since the peaks of time are heaped round about, and those we most love live near, languishing on mountains most separate.]

In this alpine landscape, the proximity of the beloved ones is deceptive, for treacherous gorges and valleys isolate us from them. As an image of temporality, this passage suggests that, even though we know of monumental acts (*Gipfel*) performed in the past, these events are difficult to interpret. We are irrevocably belated; Hölderlin indeed uses two absolute superlatives to describe our temporal separation. By extension, our relationship to the future is also problematic. How can we bring God to us or help usher in the millennium? The rest of the poem addresses itself to these problems.

The collective voice (*wir*) of the poem longs to be like the eagles who also live in darkness or visual estrangement but still can overcome separation by tracing in their flight "leichtgebauete Brüken" [lightly constructed bridges] (l. 8). Indeed, in the poem "Rousseau" Hölderlin again compares the Spirit to eagles as harbingers of the parousia, albeit threatening. In "Patmos" these bridges or links between the temporally disparate mountain tops are what the final voice of the hymn claims to have discovered in *bestehendes,* at least according to our first reading of the last lines. The *Wiederkehr* of the last verse of stanza one expresses this very desire to return to the present after an excursion into the past, but it will be a return enriched by the wisdom and experience of previous ages. In other words, the first stanza sketches the need and yearning for full memory—"treuesten Sinns" [a mind most faithful] (l. 14)—which incorporates within itself correct interpretation. The antithesis of the first two lines will thereby presumably be overcome. But is our second reading of the very last lines (willful confinement to an impoverished, but secure and unassailable, present not threatened by the danger of divine proximity) perhaps truer to the entire text?

With the second stanza the persona's journey, his exploration of the antithetical poles, begins. Here the expanse of their effect and their mutual boundaries are tested. The poem is then the realm where the play and interaction between limits is investigated. Through his visionary experience, the persona endeavors to make the past more immediate to the imagination. He also brings the distant east into our ken. But his route is circuitous and marked by detours, and at certain boundaries his course is deflected. The poem thus is the staking out of a site marked by dislocation and disruption. This creation of a spacing—an interval and an interim, the tracing of an eccentric course—constitutes for Hölderlin the act of writing.

The poet is first transported from the present, i.e., from his own home (l. 20). The fatherland, despite its congenial familiarity, is the locus of deficiency and decline. Its yearning brooks (l. 23) intimate faraway goals. The time of day is twilight; the woods are darkening (ll. 20–23). This setting contrasts then with the sudden illumination provided by the sight of Greece: "in frischem Glanze . . . Im goldenen Rauche . . . Mit Schritten der Sonne" [in fresh radiance, golden haze, with the striding of the sun] (ll. 25ff.). The persona is blinded at the sight. The play of presence and absence is thus sketched in a geographical chiaroscuro.

The persona's return to his dim origins begins with his *Einkehr* to Patmos:

Und da ich hörte,
Der nahegelegenen eine
Sei Patmos,
Verlangte mich sehr,
Dort einzukehren und dort
Der dunkeln Grotte zu nahn.

(ll. 51–56)

[And since I heard that one of the nearby islands was Patmos, I much longed to turn in there and there to venture towards the dark grotto.]

In contrast to the shadowless Aegean waterways (l. 49), Patmos houses the somber cave of Johannine renown. Thus, in his flight to the past, the persona passes over Greece—described in superlative, sublime terms—to alight on a poverty-stricken island which, albeit Greek, commemorates a uniquely Christian event. But why the return to a place of deprivation?

Mythologically speaking it is accurate to refer to Tmolus, Paktol, Taures and Messogis as Greece, but geographically it is imprecise. Hölderlin writes: "Doch bald . . . blühte . . . Mir Asia auf" [Soon Asia blossomed before me] (ll. 25–31), referring of course to Asia Minor. Thus, in travelling to Patmos, the persona actually retraces his steps. Patmos lies close to the gates of Asia (l. 46) or before the continent, if a person travels from west to east, as the narrator initially does.[11] In itself, this detour would be insignificant, but it is one in a series of signs betokening eccentricity, a swerving aside and missing of the mark. Is the persona perhaps even willfully evading his intended goal? Only those forced to swerve from their object of desire visit the island—those who have been shipwrecked or who mourn the loss of their homeland or a departed friend (ll. 64ff.). The persona even comments upon the odd choice of Patmos over Cypros, home of Venus:

Denn nicht, wie Cypros,
Die quellenreiche, oder

Der anderen eine
Wohnt herrlich Patmos.

(ll. 57–61)

[For unlike Cypros, rich in springs, or any of the others majestically does Patmos dwell.]

The reader finds his expectations of parousia further reversed in the course of the hymn. No specific mention is made of the divine revelation but only of John's laments (l. 73). He mourns his departed friend (l. 66). What follows then is a striking evasion of the apocalyptic vision suggested by the title and a return instead to its antecedent event—Christ's life on earth. John's exiled existence on the island symbolizes the distance of divine being—not only of the Christian God but, as the evasion of Greece suggests, also of the gods of antiquity. Yet reflection on this divine absence generates the memory of the events portrayed in the Gospels, leading up to the time of John's abode on Patmos. The narrator recounts in cursory form the Last Supper, the Passion, the scene at Emmaus, Pentecost, and then Christ's final appearance on earth—His Ascension.

What motivates, though, the chronological reversal of the last two events? Two stations in the text can be construed as referring to both Pentecost and the Ascension. In the first instance, the descent of the Holy Spirit occurs after what could be understood as a reference to the Emmaus episode:

. . . und ihnen gieng
Zur Seite der Schatte des Lieben.
Drum sandt' er ihnen
Den Geist, und freilich bebte
Das Haus und die Wetter Gottes rollten.

(ll. 98–102)

[And the shadow of the beloved one accompanied them; therefore he sent them the spirit and indeed the house shook and God's storms thundered.]

The following stanza then depicts the last appearance and subsequent departure of Christ: "Izt, da er scheidend / Noch einmal ihnen erschien" [Now in departing He appeared to them again] (ll. 106–7). The central lines of this stanza, "Denn wiederkommen sollt es / Zu rechter Zeit" [for it should return in due time] (ll. 112–13), recall the angelic commentary on the Ascension: "This same Jesus, which is taken up from you into heaven, shall so come in like manner as ye have seen him go into heaven" (Acts 1:11). But the narrator, mirroring the disciples' unwillingness to accept their exiled condition—"und lassen wollten sie nicht / Vom Angesichte des Herrn / Und der Heimath" [for they did not want to depart from the Lord's visage and their home] (ll. 95–97)—also reconstructs a second time these last signs of Christ's presence. Despite the calling of the Spirit, the disciples are tied to a happier past, the memory or shadow of which they will not give up. Indeed, because this reminiscence is so excessive, in a later version Hölderlin changes the shadow accompanying the mourners on the road to Emmaus to a "Seuche," a pestilence.

At line 129, the disciples are once again gripped by the Holy Spirit: "Die Loken ergriff es, gegenwärtig" [it gripped their locks, instantaneously]. Yet simultaneously with, or immediately following, this token of presence God departs: "Wenn ihnen plözlich / Ferneilend zurük blikte / Der Gott" [when hasting away, the Lord suddenly glanced back at them] (ll. 130–32). In both examples of this temporal doubling back, Hölderlin reverses the traditional significance of the Holy Spirit's advent. Pentecost does not betoken continuing divine presence during Christ's physical absence but instead fits into the temporal period delimited by the Incarnation and Ascension. Our final impression of the Christian story renarrated in Patmos is then informed by the divinity's departure and the ensuing night. Indeed, Hölderlin's Christ knows only the Passion and not the Resurrection. He is the deity of death: "aber nicht zu leben, zu sterben warst du gesandt" [not to live, to die you were sent] (2:132, l. 72). At the Last Supper, as His heroes of death (l. 105) gather around, Christ announces or rather pronounces His crucifixion: "ruhigahnend den Tod / Aussprach der Herr" [in quiet surmise the Lord pronounced death] (ll. 83–84). As Hölderlin's emphasis on the Passion and Ascension suggest, Christ is always the departing, not the returning, deity. Hölderlin stops where the Gospels end, halting before the story narrated in Acts, the Epistles, and, most important of all, Revelation. [12]

The narrator retraces John's steps in Jerusalem: "es sahe der achtsame Mann / Das Angesicht des Gottes genau" [the attentive man carefully observed the Lord's visage] (ll. 79–80). But he fails to enact the latter's Patmos experience. Although a spirit transports the speaker to Patmos, he does not carry him into the future. How, though, are we to read the few lines in "Patmos" that refer to the parousia—to "rechte Zeit" [true, right time] as opposed to what Hölderlin refers to in "Brod und Wein" as "dürftige Zeit" [time of dearth] (2:94, l. 122)? In the middle lines, "Denn wiederkommen sollt es / Zu rechter Zeit" [for it should return in due time] (ll. 112–13), Hölderlin circumscribes the divine with the indeterminate *es*—much as in the lines already quoted referring to the spirit: "und nicht geweissagt war es, sondern / Die Loken ergriff es" [without being prophesied it gripped their locks] (ll. 128–29). Hölderlin thereby refrains from naming the divine. [13] To identify the nature of the Godhead, to describe the parousia, would entail error—the sign of inevitable human imperfection. In Hölderlin's words, such an attempt would be "untreu, / Der Menschen Werk" [untrue, man's doing] (ll. 114–15). Just as the kingly one (*Der Königliche*) suffers and breaks the staff himself (l. 111), so does he alone determine the time of the Second Advent: "Nicht alles will der Höchste zumal" [the Most High does not ordain everything at once] (l. 161). The central lines of "Patmos" are, as we have seen, an angelic pronouncement, not a prediction of future fact by human voice. Man does not exercise any influence on the coming of the millennium.

Hurrying the parousia indeed only arouses God's wrath: "Doch es zwinget / Nimmer die weite Gewalt den Himmel" [for the wide power of heaven will not be coerced] (2:48, ll. 55–56). The Lord hates untimely change (2:225, ll. 94–96). In a letter to his brother dated June 2, 1796, Hölderlin writes of the futility of trying prematurely to curtail the limbo of existence:

Freilich sehnen wir uns oft auch, aus diesem Mittelzustand von
Leben und Tod überzugehn in's unendliche Seyn der schönen
Welt, in die Arme der ewigjugendlichen Natur, wovon wir
ausgegangen. Aber es geht ja alles seine stete Bahn, warum
sollten wir uns zu früh dahin stürzen, wohin wir verlangen.
(6:210)

[Indeed we often long to traverse out of this intermediate state
of life and death, into the infinite being of a beautiful world,
into the arms of an ever-youthful nature, from whence we
departed. However, everything takes its normal course; why
should we precipitate ourselves too soon in the direction of
what we yearn for?]

Such a move would entail approximating (*gleichen*) the Deity's om-
niscience. Hölderlin writes, though, in "Friedensfeier": "Doch
nimmer kannst du ihm gleichen" [Yet never can you be like Him]
(3:535, l. 70). Cognates, of course, of the verb *gleichen* are the noun
Gleichnis, a comparison, and the verb 'to compare,' *vergleichen.* The
poet/persona can never find a figurative language in which to speak
accurately of the Deity. The overriding of human boundaries—
crossing the bar between a symbol for the Deity and the Deity
himself—is an act of violence incurring God's punishment:

Zum Traume wirds ihm, will es Einer
Beschleichen und straft den, der
Ihm gleichen will mit Gewalt.
(2:141, ll. 113–15)

[It becomes a dream to him who tries stealthily to seize it and
punishes him who tries forcefully to be like Him.][14]

To the same effect, a later variant of "Patmos" reads: "Grausam
nemlich hasset / Allwissende Stirnen Gott" [for cruelly God hates
all-knowing minds] (180, ll. 72–73).

In "Patmos" the second reference to the parousia, specifically
to the awakening of the dead at the Last Judgment (ll. 184–85),
confirms the alterity of God and denies the poet access to divine

intentions. Human deeds (*Menschen Werk*) are thus contrasted with divine workings:

> Denn sie [die Menschen] nicht walten, es waltet aber
> Unsterblicher Schiksaal und es wandelt ihr Werk
> Von selbst, und eilend geht es zu Ende.
> Wenn nemlich höher gehet himmlischer
> Triumphgang.
>
> (ll. 176–80)

[For men do not govern, but immortal fate does and their work moves of itself and hastens towards completion. When, namely, higher the heavenly march of triumph proceeds.]

Here the prepositional phrase "von selbst," given emphasis by the enjambement, is repeated from line 111. In this context, it again implies the exclusion of the speaker's involvement. The poet-persona totally eradicates all signs of personal volition and ascribes temporal change solely to fate. Even his own activity of writing becomes effaced and deficient when confronted with the song characteristic of the millennium (ll. 182–83). Only in the future will "der frohlokende Sohn des Höchsten" [the joyous son of the Most High] be named (l. 181).[15] Song in its ultimate form, presumably in spiritual tongues, differs from German verse bound to the letter (l. 226); in the future, the "Stab des Gesanges" [wand of song] will replace the letter and even the "Stillleuchtende Kraft aus heiliger Schrift" [silently shining strength from Holy Writ] (l. 194). Sacred Scripture thus now supplants and perhaps even obstructs direct vision. In "Friedensfeier" Hölderlin tells of the difference: "wo aber / Ein Gott noch auch erscheint, / Da ist doch andere Klarheit" [but where a god as well appears, there shines yet a different clarity] (3:533, ll. 22–24).[16]

How are we to understand the paradox, however, that Hölderlin can still allege the Deity's alterity while refusing to claim knowledge of divine intention? Perhaps the above statements bear not a descriptive but a self-reflexive import. They comment primarily upon the persona's present deficient utterance rather than on the parousia. After the two major passages in "Patmos" referring to the Second Coming, the narrator suddenly reverts—halfway through lines 186 and 113—to describing once again the time of spiritual desolation, the period in which he is writing. Although Hölderlin is working with a theme that demands inspirational treatment, he cannot claim divine afflatus *and at the same time* be aware that he is writing in a belated, secular age. The moments in the text referring to God's active presence are brief, fraught with the danger of incorrect naming and useless speculation.

Hölderlin avoids circumscribing the millennium not only in "Patmos" but also at other strategic moments in his late oeuvre. "Friedensfeier," we recall, ostensibly tells of the expected coming of a messianic figure, whether or not one wishes to specify the prince of the feast as Christ. The narrator alludes to the latter's past deeds and sacrifices, but only questionably can we assert that the persona does more than herald his coming. Hölderlin indeed here projects the eschaton into an indeterminate future. The persona calls upon the "Fürst des Festes" (3:536, l. 112), but the latter has not yet arrived. Further clues in the text suggest that the parousia is as yet delayed. We cannot say, for instance, that the feast has begun; guests are on their way, "kommend" (3:533, l. 10). The present is still deficient: "eher legt / Sich schlafen unser Geschlecht nicht, / Bis . . ." [our race shall not rest, until . . .] (3:536, ll. 112–13). Furthermore, the words "verkünden" [announce] (3:536, l. 119), "Hoffnung" [hope] (3:537, l. 122), "Ahnen" [intimation] (3:537, l. 127) and "Versprechen" [promise] (3:537, l. 129) imply the retention of chiliastic expectancy and not its fulfillment. The line "bald sind wir aber Gesang" [soon, however, we are song] (3:536, l. 93) projects into the future the pure, transparent voice in which the poet desires to speak—a time when his being would be nothing but song. However minimal, a gap separates the speaker from his desideratum. If we were to speak of the ideal tense of "Friedensfeier," it would be the future perfect. The hymn takes place not so much in a visionary present as in an ideal future which is still anticipatory.

Very similarly, at the close of "Ermunterung," Hölderlin displaces the parousia by positing a future moment which prophesies another, posterior future:

> und dann erst
> . . . .
> er, der sprachlos waltet und unbekannt
> Zukünftiges bereitet, der Gott, der Geist
> Im Menschenwort, am schönen Tage
> Kommenden Jahren, wie einst, sich ausspricht.
>
> (2:35–36, ll. 18–28)

[And only then, He who reigns silently and unknown, prepar-
ing what is to come, the God, the spirit in human word, on
the lovely day will announce itself to coming years, as once
before.]

God will one day commune with yet-future generations. Even in
the pastoral conclusion to "Germanien" cited previously, Hölderlin
is careful to leave the future open and distant. After glancing into
the future, he indeed returns to the present, to "der Mitte der
Zeit" (2:152, l. 103).

After having been alerted to this undercutting of the ecstatic,
luminary instance, we find in returning to *Hyperion* a similar rhe-
torical move directly following a passage in which Hyperion claims
to have experienced in the here-and-now the perfection man usu-
ally postpones to the end of time ("die Vollendung, . . . die wir
hinausschieben bis an's Ende der Zeit" [3:52]). Hyperion calls this
ultimate experience "beauty" but in the next breath admits that he
does not yet know it; he only intimates it, this new kingdom of a
new divinity (3:53). Not only, of course, is Diotima's frail beauty
subject to the dictates of mutability and indeed of death (3:63) but
she herself also plays the role of reminding Hyperion of the futurity
of perfection: "Es ist eine bessere Zeit, die suchst du, eine schönere
Welt" [The time you search for is a better one, a more beautiful
world] (3:67). Hyperion's virtue in his paucity is to possess the
dream of an ideal state or what Diotima calls, in words that em-
phasize their illusory nature, "the phantom of golden days yet to
come" (3:67). We then encounter the same displacement and dis-
solution of the reconciliatory moment in the *Grund zum Empedokles*:
Hölderlin writes that the unifying instant disintegrates like an op-
tical illusion (*Trugbild* [4:154]). Thus the persistent postponement

of the parousia in the late hymns—magnified, as we shall see, in
the last fragments—is already latent in Hölderlin's Frankfurt
period.

Compared to the oscillations of *Hyperion* and to the trepidation
with which Hölderlin circumscribes the future in the later poems,
the attainment of parousia in early hymns seems almost facile in
retrospect. In "Hymne an die Menschheit," for instance, the tone
of jubilation sustained throughout culminates in the last line:
"Und zur Vollendung geht die Menschheit ein" [And humanity
strides to its consummation] (1:148, l. 88). In other words, no
mediative section or dialectic struggle leads up to this proclama-
tory conclusion. Likewise, although the persona at the close of
"Hymne an die Freiheit" claims to have arrived at the goal so ar-
dently fought for (1:142, l. 97), references to the maternal breast
(ll. 20, 32, 60) seem to contradict his purported coming-of-age.
Only in the 1793 "Hymne an die Freiheit" does the speaker at the
close attenuate his earlier affirmation that the days of the gods
descend from heaven again (1:160, l. 113). From his present stand-
point, the future is still distant:

> Lange schon vom engen Haus umschlossen,
> . . . .
> dort in wolkenloser Ferne,
> Winkt auch mir der Freiheit heilig Ziel!
>
> (1:161, ll. 121–26)

[Already a long time enclosed by a confining home, there in
the cloudless distance the sacred goal of freedom motions to
me.]

As long as the poet speaks of signs and tokens (*Winke*), he implies
that the pure discourse of the parousia has not yet been instated.
Indeed, in both "Rousseau" and "Friedensfeier," Hölderlin cau-
tiously refers to the parousia solely in terms of intimations. Be-
cause of its enigma, the "language of the gods," as Hölderlin calls
it in "Rousseau," testifies as much to godly silence as to meaning.

If the poet is ignorant of divine intentions and cannot claim inspiration without the danger of error, what significance can writing have? What does it mean for Hölderlin's voice, if his words are denied eschatological validity or justification? What if the *Winke* mislead, by the very fact that they are unverifiable? Although Hölderlin's writings are replete with chiliastic references, they must not be construed as naming the divine, conjuring it up, or even appointing significance to it. Hence, the reader cannot ever conclude that Hölderlin says this or that about the parousia. "Patmos" resists this type of paraphrasing. Instead, Hölderlin tests the limits to which his writing extends—to the point wherein his verse, in intimation of an overpowering parousia, halts with the words: "Vieles wäre / Zu sagen davon" [much could be said of that] (ll. 88–89), or with the question: "was ist diß?" (l. 151). At these points unanswered silence befalls both reader and writer. After such caesuras, Hölderlin turns with the interjections *but* or *yet* or, in the lines following line 151, with an extended metaphor (tropus = turn) to discover yet another limit.

Neither cognitive thought nor recollection can reduplicate and exhaust what Hölderlin in his essay "On Religion" calls "that more unending coherence of life":

> In so fern aber ein höherer unendlicherer Zusammenhang zwischen ihm und seinem Elemente ist in seinem wirklichen Leben, kann dieser weder blos in *Gedanken,* noch blos in *Gedächtniß* wiederhohlt werden. . . . Jene . . . Beziehungen des Lebens können zwar auch gedacht, aber nur nicht *blos* gedacht werden; der Gedanke erschöpft sie nicht. (4:276)

> [Inasmuch as there exists a higher, infinite relation between him and his surroundings, in his real life this association can be rehearsed neither merely in *thought* nor merely in *memory.* These connections of life can be conceived but not *merely* conceived; thought does not exhaust them.]

In other words, it seems that Hölderlin tries to approach parousia by writing truthfully of it, until he recognizes that his thoughts and statements, despite all vigilance, are in error. The writing narrator of *Hyperion* thus equally recants his positions. His fluctuations do not necessarily reside in his immediate reactions to events, which he would then record transparently. Instead, Hyperion's text registers and indeed works out the waverings of the writing persona. In corresponding with Bellarmin, Hyperion reflects upon and revises his past. Like Hyperion, the persona of the hymns discovers the limits to his writing. He then swerves aside to take up another course that corrects the first. Hölderlin successively discovers the boundaries of his discourse and, indeed, the fact that these boundaries are themselves relative, temporal, and ever shifting. In a letter to his friend Isaak von Sinclair, Hölderlin comments upon this constant alteration: "Freilich muß aus jedem endlichen Gesichtspunct irgend eine der selbstständigen Kräfte des Ganzen die herrschende seyn, aber sie kann auch nur als temporär und gradweise herrschend betrachtet werden" [To be sure, from every finite perspective, one of the independent forces of the whole must be the ruling one. But it can only be viewed as dominating temporarily and by degrees] (6:301). Hölderlin's novel thus closes by promising its continuation in another epistle which will rework, once again, Hyperion's past experiences. Hyperion's last words are "So dacht' ich. Nächstens mehr" [So I thought. More to come] (3:160). In "Patmos" the persona's detoured, eccentric journey similarly demonstrates this exploration of linguistic barriers.[17]

If we were to map this exploration in "Patmos," it would take the form of *recurring* antithetical constructions and the imagery of separation continued from the first stanza. By retaining polarities, the writer tries to stave off erring, unbounded extremes or *Ungebundenes* (2:159, l. 72) hated by God. In the remainder of this section on "Patmos," then, I want to investigate exactly how Hölderlin upholds the basic polarity with which the hymn started. He realizes that, try as he may, he cannot sublate differences. Yet he also cannot avoid catapulting himself into extremes: "Und immer / Ins Ungebundene gehet eine Sehnsucht" [a longing always seeks the unbound] (2:197, ll. 12–13).

Hölderlin sustains throughout "Patmos" both the opposition between proximity and distance and its visual correlative, light and darkness. God's visage (l. 80) signifies for Hölderlin the parousia or proximity. It recurs in lines 96, 123, and 147:

> . . . und lassen wollten sie nicht
> Vom Angesichte des Herrn
> Und der Heimath.

> Denn schon das Angesicht
> Der theuern Freunde zu lassen.

> . . . und selber sein Angesicht
> Der Höchste wendet
> Darob.

> [And they did not want to depart from the Lord's visage and their home.] [For already to leave the visage of dear friends.] [And even He who is highest turns his countenance from it.]

In all three cases Hölderlin contrasts visage with separation. The dispersion of the apostles represents the symbolic counterpart to visual immediacy: "Doch furchtbar ist, wie da und dort / Unendlich hin zerstreut das Lebende Gott" [Yet horrible it is, how God infinitely disperses here and there the living] (ll. 121–22). Reminiscent of the alpine landscape of stanza one, the mountains now stand between the disciples and mark separation from a meaningful past: "Und fernhin über die Berge zu gehn / Allein" [And to go far away over the mountains, alone] (l. 125).[18] As a result, the disciples become an eternal enigma to one another (l. 140).

Parousia is also associated with visual illumination, as in the Acts account of the tongues of fire over the heads of the apostles. Apocalypse indeed means "uncovering or disclosure." But in "Patmos," the pentecostal appearance of God in thunder (*Ferndonnernd*) gives way to the extinguishing of Christ, the sun: "Izt, da er scheidend / Noch einmal ihnen erschien. / Denn izt erlosch der Sonne Tag" [Now in departing, He appeared to them again. Now the day of the sun expired] (ll. 106–8). The evening announced at Christ's death—"Doch trauerten sie, da nun / Es Abend worden" [Yet now they grieved, as the evening descended] (ll. 91–92)—becomes the long night of separation. From here the narrator continues to describe the state of absence as it extends from the Ascension to the time of the hymn's composition: "Von nun an, / Zu wohnen in liebender Nacht" [from henceforth to live in loving night] (ll. 116–17).[19] Why, though, is the night "loving"? Why does Hölderlin shun the divine light?

The image of the lightning bolt helps provide a response to the above questions. The sign substituting for parousia, the lightning in the thundering heavens (l. 204), overwhelms its perceiver.[20] As sudden divine radiance is blinding, leading to total darkness, so the speaker prefers a more familiar, mildly illuminated setting (ll. 21, 194). Speaking on behalf of those with "timid eyes," the persona in "Patmos" wishes to avoid potentially devastating spiritual illumination:

> Es warten aber
> Der scheuen Augen viele
> Zu schauen das Licht. Nicht wollen
> Am scharfen Strale sie blühn.
> (ll. 186–89)

[Many timid eyes wait, however, to behold the light. They do not wish to blossom at the searing beam.]

The reference comes from Matthew 24:27: "For as the lightning cometh out of the east, and shineth even unto the west; so shall also the coming of the son of man be." Indeed, Hölderlin writes in "Einst hab ich die Muse gefragt" that the last sign is the lightning bolt:

> Das lezte aber ist
> Das Himmelszeichen, das reißt
> . . . Menschen
> Hinweg.
> (2:220, ll. 11–14)

[Last, however, is the sign in the heavens that tears men away.]

According to Hölderlin's use of the biblical metaphor, divine prox-
imity, visualized in the lightning bolt, annihilates the subject by
consuming him in fire.

Other late texts by Hölderlin may help us at this juncture to
elaborate upon the distinction between light and darkness in "Pat-
mos." Regarding the myth of Semele, Hölderlin wrote to Böhlen-
dorff on December 4, 1801, that of all he could perceive of God
this one sign seemed predestined for him (6:427). God reveals
himself to man in moments of searing illumination which are si-
multaneously signs of His destructive wrath. In "Wenn aber die
Himmlischen," Hölderlin writes of the marked foreheads of the
mountains:

> Denn es traf
> Sie, da den Donnerer hielt
> Unzärtlich die gerade Tochter
> Des Gottes bebender Stral.
>
> (2:222, ll. 5–8)

[For the Lord's trembling glare struck them, as the thunderer
and his upright daughter ungently met.]

The violent conception of Bacchus, destroying the mother, occurs
"vergessen / . . . im Zorne" [forgotten, in anger] (ll. 15–16).
That God's wrath strikes suddenly in unexpected illumination sug-
gests that, until then, the human being had lived in darkness and
hence unavoidable error.

Other instances of the Semele myth in Hölderlin's late writing
can elucidate the question of error. A reading of the last frag-
mented lines of "Wie wenn am Feiertage" hinges on the signifi-
cance of the Semele passage.[21] Only when the speaker follows
the logic of his metaphor and recognizes the danger inherent in
the birth of both Bacchus and poetry does his authoritative voice be-
gin to break down. Just as Semele desired "sichtbar / Den Gott
zu sehen" [visibly to perceive the Lord] (2:119, ll. 50–51), so is
the poet cast into darkness when he aspires "die Himmlischen zu
schauen" [to behold the heavenly ones] (2:120, l. 70). In one

version of "Friedensfeier," on the other hand, parousia does not
consume when diminished or apportioned:

> Zu schwer ist jenes zu fassen,
> Denn wäre der es giebt, nicht sparsam
> Längst wäre vom Seegen des Heerds
> Uns Gipfel und Boden entzündet.
>
> (2:134, ll. 59–62)

> [Too difficult is it to grasp that, for if He who gave it were not
> frugal, summits and ground would long have been ignited
> from the hearth's blessing.]

In being mindful of human frailty, the Deity does not grant total,
all-encompassing vision. In other words, He withholds and delays
presence. The initial line of this passage from "Friedensfeier" re-
sponds to the beginning of "Patmos": not only is God difficult to
grasp, but the parousia is also unattainable in full measure. Indeed,
in the late "Einst hab ich die Muse gefragt," Hölderlin writes that
he will refrain from mentioning the Most High, for no mortal can
fathom Him (2:220, ll. 4–5). The poetic voice in "Dichterberuf"
also comments upon its temporary silencing:

> Wo wunderbar zuerst, als du die
>   Loken ergriffen, und unvergeßlich
> Der unverhoffte Genius über uns
>   Der schöpferische, göttliche kam, daß stumm
>   Der Sinn uns ward und, wie vom
>   Strale gerührt das Gebein erbebte.
>
> (2:46, ll. 19–24)

> [Where wonderfully at first, when you seized us by the locks,
> and unforgettably the unhoped-for spirit, creative and divine,
> descended upon us, our senses fell silent, and, as if moved to
> the bone by the flash, we trembled.]

In view of the significance of fire for Hölderlin's writing, the
pentecostal event of "Patmos" is ominous: "und die Wetter Gottes

rollten / Ferndonnernd" [and the Lord's storms rolled, thundering into the distance] (ll. 102–3). Furthermore, according to the constellation of images, vision/anger/thunder, the lines in "Patmos" reading "Im Zorne sichtbar sah' ich einmal / Des Himmels Herrn" [visible in anger I once saw the Lord of the heavens] (ll. 171–72) seem to be another, indirect allusion to the Semele myth. Indeed, the preceding lines refer to the work of the poet-speaker, who is analogous to Semele, as we have seen in "Wie wenn am Feiertage." In order then to distance the danger of incineration—and, perhaps with it, salvation—advent of the spirit is displaced and locked into a period of divine presence radically separated from and closed to the present. We can conclude that Hölderlin consistently sustains the severing interval between deity and man.

As "Wie wenn am Feiertage" suggests, the poet incurs the heavens' wrath by the very fact of his writing, by trying to enclose the divine in language (2:119–20, ll. 50–60).[22] The problem must now be addressed, as it arises in Hölderlin's works, of language's role in delineating the opposition between parousia and temporality. In the later fragmented poems, the dangers of incorrect exegesis—the failure to perform the closing lines of "Patmos"—become even more pronounced, almost inevitable: "Oft aber wie ein Brand / Entstehet Sprachverwirrung" [often, however, like fire, confusion of tongues arises] (2:253, 35–36). "Die Titanen," for instance, closes with the apocalyptic image of God approaching in anger (2:219, l. 83). Although Hölderlin recognizes the need for correct exegesis, as at the close of "Stimme des Volks" (2:53, ll. 71–72), he elsewhere also acknowledges that divine signs remain uninterpretable: "wenn einen dann die heilige Wolk umschwebt, / Da staunen wir und wissens nicht zu deuten" [when holy clouds then surround one, we are astonished and know not how to interpret it] (2:128–29, ll. 105–6). Although "Gott rein und mit Unterscheidung / Bewahren" [to keep God pure and differentiated] is the task of the poet, a misinterpretation or "Fehler / Des Zeichens" [error of the sign] (2:252, ll. 12–13, 15–16) brings down God's judgment. Is all sign, though, error?[23]

On various occasions Hölderlin suggests that, whenever

language *claims* to describe eschatological or ultimate presence, it errs and brings down the wrath of God—at which point his poem ends, as in "Wie wenn am Feiertage" and "Die Titanen." As a result, language has the function of distancing God, of descrying the limits within which it can sustain itself. The poet desires to remain within the interim because of the dangers of stepping beyond its bounds. The frequent references to *bleiben* in the late Hölderlin testify to this need for measure, restraint, and even forced restriction.[24] The danger is not simply and purely annihilation of the self or consummation by an all-encompassing divinity, all of which would imply the attainment of parousia. Rather the peril lies in inescapable error, in a language untrue to its purpose. This oversight then elicits divine retribution—the reinstated sign of God's alterity. And yet the very fact that Hölderlin so often abruptly ends a poem with the allusion to lightning suggests that this sign, like all others, also misleads: as a sign it is given to error. Hölderlin recognizes that he still misrepresents God. His language reaches yet another barrier—at which point he falls silent.

The legitimate persona of the Hölderlinian poem therefore does not hubristically strive to control God or to summon the parousia, nor is he engaged in the opposite activity: effacing and abnegating himself in order to become pure and guiltless in the process. Instead, the voice speaking in Hölderlin's poems is keenly aware of polarities, limits, and differences and conceives the poetic profession to be their careful charting. The poet preserves his "fetters":

> [U]nd doch ist etwas in uns das diese Fesseln gerne behält –
> denn würde das Göttliche in uns von keinem Widerstande
> beschränkt, so wüßten wir von nichts außer uns, und so auch
> von uns selbst nichts, und von sich nichts zu wissen, sich nicht
> zu fülen, und vernichtet seyn, ist für uns Eines. (3:194)

> [And yet there is something in us that would gladly keep these
> chains. For if the divine in us were not limited by opposition,
> we would not know of anything outside ourselves and therefore
> of ourselves. And not to be cognizant of ourselves, not to be
> sensate, would be the same as being annihilated.]

The poetic word forces God's retreat by consistently pointing to its own insufficiencies. If Hölderlin categorically stations himself in a temporal space before the parousia, then the actual references to an ideal future state express not so much "utopic intentionality"[25]— whereby a poetic self would project potentially erroneous desires onto the future—as a very cautious exploration of possibilities, ready to be recanted at any subsequent point in the text. Hölderlin's "future perfect" is open to relativization and reformulation; it is always anticipatory and unfulfilled. Hölderlin delays and circumvents the parousia in order to keep on writing. He paradoxically creates a lacuna which can, in turn, generate language.

Let us return to "Patmos" to see how Hölderlin investigates this paradox. Whereas he begins by hoping to join the pinnacles of time in a continuous history, he discovers instead in his detoured flight to the past that "Abgründe der Weisheit" are "unverwandt" [the depths of wisdom are unconnected]. Nonetheless, in the valleys of the mountains living images (*lebendige Bilder*) grow green (ll. 118–20). Our best knowledge of the world is fragmentary, or as isolated and opaque as the disciples reciprocally were after the *dispersio*. Yet, if we look upon the vertical imagery in "Patmos" as a token of the closeness to or distance from a celestial being, then this last phrase implies that language, however insufficient, grows at a remove from divinity, in the valleys. Indeed, language thus is only possible after the departure of the gods. The verdant imagery of these lines links them to later verses which confirm our reading:

> [wenn] . . . selber sein Angesicht
> Der Höchste wendet
> Darob, daß nirgend ein
> Unsterbliches mehr am Himmel zu sehn ist oder
> Auf grüner Erde, was ist diß?
>
> (ll. 147–51)

[When even the Most High turns His countenance away, because nowhere is an immortal to be seen in the heavenly skies or on the green earth, what is this?]

Hölderlin answers the question raised by the divine's absence by reflecting on his own language, as represented in the symbol of the sown/threshed grain.

Hölderlin is acutely aware of the temporal remove separating his copied image from its original (*wie er gewesen*). In the "Wurf" [cast] l. 152) separating the two, much is dissipated: "von der Rede / Verhallet der lebendige Laut" [from speech the living sound dies away] (ll. 159–60). In a later version, the loss becomes dreadful: "Ein furchtbar Ding, Staub fällt" [a terrible thing, dust falls] (178, l. 155). The "living images" then are susceptible to the death of inspiration. Indeed, lines 119–20 were deleted from later versions. When images aspire to imitate mimetically and then replace the original, they not only falsify the source but also delude the interpreter. In the section following stanza eleven, Hölderlin depicts the poet's having just represented God, when a person described as a servant (*ein Knecht*) falls upon him and tries to imitate in turn the inanimate copy:

> Wenn aber einer spornte sich selbst,
> Und traurig redend, unterweges, da ich wehrlos wäre
> Mich überfiele, daß ich staunt' und von dem Gotte
> Das Bild nachahmen möcht' ein Knecht —
>
> (ll. 167–70)

[When, however, one quickened his steps and, speaking sadly, fell upon me on the way, so that I, defenseless, was taken by surprise and [he], a servant, wanted to copy [my] image of God.]

Error is thereby magnified. The result of the encounter is signified in the text only with an evasive dash. The *wenn*-clause is not completed. Is Hölderlin here warning his reader, who might be "speaking sadly,"[26] from mistakenly deriving consolation from the poet's verse?

For Hölderlin, the poet's discourse is always incomplete. His ellipses, with which the late fragments abound, are a function of such necessary silence which nonetheless seems to resonate with attentive expectancy and, perhaps, hope. The sovereignty of silence teaches Hölderlin to locate his verse in the realm of the figurative, forming hypothetical, postulative clauses. Indeed, "wie wenn" is a favorite construction of Hölderlin. Extended "(wie) wenn" clauses—especially at the beginning of "Wie wenn am Feiertage" and "Am Quell der Donau"—are so long that they seem to defy completion and certainly avoid it. They testify to Hölderlin's almost exaggerated care to spell out all the circumstances surrounding a situation. Such prolonged conditional phrases act as absolute metaphors by threatening to omit their referent, for when will all conditions be met? In a statement sounding very similar to Novalis, Hölderlin writes that we can only stipulate preconditions. We cannot create perfect coherence: "Und dann sind die Geseze jenes unendlichern Zusammenhangs, . . . doch immer nur die Bedingungen, um jenen Zusammenhang möglich zu machen, und nicht der Zusammenhang selbst" [for the laws governing those more infinite relations are only the conditions which make the relations possible; they are not the cohesion itself] (4:277). Hölderlin's language thereby extends itself into the future.

Retrospectively, then, we can say that the phrase "living images" tries and yet fails to bridge chiastically the pairs of opposites: living/dead and spirit/letter. Hölderlin thus writes in *Hyperion* of the impossibility of a literal revelation, which would bring about death: "Das Heilige muß Geheimniß seyn, und wer es offenbaret, er tödtet es" [Whatever is holy must remain a secret; whoever reveals it kills it] (3:277). In other words, Hölderlin recognizes the perennially deficient (i.e., figurative) status of the letter. The letter is not therefore "evil" or "wrong"—"Und nicht ein Übel ists, wenn einiges / Verloren gehet" [for it is not bad if something is lost] (ll. 157–58)—for words still structure the poet's sole, albeit unavoidably erring, discourse. Although language presupposes separation from God, it still can comment upon this distance and indeed discovers its purpose in doing so.

Hölderlin's is a discourse which thus arises in the night of separation and which, in fact, vigilantly sustains the duration of this interim. Precisely because Hölderlin stations himself within a prolonged interregnum, he refuses to speculate about any categorically different future. His discourse cannot fill the gap. Instead it extends it.

In the phrase "Zu lang, zu lang" that recurs throughout the poems written after the turn of the century, Hölderlin acknowledges that the parousia is protractedly delayed (2:7, l. 29; 9, l. 13; 47, l. 45). The words reappear in "Patmos": "Zu lang, zu lang schon ist / Die Ehre der Himmlischen unsichtbar" [too long, far too long has the honor of the heavenly ones been invisible] (l. 212). This situation of God's absence (*Gottes Fehl* [2:48, l. 64]) does not mean, though, that for Hölderlin God has totally disappeared: for Christ still lives (l. 205). In "Mnemosyne" he further writes: "Zweifellos / Ist aber der Höchste" [undoubtedly, the Most High *is*] (2:193, ll. 8–9). His appearance is only delayed or his present relationship to the human condition is kept as tangential as possible by the poet. Hölderlin realizes that any symbolic representation of the Father cannot substitute for presence. Indeed, by refusing to enclose the divine in language, Hölderlin attests to its unseen presence and its alterity. The discourse that implies absence is the only correct one. The divinity is totally independent of any human effort to circumscribe it. In a letter to his mother in 1799, Hölderlin writes that what is holy remains so, even if men do not notice it. Because language is so misused, the motions of the heart often cannot be expressed by means of it. Such is the case, according to Hölderlin, with many a pastor who cannot find the right words (6:310). The vigilant poet, in contrast to the inarticulate pastor, explores the separation of his word from what is holy. He is also cognizant of the uselessness of this awareness. Poetic utterance can never change the relationship between divinity and man, but it can define the dilemma more precisely.

Thus the poet guards against sliding into a discourse that would name God. But, in addition, he also receptively awaits God's possible advent: "Es warten aber . . . viele" [many, however, wait] (l. 186). For Hölderlin, the exemplary figure of patient expectation is the centaur Chiron: "Und ferne lausch' ich hin, ob nicht ein / Freundlicher Retter vieleicht mir komme" [And I listen off into the distance, to glean whether a kind savior might not come to me] (2:56, ll. 23–24). If eschatological confirmation of the speaker's faith were in vain, then his voice would fall entirely silent. If God were too distant, then poetic intentionality would be pointless. As the breaking off of many later poems suggests, this is a very real problem for Hölderlin. The correct balance between proximity and distance must then be maintained: "weil / Ohne Halt verstandlos Gott ist" [for without support, the Lord is not understandable] (2:163, l. 79).

What constitutes this stayhold (*Halt*) for Hölderlin? In circumscribing his limits or in tracing out the persona's detours in "Patmos," Hölderlin delineates a spacing and interim. He knows his site to be one of dislocation and loss, reflected in the ellipses of his verse and in his intricate syntax. Hölderlin interrupts, complicates, and even at times suspends articulated language. He discovers a speech which maintains silence. Paradoxically then, displacement serves to orient Hölderlin's poetic voice; it renders his verse unique and distinctive. By constantly correcting itself, Hölderlin's voice constitutes itself. Likewise paradoxically, we can say that the period of waiting about which Hölderlin writes is pregnant and attentive in its silence. Indeed, the word *still*, meaning both 'silent' and 'quiet,' appears with notable frequency in his verse. Hölderlin's keen sense of absence is coupled then with the posture of listening. He matches the fear of misrepresentation with a desire for presence in language. Conversely, the essay "Über die Verfahrungsweise des poetischen Geistes," which speaks of poetic inspiration, belies its evidence with tortured, unending clauses and dense argumentation. Such duality pervades Hölderlin's writing and indeed characterizes it.[27]

Therefore, Hölderlin is preeminently preoccupied not only with detaining the parousia but also with defining its antithesis— "dürftige Zeit" [time of dearth] (2:94, l. 122) and the extent of the latter—as exactly as possible. Considering that the later works which display Hölderlin's renewed chiliastic interest were written in Swabia, one can speculate that the general spiritual climate of the land influenced the poems. Swabia, home of Andreae, Bengel, Oetinger, and Hahn, was no longer under the sway of such strong religious leaders, and chiliastic enthusiasm had dissipated. The phrase from "Brod und Wein" about the time of dearth can thus be seen to express Hölderlin's regret about the current lack of spiritual interest. But for Hölderlin "dürftige Zeit" signifies not merely a passing period of emptiness but time itself (i.e., temporality, as opposed to eternity). The poet's task then is to understand time in and through which he writes, to fathom its deficiencies, and to explain its lack of stability. The poet must strive to be "kundig des Wandels" [versed in change] (2:64, l. 23). The answer to the question about the role of the belated poet "wozu Dichter in dürftiger Zeit?" lies then in a reversal of its wording: only in times of deficiency and when time is not sacred is there a purpose in being a poet.

As evidenced in his letters, the notion of mutability preoccupied Hölderlin: "daß mir nemlich das Vorübergehende und Abwechselnde der menschlichen Gedanken und Systeme fast tragischer aufgefallen ist, als die Schiksaale, die man gewöhnlich allein die wirklichen nennt" [Whatever is transient and intermittent in human thought and system has struck me as more tragic than the destinies one usually calls the only true ones] (6:300). Here Hölderlin could have been characterizing both the rhythm of Hyperion's life as well as the ever-reopening interval separating the poet from the transcendent object of his desire. In another letter Hölderlin remarks that what always drives human beings is the striving for something intangible, different, and better. For this desire they sacrifice what is at hand (6:327). At the close of "Der Archipelagus," the persona asks to be able to understand "die Göttersprache, das Wechseln / Und das Werden" [the language of the gods, the change and becoming] (2:111–12, ll. 292–93) and to recall "[der Stille,] wenn die reißende Zeit . . . / Zu gewaltig das Haupt ergreifft" [silence, whenever time rushing by grabs the mind too forcefully] (2:112, ll. 293–96). In the second version of "Dichtermuth" the poet-persona admits to being subject to temporality. He refers to poets as the ephemeral ones in time fleeting by (2:64, l. 18). And in "Stimme des Volks," discontinuous, secular time leads man "In Eile zögernd" [in haste hesitating] along "die geschwungnere Bahn" [the more arched path] (2:50, ll. 47ff.).

In all three poems just cited, the persona's recognition of the sway of temporality occurs towards the end. Similarly in "Patmos," the persona paradoxically recognizes in his journey to the past that the past, like the future, is hermeneutically closed to him. The persona turns instead to meditate in the second half of the poem on present destitution, as symbolically portrayed at the outset in the landscape of his homeland. This return to present time and the corresponding rejection of soteriological speculation also informs the earliest version of "Der Einzige." Referring to Christ, the poetic persona admits:

> Es hindert aber eine Schaam
> Mich dir zu vergleichen
> Die weltlichen Männer.
>
> (2:155, ll. 60–62)

[Yet a shame hinders me from comparing you with worldly men.]

The persona must restrict his writing to secular themes (2:156, ll. 104–5). In "Patmos" the sacrifice (l. 217) that the gods demand is this acceptance of the human condition and its mutability. In the words of "Der Rhein," one must tolerate inequality (*Ungleiches dulden* [2:145, l. 120]). Yet at the same time, the heavenly ones exact critical vigilance against susceptibility to error and misinterpretation: "Wenn aber eines versäumt ward, / Nie hat es Gutes gebracht" [for if anything is neglected, it never bade well] (ll. 218–19). The two requisites, though, are mutually exclusive and condemn Hölderlin before the fact, because error—given the irreparable opposition between human time and God's advent—is unavoidable. Hölderlin writes:

> Nie treff ich, wie ich wünsche,
> Das Maas. Ein Gott weiß aber
> Wenn kommet, was ich wünsche das Beste.
>
> (2:155, ll. 89–92)

[Never do I strike, though I would, the right measure. But a god knows, when it comes, what I wish for, the best.]

Since error is prior to discourse, it cannot ever be pinpointed. Even recognition of error is subject to error itself. The only possible exit from this labyrinth, then, is the future.

Therefore, when the time of absence becomes all pervasive, induces inertia, and threatens to erase even the thought of parousia, the limits within which the poet writes become constricting. As the ending of "Patmos" inherently suggests, we cannot exclude the possibility that language can become petrified and fixed when the spirit departs. Although writing arises in divine absence, it can also become endangered by the extended void—by the lack of any *possibly* correct referent. The watchful poet never abandons faith in the *potentiality* of his language, the belief that it might evoke presence. The poet can slacken in his vigilance thus in two ways: he can harbor the delusion that he can grasp God in his fullness or he can forget the very existence of divinity. In either case, the poet's word becomes *fest,* an empty letter devoid of spirit.[28] In the first instance, the letter indeed must be "tended" in order to prevent a misleading, paralyzing attachment to parousia—or, as expressed in "Patmos," to visage and spirit.[29] In the second case, the letter must be tended, so that it gives rise to future writing and extended interpretation. Hölderlin wrote to his brother Karl:

> Ja! wer das Wort mißbraucht, wer Wort verfälschet oder nicht hält, der fehlet wohl sehr, aber gewiß der auch, der es zu wenig braucht. . . . Künftig, je mehr wir sprechen und fühlen werden, wie kalt das Wort ist, um so mehr werden wir Seele und Treue hineinzulegen suchen, um so mehr wird alles in uns lebendig werden, was gut ist. (6:420)

> [Yes! Whoever misuses a word, distorts or does not keep it, gravely errs; but certainly also whoever uses it too little. In the future, the more we speak and realize how cold language is, the more we shall try to infuse it with soul and fidelity. Everything that is good in us will come to life all the more.]

In other words, "Gottes Fehl hilft" [the Lord's absence helps] (2:48, l. 64). Divine absence felicitously permits the writing of

Hölderlin's extended and—like those of Novalis—fragmented texts.

The Revisions: "Patmos" and "Brod und Wein"

. . . a future that remains harassed forever by a relapse within the inauthentic. It can know this inauthenticity but can never overcome it.
—Paul de Man, "The Rhetoric of Temporality"

La fin toujours imminente, aucune transition entre être et ne plus être, la rentrée au creuset, le glissement possible à toute minute, c'est ce précipice-là qui est la création.
—Victor Hugo

Hölderlin thus circumspectly delays the parousia. Every time his writing comes too close to a possibly false depiction of divine return, he swerves aside to correct his former statement. This process of emendation not only is evidenced *within* any given poem, as in "Patmos," but is carried beyond its formal boundaries into later versions as well. Hölderlin *defers* the parousia and also writes so that each approximation *differs* from the preceding circumscription; as we shall see, Hölderlin's manuscript is a palimpsest of variants. For Hölderlin, the written text must forfeit its authoritative, completed status to future revision. In light of these corrections, we can assume that the notion of the poem as a self-contained, organic whole would have been foreign to Hölderlin. What matters instead is correct utterance and vigilance against error.

In the later versions of "Patmos" and "Brod und Wein," Hölderlin reformulates those phrases about divine proximity that could be construed as too presumptuous. In approaching the late Hölderlin, we enter a hotly debated area of research. Hölderlin's madness has been hastily glorified, as by D. E. Sattler, and even wholly denied, as by Pierre Bertaux. Their fierce polemic has generally led critics outside the Marxist arena to avoid the late fragments.[30] By dealing with the revisions here, I do not claim either to offer intact close readings or to judge the poetic qualities of the revisions as superior or inferior to Hölderlin's former work. Neither project could or should be undertaken. Instead I am interested in seeing how the later rewritings confirm a writing of nonclosure present in the earlier versions. The variants extend the impetus motivating their "original."

This statement pertains particularly to "Brod und Wein"—a poem interpreted and reinterpreted, but negligibly in terms of its rewritings. Sattler and Groddeck must be thanked for bringing the 1804 corrections to the attention of scholars through their Frankfurt edition. But we need not share their assumption that this version is the ultimately correct one. In reconstructing the "final version" they commit Friedrich Beißner's error, with respect to "Patmos," of differentiating among the various attempts, fragments, and preliminary steps towards a new version. Such categorization must be arbitrary in manuscripts that, at most, offer a series of variants. On the other hand, the revisions are by no means insignificant because they alter poems that already display in themselves extraordinary lucidity and coherence. The changes neither detract from the earlier poem nor enhance it: they merely instate a difference and, furthermore, point to Hölderlin's heightened awareness of the distance between his word and the divine.

In the revisions of "Patmos" and "Brod und Wein," Hölderlin not only returns to the problem of the parousia's rendition but also develops it further. He reformulates anew the relationship of his writing to a postulated advent. While correcting those earlier moments which were misleading, Hölderlin paradoxically recapitulates the same basic theme of delaying the apocalypse. This vigilant redefinition of limits is already familiar to us from other writers on the apocalypse. Oetinger and Jung-Stilling reworked Bengel's prophecy. Novalis responded to Lavater. Furthermore, the author of *Heinrich von Ofterdingen* reformulated in constantly new guises fairy tales about the golden age, thereby resisting its ultimate, nonfictional arrival. Hölderlin's work likewise exemplifies this combined aspect of deferral and difference in circumscribing parousia.

First let us return to "Patmos" and then, in conclusion, to the 1804 version of "Brod und Wein" to confirm our findings. The most striking correction in the later versions of "Patmos" is the deletion of the first line, "Nah ist" [near is]. Hölderlin replaces it with the phrase, "Voll Güt' ist. Keiner aber fasset / Allein Gott" [Full of goodness is; no one, however, can by himself grasp God] (2:173, ll. 1–2). This announces the theme of Christ's ineffable kindness, as opposed to "das Zürnen der Welt" [the wrath of the world] (175, l. 87). How is the discrepancy between a benevolent Deity and the existence of evil in His creation to be reconciled? In his initial statement, the persona relinquishes any claim to answer such questions by himself. Hölderlin thereby stipulates more precisely the barriers blocking full comprehension of the Deity. In his "Patmos" revisions, Hölderlin further explores this problem of true recognition, or *Erkenntnis.*

If the Deity is therefore no longer near, how is Holy Writ, the testimony of His presence, to be interpreted? Or is it, as one of the revisions of "Patmos" intimates, an "uneßbare . . . Schrift" [inedible script] (185, l. 144)? As if trying to extrapolate from the prescriptive last lines of "Patmos" as written for and presented to the Landgraf of Homburg, the poet-persona reflects on what constitutes his material, or *Fabel:* "Johannes. Christus. Diesen möcht' / Ich singen" [John, Christ, to these I would sing] (181, ll. 151–52). Yet the choice of a Christian theme is not without danger, precisely because of the alterity of the Christian God:

> Anders ists ein Schiksaal. Wundervoller.
> Reicher, zu singen. Unabsehlich
> Seit jenem die Fabel.
> (181, ll. 156–58)

[It is different, a fate, more wonderful; richer, to sing; unfathomable is the story ever since Him.]

This *Fabel* excludes the possibility of comparative utterance: "Schwer ists aber / Im Großen zu behalten das Große" [However, it is difficult adequately to contain what is great] (181, ll. 146–

47). Indeed, the revision breaks off at the line, "Wenn einer / Für irrdisches prophetisches Wort erklärt" [when one interprets prophetic utterance as earthly] (181, ll. 74–75). Incomplete, the *wenn* clause implies that prophecies cannot be adequately cloaked in comprehensible, human terms. Furthermore, *einer* does not refer to anyone but rather to the single one, John the Divine, and to the initial words of his Gospel. However oblique, this reference to John as a writer is yet the most direct of all the Patmos versions. What, though, makes John's prophetic vision or Revelation so privileged that the poet-persona cannot imitate it and falters even when trying to mention it?

Already in the first version, Hölderlin describes John as *achtsam* (182, l. 167), which means not only 'attentive' but also 'careful and discriminatory.' Christ is given the similar attribute of "wohlauswählend" [having well chosen] (182, l. 171). In the immediately preceding lines, 162 to 166, Hölderlin writes of the mortal danger of not sufficiently recognizing and weighing the delicate import of the history of salvation before beginning to write about it:

> Begreiffen müssen
> Diß wir zuvor. Wie Morgenluft sind nemlich die Nahmen
> Seit Christus. Werden Träume. Fallen, wie Irrtum
> Auf das Herz und tödtend, wenn nicht einer
>
> Erwäget, was sie sind und begreift.

[But first we must understand this: ever since Christ, names are like a morning breeze, become dreams, fall like error upon the heart and are deadly, unless one weighs what they are and understands.]

Returning to the notion of trepidation, while relinquishing his claim to full comprehension, Hölderlin later condenses these lines to "Schauen, müssen wir mit Schlüssen, / Der Erfindung vorher" [We must look beforehand with the inferences of invention] (186, ll. 162–63). The poet dare not be too audacious—"Daß aber / Der Muth nicht selber mich aussezze" [May courage not expose me]

(182, ll. 161–62); nor must he be too hasty—"Zu meiden aber ist viel" [Much is to be avoided] (182, l. 185). In other words, insight is necessary. Indeed, in "Friedensfeier" Hölderlin writes, referring to divine gift: "Tiefprüfend ist es zu fassen" [It is to be grasped upon deep examination] (3:535, l. 60).

Even if Christ possessed discernment (182, l. 176), are not those living in the time of his absence barred from it? Hölderlin asks:

> wenn aber die Ehre
> Des Halbgotts und der Seinen
> Verweht und unerkenntlich . . .
> . . . was ist diß?
>   (177, ll. 145–51)

[But what does it mean, when the honor of the demigod and of those who belong to Him [has] dissipated and [is] unrecognizable?]

Hölderlin thus replaces the earlier "wo zweifach / Erkannt-. . ." [doubly recognized] with "wo zweifach / Besorget . . ." [doubly provided for] (177, ll. 126–27). In the late version of "Brod und Wein," he implies moreover that *Erkenntnis,* meaning here 'revelation,' would overwhelm reason:

> Aber, wie Waagen bricht, fast, eh es kommet, das [Schiksaal
> Auseinander beinah, daß sich krümmt der Verstand
> Vor Erkenntnis.
>   (FHA 261, ll. 136–38)

[But like scales, fate almost falls apart before it arrives, with the result that reason cringes before recognition.]

Likewise, in a sketch to a later version, Hölderlin qualifies the persona's rapture to Greece as "unermeßlicher, denn ich vermuthet" [more immeasurable than I had conjectured] (173, l. 17). What Christ was able to recognize was "the wrath of the world," which in an earlier version Hölderlin called *karg* [meagre] (182, l. 175) but in the end changed to "begrifflos . . . nahmlos" [without concept and name] (186, l. 175). With the revision, Christ's insight assumes a superhuman quality, one transcending the categories, or *Begriffe,* with which the mind operates. How then is the presence of evil in God's creation to be understood? In other words, how can the poet follow the dictum that he must first understand (*Begreiffen* [182, l. 162]), when his object is *begrifflos?* Indeed, in one version even Christ falls silent: "und zu schwaigen, da / Ers sahe, das Zürnen der Welt" [and to say nothing, when He saw the wrath of the world] (175, l. 87). The thematics of ineffability become more and more pronounced with the successive variants.

The contrasts multiply. Compared with the poet's voice of trepidation, divine utterance is like fire "tödtlichliebend" [mortally loving] (185, l. 145). The signs of divine volition become more destructive, unmitigated, and unimpeachable. "Zerstört" [destroyed] replaces the milder "zerstreut" [scattered] in line 122, and the word *true* is inserted: "Doch furchtbar wahrhaft ists, wie da und dort / Unendlich hin zerstört das Lebende Gott" [Yet it is horribly true, how God infinitely destroys here and there the living] (176, ll. 121–22). In a still-later variant, God's apocalyptic voice, "Ergrimmt" [furious] (177, l. 149), proclaims judgment:

> Von Gott aus nemlich kommt
> . . . Offenbarung, die Hand des Herrn
> Reich winkt aus richtendem Himmel.
> (180, ll. 67–69)

[From God comes revelation; the rich hand of the Lord gestures from a judging heaven.]

Such manifestations of divine will are overpowering, uninterpretable, inedible. Thus the references to the massacre of the innocents (181, l. 142) and to the beheading of John the Baptist (181, l. 143) appear as daringly opaque signs of inexplicable violence. Yet, paradoxically, as in the exemplary case of Christ, suffering does not silence His voice of affirmation "wohlredend im Verschwinden" [speaking well as He disappeared] (185, l. 143). Exegesis, though, falls silent before Scripture. "The fixed letter" is too otherworldly to be humanly "tended." In other words, the sacred text only confirms the separation of man from his gods: it fails to mediate.

Hölderlin presents his reader here with opposing categories of voice. The voices of God (185, l. 146) differ qualitatively from the poet's utterance. What, though, in the revisions motivates the distinction? Hölderlin describes John of Patmos not only as *achtsam* [attentive] but also in a later version as *Rein* [pure] (180, l. 73). Christ's word is white as snow (186, l. 174), and his face emits a purity that is as chaste as a sword (186, ll. 165–66). Conversely, in describing the time of divine absence, Hölderlin writes that "Unschuld angeborne / Zerrissen ist" [inborn innocence is rent] (180, ll. 66–67). Man cannot earn purity, it must be granted: "Nemlich rein / Zu seyn, ist Geschik" [For to be pure is destiny] (182, ll. 182–83). By introducing distortion, suffering brings about the loss of purity: "Nemlich Leiden färbt / Die Reinheit dieses" [For suffering colors the purity of this] (186, ll. 164–65). Paradoxically, suffering mars absolute presence, although it is an integral chapter in the Christian occidental story—"Viel aber mitgelitten haben wir, viele Maale" [much have we suffered along, many times] (179, l. 25).[31] In a later version the secondary meaning of *Maale* evoked the word *Merkzeichen*: the sign of suffering is a scar (184, l. 25). The paradoxes multiply in the late "Brod und Wein," where parousia itself induces affliction: "Auch Geistiges leidet, / Himmlischer Gegenwart" [Even the spiritual suffers in the presence of the divine] (FHA 261, l. 109). The corrections made to "Patmos" underscore the differences between divine perfection and human frailty, the impossibility of inspired voice. All references to purity and suffering, unique to the late version, reemphasize the boundaries separating God from man and hence the poet's inability to renarrate the parousia. We can conclude that the task of sublating such differences and arriving at a full realization and understanding of Scripture seems too great for Hölderlin to have accomplished. A late fragmentary poem, "Einst hab ich die Muse gefragt," reveals how characteristic "Patmos" and its rewritings are for the late Hölderlin. Here he again willfully inscribes an interval separating himself from divinity: "Denn nimmer, von nun an / Taugt zum Gebrauche das Heilge" [For from now on the holy will never be suited for use] (2:221, ll. 34–35). And as lines from "Friedensfeier," "Der Einzige," and above all "Brod und Wein" suggest, the proper discourse for parousia presented an insurmountable problem for the mature Hölderlin: "Lang und schwer ist das Wort von dieser Ankunft aber / Weiß ist der Augenblik" [The word of this arrival is slow and heavy, but the moment is white] (FHA 260, ll. 87–88).

The 1804 corrections made directly to the 1803 Homburger-Folioheft copy of "Brod und Wein"—the copy used by Beißner as the authoritative version—signal once again Hölderlin's heightened attentiveness to the problem of the parousia's depiction. Many of the themes and images encountered in "Patmos" reappear in both versions of "Brod und Wein," facilitating for us an entry to the texts. For Hölderlin alters precisely those themes common to "Patmos"—the play between light and darkness, the Semele metaphor, and the self-reflexive sign.[32]

The finished version of "Brod und Wein" is an elegy on the delay of the parousia; it is consciously written in the interregnum, looks back to the time of the gods' presence, and ever so tentatively intimates their return. The poem poses to itself the problem of the correct posture to maintain during the time of dearth. How and why does poetry function during the interim? In the course of the poem, this period of waiting—symbolized in the image of the night—is recognized to be privileged or, in Hölderlin's words, "holy" (2:91, l. 48; 94, l. 124; 48, l. 53; 212, l. 48). In fact, in the concluding stanza a reconciliation is effected between night and day, i.e., between time as marked by the gods' absence and sacred time with signs of their presence. What permits this balance and how is it upset in the revisions?

The first stanza begins in a time of reflection on nonbeing. The night descends—or, in Hölderlin's terms, rises like the moon—upon a town resting from the activity of the day. The oncoming of the night betokens temporality or measurable, passing time: "Und der Stunden gedenk rufet ein Wächter die Zahl" [And mindful of the hours, a watchman calls out the time] (2:90, l. 12). The coming of night, in a way reminiscent of Novalis's *Hymnen an die Nacht*, marks a special time that fosters meditation and thus poetry: "das strö-mende Wort" [the streaming word] (l. 34). Although night is the time of sleep and forgetfulness, it paradoxically also awakens me-mory—the key therefore to the beatific past Hölderlin is about to narrate. In recalling the past, the speaker remains awake, holding (figuratively speaking) a vigil for the approaching dawn. The night grants "Heilig Gedächtniß auch, wachend zu bleiben bei Nacht" [Holy remembrance, to keep alert at night] (l. 36).

The question we have raised in this chapter in reference to the late Hölderlin is why he delays the parousia. Does he in fact do so in the standard version of "Brod und Wein"? The dilation presum-ably depends upon the reason for the gods' initial departure. This is not to say that alleviation of this originary problem would bring about their return. In an early essay entitled "Was heißt und zu welchem Ende studiert man Universalgeschichte" [What is univer-sal history and to what purpose is it studied?], Schiller had already stipulated that return to a previous state, indeed to the golden age of Greek history, was not only impossible but undesirable (NA 17:375). Schiller then writes in *Ueber naive und sentimentalische Dichtung* that a future idyllic state would be characterized by its difference from its originary parallel (NA 20:472). Repetition of the past would not only glorify immaturity, it would also encour-age the dormancy of human striving. But just as the past is barred to us, Hölderlin would add, so too is the future. The preconditions for future parousia escape us, though perhaps the cause of the gods' absence does not. Although knowing what made the gods depart might not help us bring on the future, it could help us define our current state. "Brod und Wein" concerns itself less with the prob-lem of an indefinitely suspended parousia than with understanding the time of dearth.

Surprisingly, then, the precise moment of the gods' flight can-not be ascertained in the elegy. After two stanzas celebrating the illumination afforded by the gods' cohabitation with men, their absence is suddenly (as if accidentally) noticed: "Aber wo sind sie?" [But where are they?] (l. 99). For a time as well, their presence had been unobserved, unheeded (l. 88). Indeed, in retrospect the spiritual plenitude brought by the gods appears transitory and precarious, for man hardly realizes how and when it left. What, the reader asks, signals not the moment of the recognition of loss but its cause? After two stanzas of describing the gods' habitation with mankind, Hölderlin writes: "nun aber nennt er sein Liebstes, / Nun, nun müssen dafür Worte, wie Blumen, entstehn" [Now, however, he names what he most loves, now words like flowers must arise for it] (ll. 89–90). Having earlier observed in Hölderlin the danger latent in naming divinity, we now notice the forcefulness and even violence expressed in the verb *müssen,* repeated in the second line of stanza six. The gods have thus disappeared at the moment (*nun*) that man tries to control them by naming them and by stipulating what would *not* be appropriate for their worship. The introduction of negations is striking in the line following the above passage: "Nichts darf schauen das Licht, was nicht den Hohen gefället" [Nothing that displeases the high ones is permitted to see the light] (l. 93). In *Hyperion* Hölderlin tells how divinity disappears the moment man tries to grasp it and make it his own (3:203). What appears to be close is then, in reality, distant. In the 1804 version Hölderlin becomes much more precise in pointing to the disrupting cause of absence: "ein Aergerniß aber ist Tempel und Bild" [A vexation, however, is temple and image] (FHA 260, l. 108). The image implies the absence of that to which it refers. It both marks and causes absence.

But why only in the later version is this cause clearly stated? What motivates the indirectness of the standard text? The answer lies in the title of the elegy. According to my reading of "Brod und Wein," what causes the gods' departure at the same time betokens their former presence *and* promises their return. Hölderlin writes that the last of the gods, a "stiller Genius" (l. 129) who is at once Christ and Dionysus, before departing leaves behind a sign that he will return:

Ließ zum Zeichen, daß einst er da gewesen und wieder
Käme, der himmlische Chor einige Gaaben zurük.

(ll. 131–32)

[Leaves behind, as a sign that he was once there and will come
again, some heavenly offerings.]

The two gifts are the symbols of bread and wine. They serve to
remind man of the gods, "die sonst / Da gewesen und die kehren
in richtiger Zeit" [who once were there and who shall return at the
proper time] (ll. 139–40). The act of recollecting, we remember,
characterizes the interim spent in attentive waiting. The sign gives
memory its existence. Yet reciprocally, the sign—the attempt at
representation—is what makes memory necessary in a time
marked by absence. Thus bread and wine are not only treasured
symbols of divinity but also, however paradoxically, signs betoken-
ing a lack or dearth.

Inasmuch as they symbolize light, bread and wine permit the
speaker in the final stanza to set the images of light and darkness
side by side: "Ja! sie sagen mit Recht, er söhne den Tag mit der
Nacht aus" [Indeed, they justly say, he reconciles day with night]
(l. 143). The wine god brings the trace of the flown deities down to
the darkness of the earth (l. 148). The god is also called a
torchbearer who descends to the shadows (l. 155). Images of light
appear in the penultimate distich. Although night is the time of
the sleep of forgetfulness (l. 115), clearly even this slumber is not
without its comforting dreams: "Sanfter träumet und schläft"
[More gently sleeps and dreams] (l. 159).

In the revision this balance between light and darkness is up-
set, and night imagery predominates. Indeed, according to Grod-
deck, "The Night" was the final title Hölderlin planned to give his
elegy.[33] The first change in the body of the text is made in line 14,
where *Ebenbild* replaces *Schattenbild*:

Sieh! und das Ebenbild unserer Erde, der Mond
Kommet geheim nun auch; die Schwärmerische, die Nacht
[kommt.

[Behold! the copy of our earth, the moon, also secretly now comes; the visionary one, the night comes.]

With this shift, Hölderlin suddenly establishes a more intimate relationship between the moon and earth or between darkness and the present human situation. Hölderlin then introduces an unsettling note in the fifth stanza which was previously devoted to a depiction of illumination. Line 80 now reads: "reißt hin ewig in Nacht das Geschik" [fate rips eternally into the night]. Hölderlin then removes the references to light from the last verse. He retracts the image of the torchbearer, and with the phrase "es ruhn die Augen der Erde" [the eyes of the earth rest], he revokes the previous line wherein the awakening eye perceives the light. Furthermore, the very last line ends with the word *night*.

The new ratio in the light-dark dichotomy alerts us to a fundamental shift. But of what is the emphasis on night an index? What, more precisely, is the difference between our two texts? We can address this question, as in "Patmos," by focusing on the moments where the persona reflects upon the nature and preconditions of language. Given the fact that night intimates both the anteriority of illuminating presence and belated time—"Aber Freund! wir kommen zu spät" [But friend! We come too late] (l. 109), how does the notion of the sign respond to the problem of transiency? In other words, how do the two versions differ in the value they ascribe to the sign (l. 131)?

From the first version, we concluded that the longing for stabilization is stilled by symbolic language. Bread and wine are left by the gods as tokens of their former presence. The ivy and fir likewise function as the trace of the flown deities (ll. 145–47). Time can only claim ontological stability through the sign's acting as a reminder of the past and as a promise for the future. The sign preserves the presence of the *deus absconditus*. Symbols counteract the insignificant passage of time by endowing existence with *Bleiben* [abiding, permanence] (l. 147) or "im Finstern . . . einiges Haltbare" [in the darkness something to hold onto] (l. 32). But, as we observed in "Patmos," notions of *bleiben, fassen,* and *vest* may conceal the latent threat of dormancy and petrification in an otherwise protean

language. Awareness of this danger might have been one of the
factors leading Hölderlin to revise the finished copy of the elegy.
Indeed, perhaps Hölderlin also recalled the poem Hegel dedicated
to him in 1796 entitled "Eleusis," in which the words occur:

> es blieb
> kein Zeichen deiner Feste, keines Bildes Spur!
> . . . .
> Wer gar davon zu andern sprechen wollte,
> Spräch' er mit Engelzungen, fühlt der Worte Armuth,
> . . . .
> daß die Red' ihm Sünde deucht.
>
> (StA 7:235)

[No sign of your festival, no trace of an image remained.
Whoever would speak to others of it, were he to speak in the
tongue of angels, feels the poverty of words, that speech seems
sinful.]

In the official version of "Brod und Wein," the word serves
during the time of parousia accurately to name divine presence.
Hölderlin refers to "die fernhintreffenden Sprüche" [oracles that
strike the distant mark] (l. 61) and "das uralt / Zeichen" [the
ancient sign] as "treffend und schaffend" [striking, creating] (ll.
69–70). Upon recognizing the celestial father, people name him:
"Vater Aether! so riefs und flog von Zunge zu Zunge" [Father
Aether, so they cried, and from one tongue to the next it travelled]
(l. 65).[34] We have already commented on the passage wherein
names must spring up like flowers (ll. 89–90). But in apposition
to our initial reading that privileged the verb *must,* we can also say
that creation of the word is analogous to organic growth: words
naturally spring from the heart like flowers. But for the forced
willfulness latent in the auxiliary verb, we could say Hölderlin
implies that the sign innately corresponds to its signified.
Culminating then the succession of exemplary, *treffende* signs is the
appearance of the winegod/Christ/Dionysus as the divine logos
who unites the celestial and earthly realms. He bears the stamp of
the divine on human form: "Oder er kam auch selbst und nahm des

Menschen Gestalt an" [Or he came himself and assumed human form] (l. 107).

All but the last of the above passages are deleted in the 1804 version. Furthermore, the phrase already cited follows line 107: "ein Aergerniß aber ist Tempel und Bild" [a vexation is temple and image]. Metaphoric language, arising in the night of absence and susceptible to temporal mutation, distorts its referent. As analogies fail, so does language break down. In the new stanza seven, Hölderlin writes: "Aber doch etwas gilt, allein" [But something yet is valid, alone] (l. 123). He then reverts to the parataxis and disarticulated listing so characteristic of the fragments that precede the period of Hölderlin's mental darkness: "Die Regel, die Erde. / Eine Klarheit, die Nacht" [law, earth, a clarity, night] (ll. 123–24).[35] Already in the earlier version, Hölderlin suggests that, in divinizing his own power to make comparisons, man is unfaithful to the gods: "und fast ward ihm Unheiliges heilig" [the unholy almost became holy for him] (l. 79). To recapitulate, we have seen how the verb *müssen* in line 90 implies that man is beginning to force attributes onto the gods and, consequently, to force their retreat. Language begins to exclude parousia. Our initial reading of the destructive moments latent in the formal version of "Brod und Wein" becomes confirmed in the revisions or, more precisely, in the elisions.

Although in the later version the body of stanza eight remains the same, the very retention of the images of bread and wine is rendered problematic. In other words, the title loses its significance. In the earlier version, bread and wine not only mediate between past, present, and future but also furnish a vertical axis or "Jacob's ladder" between heaven and earth:

Brod ist der Erde Frucht, doch ists vom Lichte geseegnet,
Und vom donnernden Gott kommet die Freude des Weins.
(ll. 137–38)

[Bread is the fruit of the earth, yet it is blessed by the light.
And the joy of wine comes from the thundering god.]

Yet with the omission of the first two lines of stanza seven—"Zwar leben die Götter, / Aber über dem Haupt droben in anderer Welt" [Indeed the gods live, but above us in another world]—even the transcendent existence of the gods is questioned, and hence the vertical relationship breaks off. Their descent is impossible.

We already noted that in the original version the sign both hides and replaces an absent signified. Hölderlin writes about the necessity of this compensation in *Hyperion*:

> Ich weis, daß nur Bedürfnis uns dringt, der Natur eine Ver-
> wandschaft mit dem Unsterblichen in uns zu geben und in der
> Materie einen Geist zu glauben, aber ich weis, daß dieses
> Bedürfnis uns dazu berechtigt, ich weis, daß wir da, wo die
> schönon Formen der Natur uns die gegenwärtige Gottheit ver-
> kündigen, wir selbst die Welt mit unserer Seele beseelen, aber
> was ist dann, das nicht durch uns so wäre wie es ist? (3:192)

> [I know that need forces us to relate nature to the immortal in
> us and to believe spirit infuses the material, but I also know
> this need justifies us in doing so. I know that when the beau-
> tiful forms of nature proclaim the immanent divinity in us, we
> animate the world with our souls. But what is there, that
> would not be the way it is because of us?]

Here Hölderlin tells us that all signs are anthropomorphic and arbitrary. Bread and wine, the beautiful forms of nature, are no different. They cannot be privileged exceptions to the erring word, as the authoritative version wants to suggest. In the rewriting, bread and wine thus become the "inedible" sign to which the one version of "Patmos" alludes. Hölderlin revises his elegy in accordance with the realization that writing has nothing to do with the immortal, spirit, or divinity. He does not and cannot mediate divinity by inscribing it into human history.

The major change in the relevance of the title leads us to surmise that, with the revisions, Hölderlin's elegy no longer coheres. The lack of unity, though, does not make the revisions less meritorious of investigation. Indeed, this retouched manuscript displays the wounds and mutilations Hölderlin then writes about in the "Maale" [stigmas] of "Patmos" and the "Narben" [scars] of the late "Brod und Wein" (StA 2:179, l. 25; FHA 261, l. 109).

The most notable textual lacerations concern allusions to the deity. Hölderlin hesitates to delineate or apostrophize the gods, even in the middle trias which purports to narrate their presence. The reference to Father Aether is removed from the last stanza, and the exclamation to the Father from the fourth. In lines 65 and 68, "Vater Äther" becomes "verzehrend" [devouring]. Naming becomes elliptical. For instance, Hölderlin replaces "die Himmlischen" [the heavenly ones] with the more general designation "Himmlisches" [the heavenly] (l. 71) and in the next stanza with the yet-more-imprecise "es" (l. 73).[36] Likewise, in line 95, he substitutes "deß" [of that] for "der Himmlischen" [of the heavenly ones]. The delicate art of naming the gods described in lines 75 and 76—"kaum weiß zu sagen ein Halbgott / Wer mit Nahmen sie sind" [a demigod hardly knows how to call them by name]—is also omitted.

As the poet-persona becomes more and more reluctant to call upon the gods by name, signs of his fear of divine wrath increase. References to the Semele myth of being consumed by God's presence accumulate in the revision. In the finished version, the two allusions to Semele are indirect. According to Greek mythology, Dionysus throws a wine sop to Cerberus when he descends to rescue his mother. Thus the last line "Selbst der neidische, selbst Cerberus trinket und schläft" [Even the envious one, even Cerberus drinks and sleeps] betokens a reversal of the more familiar myth of incineration. But in the 1804 text, the specific reference to Cerberus's drinking is omitted: "Die allwissenden auch schlafen die Hunde der Nacht" [Even the omniscient dogs of the night sleep]. In the standard version the "thundering god" brings the gift of wine. But in the revisions the destructive implications of this image of fiery divine presence become more pronounced. The verb *verzehren* [to devour; to consume] is used three times in stanza four and is associated with the image of flames: "Vater Aether verzehrt und strebt, wie Flammen, zur Erde, / . . . aber wie Flammen / Wirket von oben" [Father Aether devours and tends like flames towards the earth . . . but like flames coming from above] (ll. 65–

68). Further references to fire and heat accumulate in lines 76, 78, and 110: "Auch Geistiges leidet, / Himmlischer Gegenwart, zündet wie Feuer, zulezt" [Even the spiritual suffers in the presence of the divine, catches finally like fire]. Even the deity himself is in danger of self-consumption: "Fast wär der Beseeler verbrandt" [The inspirer would almost be consumed] (l. 158).[37]

As nearness to the gods is fraught with too great a danger, Hölderlin delays their advent and extends the period of night indefinitely. Most important, perhaps, is the omission in stanza seven of the reference to the gods' coming in thunder (l. 119). Similarly Hölderlin changes "Dorther kommt und zurük deutet der kommende Gott" [from which the coming god comes and to which he points back] to "Dorther kommt und da lachet verpflanzet, der Gott" [whence the god comes and, transplanted, laughs] (l. 54). The deity is no longer coming nor to come. When the verb *to come* is indeed used, as in lines 66 and 71, it marks a past event. And as already noted, line 155 referring to the approaching torchbearer is replaced. The answer in the revision to the question of the poet's role in times of dearth would therefore no longer be to celebrate like priests the god present in the bread and wine. On the contrary, writing now serves to make itself increasingly aware of the distance of divinity and indeed to uphold the separation.

Admittedly, I have commented little on the new version itself but instead on an unseen text lying between two texts, *i.e.*, on their difference. Taken together, the changes made on the references to night, Semele, and the verb *to come* are significant. Hölderlin was obviously dissatisfied with specific aspects of the original elegy and endeavored to modify them. However, the newly constituted text number 6, as Sattler calls it, is only questionably a textual whole. We need to read it instead as it was actually written into the finished version of the Homburger Folioheft and to be constantly attentive to the difference between the two versions. Otherwise we run the risk of overlooking the weaknesses that Hölderlin felt were in his former writing. Ironically, it is almost true that the emendations are only meaningful in relation to the omissions. The alteration refers to an absent text, just as for Hölderlin the sign evokes the absent god. Yet, paradoxically, the new text cannot exist without this implied presence of an absent Other.

Given the existence of a third, palimpsest-like text which combines two other texts, we can infer that Hölderlin was probably not so much intent upon constituting a new poem as in rectifying the old, at least in the case of "Brod und Wein."[38] The implications of such a conclusion are threefold: First, they help to facilitate an entry to an otherwise very opaque area of research—Hölderlin's late oeuvre. Second, the revisions help us to remain attentive in the earlier versions to the self-reflexive moments (*e.g.*, line 90 of "Brod und Wein,") which anticipate and try to forestall error. And third, by rewriting, Hölderlin attests to the very problem he struggles with in both versions—the inability of the signifier to remain stable within the flux of temporality or, in other words, to be true to its absent signified.

In Retrospect

> Und darum ist der Güter Gefährlichstes, die Sprache dem Menschen gegeben.
> —Hölderlin

What if we were to align "Mnemosyne," "Brod und Wein," and "Patmos"? The image of slumber, indeed cradling, in "Mnemosyne" symbolizes the indefinitely extended and unperturbed waiting for the future that we saw in the finished version of "Brod und Wein." Referring to the gods, Hölderlin writes in the latter poem: "Traum von ihnen ist drauf das Leben. Aber das Irrsaal / Hilft, wie Schlummer" [Life then is a dream of them. But error helps, like slumber] (93, l. 115). With his characteristic turn of phrase, *aber,* Hölderlin warns us in "Patmos": "Wenn aber eines versäumt ward, / Nie hat es Gutes gebracht" [For if anything is neglected, it never bade well] (171, ll. 218–19). The dreamlike unreality of the interim is not, in other words, innocent. It signifies a repression of error. We recall a revision of "Patmos":

> . . . Wie Morgenluft sind nemlich die Nahmen
> Seit Christus. Werden Träume. Fallen, wie Irrthum
> Auf das Herz und tödtend.
>
> (182, ll. 163–65)

{Ever since Christ, names are like a morning breeze, become dreams, fall like error upon the heart and are deadly.}

The dreams of "Brod und Wein" have become fatal. The sleep of forgetfulness is now the sleep of death—unless the poet maintains a degree of attentiveness and awareness. We have seen in the emendations to "Patmos," however, that Hölderlin is only conscious of the fact that he can neither display nor acquire divine insight.

Have we then answered the questions with which this chapter opened? The revisions of "Patmos" suggest, in retrospect, that its original ending prematurely closes the text. The references to *bestehendes* and *Der veste Buchstab* appear as a last desperate attempt by Hölderlin to affirm continuity despite the metaphoric logic of the body of his poem. Although in the imaginative flight to Greece, Patmos, and then Palestine, Hölderlin tries to link the pinnacles of time and mend the loss of memory, he encounters only the inexorable problem of ruptured, discontinuous time in the departure of Christ and the ensuing night of the dead letter. Whenever the divine sign appears in the heavens, it reinstates difference and exteriority and is menacingly opaque and *deutungslos*. The revisions return to the unresolved problem of divine alterity and of the uninterpretable script that resists being *gepfleget*. In a belated age, the poet's discourse is perforce secular, repeatedly falling short of its unimaginable, sacred referent. If indeed Hölderlin attempts to look, in the words of "Mnemosyne," forward and backward in time, the act is not performed without due trepidation and self-reflection. Hölderlin evades any statement that could be construed as preempting the parousia.

Hölderlin's voice therefore sustains itself by not overstepping its bounds—by not letting itself be all-consumed by divine love or deadened by its perceived absence. Hölderlin traces instead the trajectory of the self that lies between the poles of *Nah ist* and *schwer zu fassen.* If we go on to analyze Hölderlin's psychological state, we can say that he checks both self-deification and total self-destruction.[39] He thereby maintains a tenuous balance: through his use of language, Hölderlin guarantees himself psychological stability. Writing becomes a therapeutic exercise in acknowledging limits. Indeed in the essay "Reflexion," Hölderlin speaks of the necessity of patience and renunciation: "Überhaupt muß er sich gewöhnen, nicht in den einzelnen Momenten das Ganze, das er vorhat, erreichen zu wollen, und das augenbliklich unvollständige zu ertragen" [One must become used to not expecting to reach in single moments the entirety one envisages, and to bear the momentarily incomplete] (4:234).

We have noticed, however, in the later Hölderlin an ever-keener awareness of the inevitability of imbalance. The fear of naming and thereby preempting the deity becomes more pronounced and eventually leads to a radically fragmented poetry and from there to silence. After 1804 Hölderlin indeed either does not respond at all to his interlocutors or responds in a painfully self-effacing manner.[40] What we encountered in this chapter were earlier symptoms announcing such illness. Now, though, the limits of language are no longer explored by a self intent upon sustaining equilibrium: the limits have finally been transgressed. The tie between language and parousia in Hölderlin's late but still-creative period not only has thematic interest but also affords some insight into the question of his eventual madness and loss of self.

On final analysis, Hölderlin's relationship to language and to parousia radically differs from that of the Romantics. The latter recognize the fictive, utopic nature of their discourse, playfully invent new apocalypses, and thereby knowingly postpone any veritable end. They accept the fecundity of symbolic, poetic discourse. Hölderlin, on the other hand, reverts to a more traditional view of the apocalypse as the unfathomable, approaching *novum*.[41] For him, symbolic discourse gravely errs in both its effort and inability to circumscribe *adventus*. And yet, if the searing, annihilating apocalypse is to be staved off, then writing must continue despite all its deficiencies. The poet's demise would occur at the very moment when the divine would break into human time. Therefore, the blind bard pleads: "O nimmt, daß ichs ertrage, mir das / Leben, das Göttliche mir vom Herzen" [O take, that I might bear it, life from me and the divine from my heart] (2:55, ll. 51–52).[42]

Hölderlin delays the parousia by consciously creating a lacuna—by reflecting on the tenuous status of his language. In the words from the essay "Über die Verfahrungsweise des poetischen Geistes," writing consists of groping towards the least possible deviation, "nach *den sichersten und möglich untrüglichsten Kennzeichen*" [towards the most sure and least possibly deceiving signs] (4:261). The interim in which Hölderlin writes is thus neither one of verbal effluence and self-assurance, as with Novalis, nor one of total pessimism, as in Jean Paul's "Rede des todten Christus." Instead, Hölderlin writes in the interim acknowledging the very necessity of insufficiencies for his continued writing. As Michel Foucault has remarked in response to Laplanche's *Hölderlin et la question du père*, language both comes "from a place of which no one can speak," from the death of God, and "directs its speech towards this absence."[43] Despite their differences, then, both Hölderlin and the Romantics relate the apocalyptic theme to poetic self-reflexivity. Stated more precisely, both are attracted to the notion of a delayed parousia because it preeminently exemplifies the complexities of poetic enunciation.

Afterword

With hope it is, hope that can never die,
Effort, and expectation, and desire,
And something evermore about to be.
—Wordsworth, *The Prelude*

Daß du nicht enden kannst, das macht dich groß,
Und daß du nie beginnst, das ist dein Los.
—Goethe, "Unbegrenzt"

In order to keep on writing, both Hölderlin and Novalis delay endings, especially the apocalyptic ending. This is not to say that chiliastic imagery disappeared from their texts. On the contrary, its marked presence has even misled interpreters into simplifying its function. As we have seen, scholars have all too often reduced the narrative structures of texts by Novalis and Hölderlin to a triadic history of salvation. Yet, although both authors used apocalyptic imagery in their texts, they also undermined in various ways the teleological structure implied by such imagery. Hölderlin maps temporal detours in "Patmos" and its revisions. Novalis structures *Heinrich von Ofterdingen* as an endless, decentered *mise en abyme*. In their short texts Jean Paul and Günderrode, like Hölderlin in his late oeuvre, explore self-reflexive dead ends. The Romantic novel—whether it be *Heinrich von Ofterdingen,* the *Nachtwachen,* or one we have not studied, like Brentano's *Godwi* or Schlegel's *Lucinde*—stratifies sequences of abruptly interrupted narratives.

This generation of writers, unlike its preceding ones, no longer perceived itself as participating in a temporal continuum. Time was neither progressive nor teleological. If the future were conceivably to extend the present, then it could do so only to establish and confirm a pattern of constant reversals and unexpected upheavals. With an acute sense of the temporality of their own writings and the necessity of self-corrective, fragmented, and repetitive form, authors such as Hölderlin and Novalis postpone and interrupt conclusions, endings, and hence any definitive statement on the parousia. The events of the French Revolution reinforced this awareness of the telos as a u-topic fiction. Chiliastic hopes had been dashed, and one could prognosticate (like Hölderlin or, more notably, Kleist) only the advent of repeated crises.

The recurring ironic, self-reflexive moment in Hölderlin and Novalis serves to remind the reader that the discourse in their narratives is purely imaginary. A writer of the time uses chiliastic and eschatological motifs precisely because they generate poetic self-reflection *ex negativo*. By extending the interim, Hölderlin and Novalis sound its linguistic expanses and confines. They paradoxically deploy metaphors of the golden age in order to refute closed orders and to reflect instead upon time, the medium in which they write. Time is for them secular and destitute. Hölderlin and Novalis confirm what Lessing concludes in *Laokoon*—that language is a medium which, unlike the visual arts, unfolds itself diachronically. But they also see language preforming our sense of time. Through the sign that points elsewhere, language evokes not what is absent but absence itself. Thus, by means of the sign which arouses recollection, it creates the past but does not recreate what has passed. And by the same token, we could almost say in a Benjaminian sense that the sign intimates the existence of a future where it will recover meaning. This postponement of accomplished referentiality is what we mean by the term *nonclosure*. The subject matter of Novalis's tales and Hölderlin's hymns is what is not, yet is to come. The discourse of past or future is thus fictive; in Hölderlin and Novalis, it is aware of being so.

Novalis, much more so than Hölderlin, explores the fecundity of an imagination that ceaselessly creates displacements, recognizing them as playful constructs. Novalis thrives on distraction. Hölderlin, on the other hand, alerts us to the reverse side of the fictive apocalypse. The writer necessarily falters and continually falls short of his exalted subject matter. He has no alternative but to bring to mind his deficiencies. Hölderlin's self-reflection is self-critical, suspicious, and uncertain of its results—though not to the point of nihilism. Hölderlin must delay the parousia in order to continue writing in a vein that can make some claim to veracity, i.e., a vein acknowledging that at some point in the future it probably will be proved inadequate. A discourse avoiding erring extremes could only be found in witnessing the succession of these extremes while remaining open to an ever-delayed parousia. When the latter arrives, it will presumably alleviate the necessity of discursivity.

By constantly deferring the parousia, Hölderlin reminds us that the self-reflection operative in his texts does not mean the self is in control of its narrative. For Novalis too the self, above all in the character of Ofterdingen, is a categorically deficient entity. We initially saw the contemporary of Hölderlin and Novalis, Jean Paul, similarly exposing the aporiae of the self-reflexive imagination which cannot discover an exit from labyrinthine conjectures about the Deity and thereby arrive at a divine telos. In the "Rede des todten Christus," the search for God never ends. These writers therefore situate both the act of narrating and the narrated time of their works in the extended interim between the no-longer and the not-yet. The narrating self must always project perfect mastery of its text onto the future.

Deferral thus entails displacement—both of the self and of the eschaton it never fully circumscribes. Novalis constantly varies his portrayal of the golden age in his fairy tales. Each reformulation does not so much supplant or improve upon a preceding version as merely offer another rendition and, in doing so, intimate that yet another is to follow. Novalis's oeuvre thus presents its reader with an ongoing, discontinuous, nonteleological series of narratives. As with Hölderlin's emendations, not only does each recasting differ from the others, but the activity of writing as such also becomes one of unending revision or, in Novalis's terms, of extended writing *cum* reading.

We initially observed how writers in the Pietist tradition never

ceased to speculate about the apocalypse, although the time of the
end was unpredictable and all commentary on Revelation might
well prove incorrect. Indeed, the *mysteriosum* invited unveiling. As
with the writers around 1800, each new exegete endeavored to
speak more correctly about the apocalypse; as a result of this effort,
each incorporated self-reflexive observations on the nature of lan-
guage into his scriptural interpretations. Thus, although writers at
the turn of the nineteenth century radicalized this pattern of revi-
sion and deferral, it was encoded in the theme of the absolute
ending. Paradoxically, the Romantics were fascinated with endings
at the same time that they eschewed them.

But that is where their tie to former teleologies stops. The
writing of this period can be characterized as a cultivated deviation
not only from every foregoing utterance but also from a particular
past—from traditional millenarianism and the Enlightenment's
temporalization of it. Indeed, Hölderlin upsets inherited salvation
history, with its sequence of the *status* of Father, Son and Holy
Ghost, to place the spirit's advent not at the end of time in Joachite
fashion but before the Ascension. However, Hölderlin's writing
enacts more than what could be termed secularization or even radi-
cal rupture from chiliastic tradition. His and Novalis's writing is
one of sustained deviation and displacement per se—one best ex-
emplified with regard to the notion of the apocalyptic ending.

By infinitely prolonging the delay, Hölderlin and Novalis
create a void. But lest we construe their absenting of God to be a
"desacralization" rather than a "secularization," we must remember
that this void longs to be filled. Schleiermacher defines religion
itself as unending desire for the unattainable and ineffable abso-
lute. Our sense for the immeasurable (*das Unermeßliche*) points us
only to what is even more infinite and hence incalculable (*auf eine
andere und höhere Unendlichkeit* [StW 298]). Punning on his friend's
name, Novalis then alludes in the *Europa* essay to the way in which
Schleiermacher fashions a veil for what is holy (N 2:747). Jean
Paul, elaborating upon Novalis's image of the veil, writes about its
self-extension. He ends the "Traum über das All" with the image
of the unending text or the "Gewebe des Isis-Schleiers, der über

die Schöpfung hing, und der sich verlängerte, wenn ihn ein End-
licher hob" [the weaving of the veil of Isis, that was draped over
creation and that extended itself, whenever a mortal lifted it] (SW
15:116).

Once cast, the veil, of course, was not to be raised by subse-
quent generations. Repeated return to the myth of the absconded
deity suggests that the scenario sketched by Hölderlin, Hegel,
Jean Paul, and Schiller needed to be reenacted. The void longed to
be filled. In the wake of the Romantics the apocalypse lacks the
finality it should signify and becomes instead unending. Jean
Paul's black apocalypse, for instance, is renowned in European lit-
erary histories for its reworkings. Upon Mme. de Staël's translation
of the dream into French, Vigny, Hugo, and, most important of
all, Nerval in his sonnet "Le Christ aux Oliviers" borrow Richter's
imagery. Heidegger traces for us the tradition of the death of God
in his essay "Nietzsches Wort 'Gott ist tot.' "[1] These repeated at-
tempts at recasting a version of the apocalyptic end alone attest to
its fundamental unnarratability and hence its postponement. In-
deed Nietzsche recounts an anecdote not about the delayed apoc-
alypse itself but about the delayed *telling* of the event of God's
demise: "Diess ungeheure Ereigniss ist noch unterwegs und wan-
dert, – es ist noch nicht bis zu den Ohren der Menschen
gedrungen" [This immense event is still on its way and travels—it
has not yet reached human ears].[2]

The *Disappearance of God*, the title of an early book by J. Hillis
Miller, is not only a weighty theme in nineteenth-century intellec-
tual history; it has import for problems of narration in nineteenth-
century texts, in particular for the novel. Miller's own recent work
on disrupted narratives and their evasion of closure can be traced
back to this earlier thematic interest. Indeed, it preforms his later
development. And Miller is not alone. Recently there has been a
wave of major investigations on the nineteenth-century aborted
narrative ending—inverse studies of Frank Kermode's *Sense of an
Ending*. Manfred Frank, for instance, has written on the European
context of the unending journey in a work entitled *Die unendliche
Fahrt*. D. A. Miller has examined the problem of closure in Austin,

Eliot, and Stendhal in his *Narrative and its Discontents*. Marianna Torgovnick likewise published in 1981 with Princeton University Press a work entitled *Closure in the Novel*.[3]

Our present study has hoped to contribute to this ongoing discussion on nonclosure. The problems of digression, curtailed development, and repetition that appear later in the nineteenth-century novel have their theoretical roots in the texts written shortly following the French Revolution. As we have seen, many writers of the generation are sceptical of a unilinear récit, above all when it claims to outline progressivity. The discourse of a Novalis is one of a prolonged sheer play of language attentive to contextuality. Novalis shows a predilection for narrative strata, layers, mirrorings, and series instead of chronological narration.[4] Hölderlin's hymns likewise chart out the deflections away from parousia.

It follows that censorship of continuity and synthesis by Novalis and Hölderlin entails the critique of the myth of the subject who claims to instate them. The question of the self which the nineteenth-century novel of education sketches indeed is programmed in the so-called ego philosophy of Fichte. Novalis, then, as we have seen, alters his predecessor by bringing to the fore and then making perpetual the division of the self from the nonself or from its object of desire. And we have read the rhythm of Hölderlin's writing in precisely the same terms. With every inflection, Hölderlin's voice recants itself, reinstates difference, and thereby holds teleological narrative drive in suspension. Above all then, it is Novalis's and Hölderlin's reflection on discourse—its temporality and repeated induction of crises evading resolution—that leads the way to the extended, intricate discourse of the nineteenth-century narrative which likewise resists closure. Belying the widespread clichés on what constitutes the Romantic movement, our two writers refuse to idealize the language that they wield. For them, writing cannot be extricated from constant historical flux.

With such summarizing remarks about the evasion of closed order, we return full swing to the problem of philosophies of history in the Age of Idealism—the problem with which we began by citing Schelling. The link between the use of apocalyptic imagery and reflection on the temporality of language is, of course, paradoxical and unexpected. Apocalyptic imagery is usually employed to depict the end of time. The paradox appears even more pronounced when we remember that this sensitivity to the temporality of language becomes linked around 1800 to the notion of teleological history. In other words, poetics, as for instance in Schiller's *Ueber naive und sentimentalische Dichtung* and in Friedrich Schlegel's *Studium-Aufsatz,* becomes inextricably bound to the philosophy of history. In this present study, though, we asked how language, being a temporal medium, could possibly relate to a telos. Let me tentatively explore this paradox.

In the late eighteenth century, interest was burgeoning in a philosophically grounded poetic self-reflexivity. In the wake of Kant's third *Critique,* the aesthetic became not only a central philosophical issue but moreover the final, synthesizing element in philosophical systems. Because it was considered able progressively to record, reconcile, and sublate binary oppositions, the aesthetic consciousness occupied a privileged teleological position in various philosophies of history written around the turn of the nineteenth century. Following Lessing's lead, poetry was seen to be the art that embodied and incorporated within itself dialectic, temporal change. As we have already observed, Szondi was the one to sight this move away from a normative to a speculative, Idealist poetics. As he has so excellently documented, poetics became inextricably bound to the idea of time's unfolding—to the philosophy of history. No longer were extraneous, inherited rules and codes of taste to judge a work. Instead, contemporary, "sentimental" art (to use Schiller's term) intrinsically possessed absolute value as an expression of modernity, especially in its awareness of temporality or, in other words, of distance from an origin.

But a problem lies with making (as Schiller does) the moderns' awareness of temporality and, above all, the Kantian insight into the ephemerality and subjectivity of the aesthetic judgment the basis for hierarchy and progression. We can be cognizant of our distinctiveness from the past without concluding that the human spirit temporally unfolds itself. In other words, temporality cannot be somehow regularized and called temporalization. In the authoritative version of "Brod und Wein," Hölderlin intimates that recognition of the distance from an origin prohibits restitution. Schiller and Friedrich Schlegel, of course, recognized the same. But it is the Hölderlin of the revisions who tells us that the memory of loss will always prevent us from seeing progress. In other words, by the very act of drawing up a philosophy of history, a writer attests to temporal disparity and endless shiftings. In the distended, unfinished, encyclopedic effort and in protracted correction, Novalis and Hölderlin respectively enact the nonrecuperative, nonaccumulative, and nonprogressive nature of writing. To reflect then on the temporality and nonteleology of language is implicitly to criticize any order that a philosophy of history tries to draw up.

The texts discussed by Hölderlin and Novalis call into question the glorification of finalizing systems and, in particular, their aesthetic resolutions. For these authors, any liaison between poetics and teleologies is fundamentally specious, because the former, self-reflexive element constantly functions as an ironic reminder of their common imaginary nature. The late Hölderlin, for instance, acknowledges that he cannot claim to portray the parousia without deceiving himself. And the Romantic poetics of Novalis contains within itself the deconstruction of the exalted ideal it claims for itself on other occasions. For Novalis the categories of origin and eschaton thus become nonsensical and mistaken.[5] As Jean Paul also perceived, self-reflexive thought never escapes its circularity to arrive at a telos or vantage point outside the circle. Nor, of course, could the telos and self-reflection ever become identical. That would be the precondition of a Hegelian philosophy of history.[6] Hegel thus appears to be not so much a response to Romantic nonclosure but—and here I risk crude over-simplification—an anachronism. The processuality of his dialectics harks back to Enlightenment *futurus*. Here, though, I myself should guard against falling into a Hegelian discourse, against outlining not a succession but the kind of hierarchy and supersession against which the Romantics reacted. It would be a different kind of study that systematically read something like Hegel's *Phänomenologie des Geistes* against the Romantics. Such a move would attempt to justify the Romantics by their anticipatory critique of Hegel—a defensive approach trying to redefine superiorities. Instead I hope to revive the former's significance for an eclectically minded generation which is, as Marquard and Blumenberg suggest, weary of authoritarian solutions.

I called this corrective and iconoclastic voice surfacing in texts written around 1800 the "future perfect." Figuratively speaking, this tense allows authors like Hölderlin and Novalis to write conscientiously, to recognize that they can state only preliminary—never exhaustive—provisions for the future. The eschaton itself lies outside their domain. Furthermore, by continuing always to hypothesize about the preconditions of an end, these writers actively stave off its arrival. The presence of this sceptical voice does not deny, however, that the structure of, say, "Brod und Wein," *Christenheit oder Europa,* or the various *Märchen* by Novalis is predominantly triadic. This structure is not the sole one; as we have seen, its use entails a venturesome self-criticism.

It is this sustained countervoice which, to my mind, needed closer scrutiny, not only in the separate works of Hölderlin and Novalis but also in the context of postrevolutionary intellectual Germany. The texts herein treated provide us with a radically new, unprecedented way of structuring the future. By consistently evading closure, the writings of Hölderlin and Novalis exemplify the discourse of iterative crises and radical temporality.

To be sure, in order to do justice to these two authors, I have risked overlooking various other Idealist, predominantly *geschichtsphilosophische* works—especially those not directly following the turn of the nineteenth century, most notably Hegel's *Phänomenologie des Geistes.* However, the critique of ends and endings in the works of Hölderlin and Novalis suggests that we could discover, though perhaps to a lesser degree, the same undermining element in other teleologically and triadically structured works of the period. We have intimated that such is the case with passages in Lessing's *Erziehung des Menschengeschlechts,* Kant's *Das Ende aller Dinge,* Schiller's *Ueber naive und sentimentalische Dichtung,* Fichte's *Über die Bestimmung des Gelehrten,* Schelling's *System des transzendentalen*

Idealismus, Hölderlin's *Hyperion,* Kleist's *Über das Marionettentheater,* and various Jean Paul texts from "Traum über das All" to the sixth "Schalttag" in *Hesperus.* This is not to mention both the Romantic fragmentation of apocalypse discussed in chapter one and Friedrich Schlegel's and Schleiermacher's frequent proximity to Novalis. But the minute work required for a thorough reading of each of these authors would rupture the parameters of this study. My apology for slighting them here lies in the lesson brought home by this investigation—that as moderns our work is destined to be prefatory. Otherwise we would have attained the perfect discourse. Friedrich Schlegel reminds us: "Das goldne Zeitalter der Literatur würde dann sein, wenn keine Vorreden mehr nötig wären" {The golden age of literature would be when prefaces were no longer necessary} (KA 2:404, no. 62).

Appendix

PATMOS

Dem Landgrafen von Homburg

Nah ist
Und schwer zu fassen der Gott.
Wo aber Gefahr ist, wächst
Das Rettende auch.
5   Im Finstern wohnen
Die Adler und furchtlos gehn
Die Söhne der Alpen über den Abgrund weg
Auf leichtgebaueten Brüken.
Drum, da gehäuft sind rings
10   Die Gipfel der Zeit, und die Liebsten
Nah wohnen, ermattend auf
Getrenntesten Bergen,
So gieb unschuldig Wasser,
O Fittige gieb uns, treuesten Sinns
15   Hinüberzugehn und wiederzukehren.

So sprach ich, da entführte
Mich schneller, denn ich vermuthet
Und weit, wohin ich nimmer
Zu kommen gedacht, ein Genius mich
20   Vom eigenen Hauß'. Es dämmerten
Im Zwielicht, da ich gieng
Der schattige Wald
Und die sehnsüchtigen Bäche
Der Heimath; nimmer kannt' ich die Länder;
25   Doch bald, in frischem Glanze,
Geheimnißvoll
Im goldenen Rauche, blühte
Schnellaufgewachsen,
Mit Schritten der Sonne,
30   Mit tausend Gipfeln duftend,

Mir Asia auf, und geblendet sucht'
Ich eines, das ich kennete, denn ungewohnt
War ich der breiten Gassen, wo herab
Vom Tmolus fährt
35　Der goldgeschmükte Pactol
Und Taurus stehet und Messogis,
Und voll von Blumen der Garten,
Ein stilles Feuer; aber im Lichte
Blüht hoch der silberne Schnee;
40　Und Zeug unsterblichen Lebens
An unzugangbaren Wänden
Uralt der Epheu wächst und getragen sind
Von lebenden Säulen, Cedern und Lorbeern
Die feierlichen,
45　Die göttlichgebauten Palläste.

Es rauschen aber um Asias Thore
Hinziehend da und dort
In ungewisser Meeresebene
Der schattenlosen Straßen genug,
50　Doch kennt die Inseln der Schiffer.
Und da ich hörte
Der nahegelegenen eine
Sei Patmos,
Verlangte mich sehr,
55　Dort einzukehren und dort
Der dunkeln Grotte zu nahn.
Denn nicht, wie Cypros,
Die quellenreiche, oder
Der anderen eine
60　Wohnt herrlich Patmos,

Gastfreundlich aber ist
Im ärmeren Hauße
Sie dennoch
Und wenn vom Schiffbruch oder klagend
65　Um die Heimath oder
Den abgeschiedenen Freund
Ihr nahet einer
Der Fremden, hört sie es gern, und ihre Kinder
Die Stimmen des heißen Hains,
70　Und wo der Sand fällt, und sich spaltet
Des Feldes Fläche, die Laute
Sie hören ihn und liebend tönt

Es wieder von den Klagen des Manns. So pflegte
Sie einst des gottgeliebten,
75   Des Sehers, der in seeliger Jugend war

Gegangen mit
Dem Sohne des Höchsten, unzertrennlich, denn
Es liebte der Gewittertragende die Einfalt
Des Jüngers und es sahe der achtsame Mann
80   Das Angesicht des Gottes genau,
Da, beim Geheimnisse des Weinstoks, sie
Zusammensaßen, zu der Stunde des Gastmals,
Und in der großen Seele, ruhigahnend den Tod
Aussprach der Herr und die lezte Liebe, denn nie genug
85   Hatt' er von Güte zu sagen
Der Worte, damals, und zu erheitern, da
Ers sahe, das Zürnen der Welt.
Denn alles ist gut. Drauf starb er. Vieles wäre
Zu sagen davon. Und es sahn ihn, wie er siegend blikte
90   Den Freudigsten die Freunde noch zulezt,

Doch trauerten sie, da nun
Es Abend worden, erstaunt,
Denn Großentschiedenes hatten in der Seele
Die Männer, aber sie liebten unter der Sonne
95   Das Leben und lassen wollten sie nicht
Vom Angesichte des Herrn
Und der Heimath. Eingetrieben war,
Wie Feuer im Eisen, das, und ihnen gieng
Zur Seite der Schatte des Lieben.
100 Drum sandt' er ihnen
Den Geist, und freilich bebte
Das Haus und die Wetter Gottes rollten
Ferndonnernd über
Die ahnenden Häupter, da, schwersinnend
105 Versammelt waren die Todeshelden,

Izt, da er scheidend
Noch einmal ihnen erschien.
Denn izt erlosch der Sonne Tag
Der Königliche und zerbrach
110 Den geradestralenden,
Den Zepter, göttlichleidend, von selbst,
Denn wiederkommen sollt es
Zu rechter Zeit. Nicht wär es gut

Gewesen, später, und schroffabbrechend, untreu,
115   Der Menschen Werk, und Freude war es
Von nun an,
Zu wohnen in liebender Nacht, und bewahren
In einfältigen Augen, unverwandt
Abgründe der Weisheit. Und es grünen
120   Tief an den Bergen auch lebendige Bilder,

Doch furchtbar ist, wie da und dort
Unendlich hin zerstreut das Lebende Gott.
Denn schon das Angesicht
Der theuern Freunde zu lassen
125   Und fernhin über die Berge zu gehn
Allein, wo zweifach
Erkannt, einstimmig
War himmlischer Geist; und nicht geweissagt war es, sondern
Die Loken ergriff es, gegenwärtig,
130   Wenn ihnen plözlich
Ferneilend zurük blikte
Der Gott und schwörend,
Damit er halte, wie an Seilen golden
Gebunden hinfort
135   Das Böse nennend, sie die Hände sich reichten —

Wenn aber stirbt alsdenn
An dem am meisten
Die Schönheit hieng, daß an der Gestalt
Ein Wunder war und die Himmlischen gedeutet
140   Auf ihn, und wenn, ein Räthsel ewig füreinander   .
Sie sich nicht fassen können
Einander, die zusammenlebten
Im Gedächtniß, und nicht den Sand nur oder
Die Weiden es hinwegnimmt und die Tempel
145   Ergreifft, wenn die Ehre
Des Halbgotts und der Seinen
Verweht und selber sein Angesicht
Der Höchste wendet
Darob, daß nirgend ein
150   Unsterbliches mehr am Himmel zu sehn ist oder
Auf grüner Erde, was ist diß?

Es ist der Wurf des Säemanns, wenn er faßt
Mit der Schaufel den Waizen,
Und wirft, dem Klaren zu, ihn schwingend über die Tenne.

155 Ihm fällt die Schaale vor den Füßen, aber
    Ans Ende kommet das Korn,
    Und nicht ein Übel ists, wenn einiges
    Verloren gehet und von der Rede
    Verhallet der lebendige Laut,
160 Denn göttliches Werk auch gleichet dem unsern,
    Nicht alles will der Höchste zumal.
    Zwar Eisen träget der Schacht,
    Und glühende Harze der Aetna,
    So hätt' ich Reichtum,
165 Ein Bild zu bilden, und ähnlich
    Zu schaun, wie er gewesen, den Christ,

    Wenn aber einer spornte sich selbst,
    Und traurig redend, unterweges, da ich wehrlos wäre
    Mich überfiele, daß ich staunt' und von dem Gotte
170 Das Bild nachahmen möcht' ein Knecht –
    Im Zorne sichtbar sah' ich einmal
    Des Himmels Herrn, nicht, daß ich seyn sollt etwas, sondern
    Zu lernen. Gütig sind sie, ihr Verhaßtestes aber ist,
    So lange sie herrschen, das Falsche, und es gilt
175 Dann Menschliches unter Menschen nicht mehr.
    Denn sie nicht walten, es waltet aber
    Unsterblicher Schiksaal und es wandelt ihr Werk
    Von selbst, und eilend geht es zu Ende.
    Wenn nemlich höher gehet himmlischer
180 Triumphgang, wird genennet, der Sonne gleich
    Von Starken der frohlokende Sohn des Höchsten,

    Ein Loosungszeichen, und hier ist der Stab
    Des Gesanges, niederwinkend,
    Denn nichts ist gemein. Die Todten weket
185 Er auf, die noch gefangen nicht
    Vom Rohen sind. Es warten aber
    Der scheuen Augen viele
    Zu schauen das Licht. Nicht wollen
    Am scharfen Strale sie blühn,
190 Wiewohl den Muth der goldene Zaum hält.
    Wenn aber, als
    Von schwellenden Augenbraunen
    Der Welt vergessen
    Stillleuchtende Kraft aus heiliger Schrift fällt, mögen
195 Der Gnade sich freuend, sie
    Am stillen Blike sich üben.

Und wenn die Himmlischen jezt
So, wie ich glaube, mich lieben
Wie viel mehr Dich,
200   Denn Eines weiß ich,
Daß nemlich der Wille
Des ewigen Vaters viel
Dir gilt. Still ist sein Zeichen
Am donnernden Himmel. Und Einer stehet darunter
205   Sein Leben lang. Denn noch lebt Christus.
Es sind aber die Helden, seine Söhne
Gekommen all und heilige Schriften
Von ihm und den Bliz erklären
Die Thaten der Erde bis izt,
210   Ein Wettlauf unaufhaltsam. Er ist aber dabei. Denn seine
                                              [Werke sind
Ihm alle bewußt von jeher.

Zu lang, zu lang schon ist
Die Ehre der Himmlischen unsichtbar.
Denn fast die Finger müssen sie
215   Uns führen und schmählich
Entreißt das Herz uns eine Gewalt.
Denn Opfer will der Himmlischen jedes,
Wenn aber eines versäumt ward,
Nie hat es Gutes gebracht.
220   Wir haben gedienet der Mutter Erd'
Und haben jüngst dem Sonnenlichte gedient,
Unwissend, der Vater aber liebt,
Der über allen waltet,
Am meisten, daß gepfleget werde
225   Der veste Buchstab, und bestehendes gut
Gedeutet. Dem folgt deutscher Gesang.

Notes

Introduction

1. On the novel and the inconclusiveness and open-endedness of the present and future it depicts, see Mikhail Bakhtin, "Epic and Novel: Toward a Methodology for the Study of the Novel," in *The Dialogic Imagination: Four Essays*, trans. Emerson and Holquist (Austin: University of Texas Press, 1981), 3–40.

2. An excellent example of the latter is Paul de Man's "The Rhetoric of Temporality" (*Interpretation: Theory and Practice*, ed. Charles Singleton [Baltimore: Johns Hopkins University Press, 1969], 173–209). Paralleling the debate between the New and the Yale Critics on Romantic form is Derrida's attack of the Structuralists' drive towards systemization and summation, cogently voiced in his early essay, "Force and Signification" (*Writing and Difference*, trans. Alan Bass [Chicago: University of Chicago Press, 1978], 3–30).

3. Maurice Blanchot, *L'entretien infini* and *Le Livre à venir* (Paris: Gallimard, 1969 and 1959). See also Michel Foucault's essay "Le langage à l'infini," on the birth of interminable, self-reflexive writing at the end of the eighteenth century. Foucault begins by referring to Blanchot.

4. Jacques Derrida, "Differance," in his *Speech and Phenomena, and Other Essays on Husserl's Theory of Signs* (Evanston: Northwestern University Press, 1973), 142.

5. On the divisibility of time, i.e., its spacing, see Derrida's *"Ousia and Grammē:* Note on a Note from *Being and Time," Margins of Philosophy*, trans. Alan Bass (Chicago: University of Chicago Press, 1982), 29–67.

6. Note that this trajectory does not need to follow a chronology in order to be end-oriented. On final analysis closure is independent of chronological accuracy, less so of the potentially destabilizing course taken by the récit (*Erzählzeit*).

7. Émmanuel Lévinas, *Totality and Infinity: An Essay on Exteriority*, trans. Alphonso Lingis (Pittsburgh: Duquesne University Press, 1969). Jacques Derrida's words on Lévinas and Blanchot could apply equally to Hölderlin: they situate themselves "within the hollow space of finitude in which messianic eschatology comes to resonate, within the expectation of

expectation" ("Violence and Metaphysics: An Essay on the Thought of Émmanuel Lévinas" [*Writing and Difference*], 103).

8. All translations are my own. Should my reader wish to consult verse translations of Hölderlin, I recommend those of Michael Hamburger (Cambridge University Press, 1980); and for whatever might not be found in Hamburger, see Richard Sieburth, *Friedrich Hölderlin's Hymns and Fragments* (Princeton: Princeton University Press, 1984).

9. The critical thinkers on temporality and narrative are too numerous and diverse to have all been given due mention in this preface. I refer my reader to the bibliography and, in particular, to Paul Ricouer on aporiae in time; Gilles Deleuze on repetition; Michel Foucault in *The Order of Things*; David Carroll on the ends of history; J. Hillis Miller and Eugenio Donato on narrative and the death of God; Peter Brooks on emplotment; Roland Barthes, Paul Veyne, Michel de Certeau, and numerous others on the temporality of historical discourse; and, of course, Frank Kermode on the sense of an ending.

10. Jacques Derrida, *Of Grammatology*, trans. Gayatri Chakravorty Spivak (Baltimore: Johns Hopkins University Press, 1974), xx.

Chapter 1   Scenes of Transition

1. Friedrich Schleiermacher, *Hermeneutik und Kritik*, ed. Manfred Frank (Frankfurt: Suhrkamp, 1977), 94.

2. Schleiermacher, *Hermeneutik*, 95.

3. See Marquis de Condorcet, *Esquisse d'un tableau historique des progrès de l'esprit humain* (Paris: Éditions sociales, 1966), 278.

4. Condorcet, *Esquisse*, 83.

5. See the chapter "Historische Kriterien des neuzeitlichen Revolutionsbegriffs," in Reinhart Koselleck, *Vergangene Zukunft: Zur Semantik geschichtlicher Zeiten* (Frankfurt: Suhrkamp, 1979).

6. Robespierre, "Sur la Constitution," in *Oeuvres complètes*, ed. M. Bouloiseau (Paris: Leroux, 1958), 9:495. Georg Büchner called Robespierre the "Blood-Messiah" in his drama *Dantons Tod*.

7. Cf. Friedrich Schlegel: "*alles Wissen {muß} in einen revolutionären Zustand gesetzt werden*" (KA 12:11). Voltaire was the first to speak of the "revolution des esprits." See Karl Griewank, *Der neuzeitliche Revolutionsbegriff: Entstehung und Entwicklung* (Weimar: Böhlau, 1955), 196.

8. Koselleck, *Vergangene Zukunft*, 88; cf. 59.

9. Koselleck writes: "Weil sich die Zukunft der modernen Geschichte ins Unbekannte öffnet, wird sie planbar, – und muß sie

geplant werden. Und mit jedem neuen Plan wird eine neue Unerfahrbarkeit eingeführt" (p. 61).

10. Quoted in Griewank, *Der neuzeitliche Revolutionsbegriff*, 249.

11. Friedrich Schleiermacher, *Dialektik, auf Grund bisher unveröffentlichten Materials*, ed. R. Odebrecht (Darmstadt: Wissenschaftliche Buchgesellschaft, 1976), 13.

12. Cf. KA 18:77, no. 592.

13. Walter Benjamin, "Der Begriff der Kunstkritik in der deutschen Romantik," in *Gesammelte Schriften*, 1:i, ed. Tiedemann and Schweppenhäuser (Frankfurt: Suhrkamp, 1974), 92. Hans-Joachim Mähl, *Die Idee des goldenen Zeitalters im Werk des Novalis: Studien zur Wesensbestimmung der frühromantischen Utopie und zu ihren ideengeschichtlichen Voraussetzungen* (Heidelberg: Winter, 1965). Wolfgang Binder has written several articles on Hölderlin and secularization; see Chapter 3 and the bibliography to this work. Meyer Abrams, *Natural Supernaturalism: Tradition and Revolution in Romantic Literature* (New York: Norton, 1971).

14. J. Hillis Miller, "Tradition and Difference," *Diacritics* 2 (1972):12.

15. Abrams, *Natural Supernaturalism*, 13.

16. Cf. Kant, GS 8:115.

17. Cf. "Das sogenannte 'Älteste Systemprogramm,'" in *Materialien zu Schellings philosophischen Anfängen*, ed. M. Frank and G. Kurz (Frankfurt: Suhrkamp, 1975), 111–12.

18. Karl Löwith, *Meaning in History: The Theological Implications of the Philosophy of History* (Chicago: University of Chicago Press, 1949), 13.

19. Gerhard Kaiser, *Pietismus und Patriotismus im literarischen Deutschland: Ein Beitrag zum Problem der Säkularisation*, 2d ed. (Frankfurt: Athenäum, 1973), 93.

20. Hans Blumenberg, *The Legitimacy of the Modern Age*, trans. Robert Wallace (Cambridge: MIT Press, 1983), 15.

21. Odo Marquard, *Schwierigkeiten mit der Geschichtsphilosophie: Aufsätze* (Frankfurt: Suhrkamp, 1973), 16.

22. I heard these terms at a lecture I attended by Jürgen Moltmann in Tübingen in the summer semester of 1981.

23. Reason functions as originator and prime agent not only in Kant's concept of the future but also in his definition of the sublime. The mind rechannels the awe back to the rational faculty, thereby claiming for itself both antecedence and superiority.

Kant's belief in progressivity thus differs from Leibniz's precisely with respect to the function of reason. The latter sees progress latent within creation, whereas the former claims that the rational human faculty acts as the prime instigator of teleological change. Cf. Leibniz: "A cumulative increase of the beauty and universal perfection of the works of

God, a perpetual and unrestricted progress of the universe as a whole must be recognized, such that it advances to a higher state of cultivation, just as a great part of our earth is already subject to cultivation and will hereafter be so more and more" (*Philosophische Schriften*, ed. J. Gerhardt [Hildesheim: Olms, 1960], 6:308). For more information on the role of reason in Kant's view of history, see Jirmiahu Yovel, *Kant and the Philosophy of History* (Princeton: Princeton University Press, 1980).

24. Cf. GS 6:122, 124, 135; 8:30, 65, 115, 334–35.

25. François Hemsterhuis, *Alexis oder Von dem goldenen Weltalter*, trans. F. H. Jacobi (Riga: Hartknoch, 1787), 115.

26. For a more comprehensive view of Herder's biblical interpretations, see Hans Frei, *The Eclipse of Biblical Narrative: A Study in Eighteenth and Nineteenth Century Hermeneutics* (New Haven: Yale University Press, 1974), 187 ff. On exegeses of Revelation at the time, see Elinor Shaffer, *'Kubla Khan' and the 'Fall of Jerusalem': The Mythological School in Biblical Criticism and Secular Literature 1770–1880* (Cambridge: Cambridge University Press, 1975).

27. John Locke, *Works* (Aalen: Scientia Reprints, 1963), 1:191–92.

28. Locke, *Works*, 192.

29. Étienne de Condillac, *Traité des sensations*, in *Oeuvres complètes* (Geneva: Slatkine, 1970), 3:80–81.

30. Denis Diderot, "Lettre sur les sourds et muets," in *Oeuvres complètes* (Paris: Hermann, 1975), 4:161.

31. Jean-Jacques Rousseau, *Émile*, in *Oeuvres complètes* (Paris: Seuil, 1971), 197.

32. As in Matt. 24:3, 27, 39; 25:31–46; 1 Thess. 2:19, 3:13, 4:15, 5:23; Rev. 19:11–21.

33. Cf. Hölderlin, StA 6:185.

34. In Old Testament theology, this distinction also helps separate prophecy from apocalypticism. See H. H. Rowley: "Speaking generally, the prophets foretold the future that should arise out of the present, while the apocalyptists foretold the future that should break into the present" (*The Relevance of Apocalyptic: A Study of Jewish and Christian Apocalypses from Daniel to Revelation* [London: Lutterworth, 1944], 35). Cf. Martin Buber, "Prophecy, Apocalyptic, and the Historical Hour," in *On the Bible: Eighteen Studies*, ed. N. Glatzer (New York: Schocken, 1968), 172–87.

35. Although its heaven is to be established on earth, this is no reason in itself to categorize millenarianism as a form of *futurus*. Because it supports faith in an *ordo novus*, millenarianism is still another form of adventism.

36. L., a.Gr. *anagoge* elevation, religious or ecstatic elevation, mystical sense; f. *an-goge* to lead up, lift up, elevate (OED). Cf. Friedrich Ohly, "Vom geistigen Sinn des Wortes im Mittelalter," in his *Schriften*

zur mittelalterlichen Bedeutungsforschung (Darmstadt: Wissenschaftliche Buchgesellschaft, 1977), 1–31.

37. See Klaus Aichele, *Das Antichristdrama des Mittelalters, der Reformation und Gegenreformation* (The Hague: Nijhoff, 1974), 51.

38. Reinhart Koselleck, *Kritik und Krise: Eine Studie zur Pathogenese der bürgerlichen Welt*, 3d ed. (Frankfurt: Suhrkamp, 1979), 132, 155, 115.

39. See Manfred Frank on how the Romantics saw consciousness contingent upon temporal succession in his *Problem 'Zeit' in der deutschen Romantik: Zeitbewußtsein und Bewußtsein von Zeitlichkeit in der frühromantischen Philosophie und in Tiecks Dichtung* (Munich: Winkler, 1972).

40. Cf. Lessing, W 8:33, and Kant, GS 8:115.

41. See Georg Friedrich Hegel, *Wissenschaft der Logik*, ed. Georg Lasson (Hamburg: Meiner, 1963), 128.

42. Cf. Goethe's ironic epigrammatic reply: "Ob die Menschen im ganzen sich bessern? Ich glaub' es, denn einzeln, / Suche man, wie man auch will, sieht man doch gar nichts davon" (HA 1:209).

43. Cf. Schiller: "Dieser Weg, den die neueren Dichter gehen, ist übrigens derselbe, den der Mensch überhaupt sowohl im Einzelnen als im Ganzen einschlagen muß. Die Natur macht ihn mit sich Eins, die Kunst trennt und entzweyet ihn, durch das Ideal kehrt er zur Einheit zurück" (NA 20:438).

44. Fichte, *Ausgewählte politische Schriften*, ed. Z. Batscha and R. Saage (Frankfurt: Suhrkamp, 1976), 216.

45. In the *Athenäum: Eine Zeitschrift*, ed. A. W. and Fr. Schlegel (Berlin: Fröhlich, 1800), 3:287, 294.

46. Marshall Brown, *The Shape of German Romanticism* (Ithaca: Cornell University Press, 1979), 38.

47. Gerhard Kurz, *Mittelbarkeit und Vereinigung: Zum Verhältnis von Poesie, Reflexion und Revolution bei Hölderlin* (Stuttgart: Metzler, 1975).

48. Ludwig Tieck, *Schriften* (Berlin: Reimer, 1828), 9:359.

49. Cf. the thematized narrative disruptures on pages 6, 15, 26, 28, 40, 94, 98.

50. Here we have the distinction between mysticism and apocalypticism. The mystics claimed authority by appealing to the divine spirit speaking through them, as through a mask. This spirit can appear at all times and at any place, each time with the same amount of fullness: one mystic does not contradict another. But the apocalyptic writer is intently preoccupied with maintaining a position superior to that of his predecessor, even if that predecessor is himself.

51. Bernhard McGinn, *Visions of the End: Apocalyptic Traditions in the Middle Ages* (New York: Columbia University Press, 1979), 5, 28ff.

52. See the title of Bengel's main work—*Erklärte Offenbarung . . . aufgeschlossen und allen . . . vor Augen geleget.*

53. Friedrich Christoph Oetinger, *Kurzgefaßte Grundlehre* (1769), 474.

54. Kaiser, *Pietismus und Patriotismus*, 171.

55. Oetinger, *Die güldene Zeit*, in *Sämtliche Schriften*, ed. K. C. E. Ehmann (Stuttgart: Steinkopf, 1864), 6:135.

56. Jung, called Stilling, *Sämtliche Schriften* (Stuttgart: Henne, 1835–37), 3:412.

57. Jung-Stilling, *Sämtliche Schriften*, 3:8.

58. Oetinger, *Philosophie der Alten wiederkommend in der güldenen Zeit* (Frankfurt/Leipzig: 1762), 13.

59. Oetinger, *Güldene Zeit*, 6:42.

60. Jung-Stilling, *Sämtliche Schriften*, 3:10.

61. See the chapter on *Das Heimweh* in Ulrich Stadler, *Die theuren Dinge: Studien zu Bunyan, Jung-Stilling und Novalis* (Bern: Francke, 1980).

62. Elinor Shaffer astutely remarks upon the paradox: "Hegel's early theological works twist and turn in their attempt to find a place for Jesus. . . . The more the theology of the age came to stress Christ as the link between man and a distant God, or, like Schleiermacher, Christ Himself as man, the more He too became cut off from God" (*Kubla Khan*, 60–61). Our topic of study is similarly paradoxical: writers at this time, although fascinated by the millennial ending, always defer it.

63. Cf. KA 12:6.

64. This trace of prolonged doubt, or uncertainty about the future, enables both the French and the Germans to use an atemporal form of the future perfect to express such a thing as probability: "Il aura manqué son train" or "Er wird wohl seinen Zug verpaßt haben."

65. Jacques Derrida, *D'un ton apocalyptique adopté naguère en philosophie* (Paris: Galilée, 1983), 77.

66. Despite the strongest voice to the contrary—that of Hegel. For elucidation of Hegel's *Sollenskritik*, see Marquard, *Schwierigkeiten*, 37.

Chapter 2   Friedrich von Hardenberg (Novalis)

1. Wilfried Malsch, *"Europa": Poetische Rede des Novalis: Deutung der französischen Revolution und Reflexion auf die Poesie in der Geschichte* (Stuttgart: Metzler, 1965), 28.

2. Hans Wolfgang Kuhn, *Der Apokalyptiker und die Politik: Studien zur Staatsphilosophie des Novalis* (Freiburg: Rombach, 1961), 17.

3. Richard Faber, "Apokalyptische Mythologie: Zur Religionsdichtung des Novalis," in *Romantische Utopie – Utopische Romantik*, ed. Dischner and Faber (Hildesheim: Gerstenberg, 1979), 79.

4. Eckhard Heftrich, *Novalis: Vom Logos der Poesie* (Frankfurt: Klostermann, 1969), 102.

5. For an essay that does not simplify the transformation, see Manfred Frank, "Die Dichtung als 'Neue Mythologie': Motive und Konsequenzen einer frühromantischen Idee," *Recherches germaniques* 9 (1979): 122–40. See also Frank, *Der kommende Gott: Vorlesungen über die Neue Mythologie* (Frankfurt: Suhrkamp, 1982).

6. Examples are legion. I shall relegate only a few to this note. Martin E. Schmid, for instance, writes: "Im poetischen *Machwerk* spricht sich die transzendente Welt aus" (*Novalis: Dichter an der Grenze zum Absoluten* [Heidelberg: Winter, 1976], 177).

Johannes Mahr comments that the poet "das vergangene Paradies zu neuem Leben erweckt und . . . gestaltet, was die Hoffnung dunkel ersehnt" (*Übergang zum Endlichen: Der Weg des Dichters in Novalis' "Heinrich von Ofterdingen"* [Munich: Fink, 1970], 267).

Hans-Joachim Mähl, the most prominent Novalis critic, likewise writes: "Die *Wunderkraft* der poetischen Fiktion . . . besteht eben darin, daß sie das Unsichtbare sichtbar, das Nichtgegenwärtige gegenwärtig macht" (*Die Idee des goldenen Zeitalters im Werk des Novalis* [Heidelberg: Winter, 1965], 341).

Cf. also Richard Samuel: "Metapher, Vergleich und Bild richten sich also immer darauf, . . . den Menschen über die Grenzen von Raum und Zeit hinweg in die Ewigkeit zu stellen" ("Heinrich von Ofterdingen," in *Der deutsche Roman*, ed. Benno von Wiese [Düsseldorf: Bagel, 1965], 284).

7. Faber, "Apokalyptische Mythologie," 21.

8. Compare Faber with Kuhn, for instance: "Im Nacherleben [des Lesers] ist die Verheißung der eschatologischen Wirklichkeit" (*Der Apokalyptiker*, 21). Heftrich writes: "Aber wo immer man auch dieses Morgenland suchen mag, *wirklich* zu finden ist es nur im Utopia des künftigen Reiches. Als Ewiges kommt dieses Reich auf uns zu, indem wir uns darauf hin bewegen" (*Novalis*, 147). And we can once again cite Mähl's disciple Mahr: "Dichtung beschreibt eine erwartete Wirklichkeit und sucht sie . . . durch die Beschreibung näherzubringen" (*Übergang zum Endlichen*, 249).

9. Cf. "Le Fragment" in Philippe Lacoue-Labarthe/Jean-Luc Nancy, *L'absolu littéraire: Théorie de la littérature du romantisme allemand* (Paris: Seuil, 1978), 57–80.

10. Cf. KA 12:392–93.

11. See Thomas McFarland for an informative presentation of the European and English Romantic concern with fragmentation, which he calls *diasparaction* (*Romanticism and the Forms of Ruin: Wordsworth, Coleridge, and Modalities of Fragmentation* [Princeton: Princeton University Press, 1981]).

12. *The Fragments of the Work of Heraclitus of Ephesus on Nature*, trans. G. T. W. Patrick (Baltimore: Murray, 1889), fragment 93.

13. Jochen Hörisch, *Die fröhliche Wissenschaft der Poesie: Der Universalitätsanspruch von Dichtung in der frühromantischen Poetologie* (Frankfurt: Suhrkamp, 1976), 203.

14. For instance, in his concluding footnote Grob writes in critical response to Mahr: "Die Bedeutung der Ironie läßt es nicht mehr zu, das Märchen als eine Präfiguration einer *realen Zukunft* zu verstehen" (*Ursprung und Utopie: Aporien des Textes. Versuche zu Herder und Novalis* [Bonn: Bouvier, 1976], 170).

Likewise Hannelore Link claims: "Novalis besitzt weder den Glauben an eine historisch gewesene 'goldene Zeit' noch den an eine realiter kommende" (*Abstraktion und Poesie im Werk des Novalis* [Stuttgart: Kohlhammer, 1971], 66).

See also Manfred Frank: "*In* der Zeit – etwa als Zukunft läßt sich ein prinzipiell Außerzeitliches weder verwirklichen noch träumen" (*Das Problem 'Zeit' in der deutschen Romantik: Zeitbewußtsein und Bewußtsein von Zeitlichkeit in der frühromantischen Philosophie und Tiecks Dichtung* [Munich: Winkler, 1972], 224).

15. See Louis Marin, *Utopiques: jeux d'espaces* (Paris: Minuit, 1973), 22.

16. See Hans-Joachim Mähl, *Die Idee des goldenen Zeitalters,* for a comprehensive history of this tradition.

17. Géza von Molnár, the first to write informatively on Novalis's reception of Fichte, comments: "Novalis takes the indirect path, the *via negativa,* to the Absolute, and this constitutes his main divergence from the approach in the *Wissenschaftslehre*" (*Novalis' "Fichte Studies": The Foundations of his Aesthetics* [Hague: Mouton, 1970], 26). Novalis, we shall see, is closer to Schelling, of whom he said to Friedrich Schlegel: "In Einem Stücke entspricht er mir mehr, als Fichte" (1:641). See also Wolfgang Janke, "Enttönter Gesang – Sprache und Wahrheit in den 'Fichte Studien' des Novalis," in *Erneuerung der Transzendentalphilosophie im Anschluß an Kant und Fichte,* ed. Hammacher and Mues (Stuttgart: Fromman-Holzboog, 1979), 168–203; William A. O'Brien, "The Richly Sown Field: Three Essays on Semiology in the Writings of Friedrich von Hardenberg (Novalis)" (Ph.D. diss., Johns Hopkins, 1981); and Richard W. Hannah, *The Fichtean Dynamic of Novalis' Poetics* (Bern: Lang, 1981).

18. Novalis, *Schriften,* ed. Samuel, Mähl, Schulz (Stuttgart: Kohlhammer, 1960), 2:361.

19. Ibid.

20. Cf. 2:98, no. 263.

21. Cf. 2:830 on the way every story refers to another story.

22. "Identität-nur-mit-sich verwandelt sich im Blick eines sie Reflektierenden zu einer *relativen,* d. h. zu einer auf Differenz bezogenen Identität" (Manfred Frank and Gerhard Kurz, "Ordo inversus: Zu einer Reflexionsfigur bei Novalis, Hölderlin, Kleist und Kafka," in *Geist und Form: Festschrift für Arthur Henkel* [Heidelberg: Carl Winter, 1977], 77).

23. Mahr, *Übergang zum Endlichen,* 192.

24. Cf. 2:141, no. 383; 673, no. 833, and the concepts of *Übergang* and *Auflösung* in Hölderlin's "Das Werden im Vergehen" (StA 4:282–87).

25. Cf. 2:673, no. 838, and *Einbildungskraft* or *Anziehungskraft* 2:96, no. 249; 94, no. 246; 98, no. 263; 134, no. 326.

26. Cf. 1:657, 2:500, no. 138; 415; 417; and Kohlhammer 2:361.

27. Cf. Schiller: "Die Zeit ist die Bedingung alles Werdens. . . . Ohne die Zeit, das heißt, ohne es zu werden, würde [der Mensch] nie ein bestimmtes Wesen seyn" (NA 20:342) and Hölderlin: "Denn die Welt aller Welten, das Alles in Allen, welches immer ist, stellt sich nur in aller Zeit – oder im Untergange oder im Moment, oder genetischer im werden des Moments und Anfang von Zeit und Welt dar" ("Werden im Vergehen," [StA 4:282]). In his notes to his translation of *Oedipus,* Hölderlin also refers to God as "nichts als Zeit" (5:202).

28. Cf. 2:181; 758, no. 47.

29. Cf. 2:77, no. 224; KA 9:413.

30. Mahr is duped by the illusion: he writes of "[d]ie Aufhebung der Zeit, die dann erreicht ist, wenn alle Gegenstände in einem ungestörten Austausch und in dauernder wechselseitiger Belebung sind" (*Übergang zum Endlichen,* 208). On the contrary, for Novalis, time is characterized by constant reciprocity, not by its sublation.

31. Cf. KA 18:77, no. 588.

32. Lacoue-Labarthe and Nancy, *L'absolu littéraire,* 64.

33. Cf. Winfried Kudszus, "Geschichtsverlust und Sprachproblematik in den 'Hymnen an die Nacht'," *Euphorion* 65 (1971): 298–311.

34. Cf. KA 2:263, no. 81; KA 2:201, no. 222.

35. Cf. 2:829; 591, no. 516.

36. Here I clearly part ways with the majority of Novalis scholars, in particular Mähl, who have carefully extracted chiliastic references in Novalis. I object not to the fact that the notion of parousia *informs* Hardenberg's writings but to the claim that his work then glorifies and embodies it. Instead, Novalis consistently resists seduction by the very thought of an end. I shall elaborate upon this crucial distinction at key turns in my discussion.

37. The "laws" of relationships operating in poetry are as unpredictable as in dream-work: "Der Traum ist oft bedeutend und prophetisch, . . . auf Associationsordnung beruht – Er ist, wie die Poësie bedeutend – aber auch darum unregelmäßig bedeutend – *durchaus frey*" (2:693, no. 959).

38. Cf. 1:652–53; 2:246, no. 50; 2:244, no. 40.

39. Cf. 2:85.

40. Paul de Man ("The Rhetoric of Temporality," in *Interpretation: Theory and Practice,* ed. Charles Singleton [Baltimore: Johns Hopkins University Press, 1969], 190) refers us to the role of allegory in Romanticism as

opposed to that of the symbol: "We have, instead, a relationship between signs in which the reference to their respective meanings has become of secondary importance. But this relationship between signs necessarily contains a constitutive temporal element; it remains necessary, if there is to be allegory, that the allegorical sign refer to another sign that precedes it."

41. Cf. the term *Brechen* (2:98, no. 257; 112; 122, no. 300; 534, no. 335; 672, no. 831). Regarding the notion of erasure, cf. also *Auflösung* (1:242; 2:512, no. 224; 565, no. 448) and the relation of *Witz* to *Auflösung* (2:240, no. 30; KA 12:392–93).

42. See John Neubauer's chapter on the foundations of *poësie pure* in his *Symbolismus und symbolische Logik: Die Idee der ars combinatoria in der Entwicklung der modernen Dichtung* (Munich: Fink, 1978).

43. Hans Blumenberg, *Die Lesbarkeit der Welt* (Frankfurt: Suhrkamp, 1981), 254.

44. Cf. 2:177, no. 555, and 2:178 on *Schweben* and free imagination.

45. Cf. KA 2:172, no. 51; 2:319; KA 18:361, no. 495.

46. I disagree therefore with the sublation of opposites Friedrich Strack sees operative in the term *Schweben:* "Der Wechselbegriff verliert seine Gegensatzstruktur" (*Im Schatten der Neugier: Christliche Tradition und kritische Philosophie im Werk Friedrichs von Hardenberg* [Tübingen: Niemeyer, 1982], 132). For the notion of reciprocity in Fichte and Schiller, cf. Jeffrey Barnouw, " 'Der Trieb, bestimmt zu werden': Hölderlin, Schiller und Schelling als Antwort auf Fichte," *Deutsche Vierteljahrsschrift* 46 (1972): 248–93.

47. Cf. 2:202, no. 651.

48. Cf. Hölderlin: "In ihrem Schmerze verläßt sie das Geliebte, hängt sich dann oft ohne Wahl an diß und das im Leben, immer hoffend und immer getäuscht; oft kehrt sie auch in ihre Ideenwelt zurük" (StA 3:203).

49. Critics such as Gordon Birrell often ignore the fact that the *Märchen* are never impersonally narrated (*The Boundless Present: Space and Time in the Literary Fairy Tales of Novalis and Tieck* [Chapel Hill: University of North Carolina Press, 1979]). Those readers interested in recent, poststructuralist interpretations of the Klingsohr tale should see William O'Brien, "Twilight in Atlantis: Novalis' *Heinrich von Ofterdingen* and Plato's *Republic*," *Modern Language Notes* 95 (1980): 1292–1332 and Friedrich A. Kittler, "Die Irrwege des Eros und die 'absolute Familie': Psychoanalytischer und diskursanalytischer Kommentar zu Klingsohrs Märchen in Novalis' *Heinrich von Ofterdingen*," in *Psychoanalytische und psychopathologische Literaturinterpretation,* ed. Urban and Kudszus (Darmstadt: Wissenschaftliche Buchgesellschaft, 1981).

50. "Die Erfüllung" opens with a description of progressive awakening: "und wie die Liebe sich / In tiefere Entzückungen verlohr, / Erwacht' ich immer mehr" (p. 365). The prose of the second part, however, begins by prolonging the dream: "Es dünkte ihm, als träume er jezt oder habe er geträumt" (p. 368).

51. Cf. the distancing of the narrator through use of the subjunctive later on: "In Heinrichs Gemüth spiegelte sich das Mährchen des Abends. Es war ihm, als ruhte die Welt aufgeschlossen in ihm. . . . Ihm dünkte. . . . Die Natur schien ihm" (pp. 298–99).

52. At a later point in the narrative, even the identity of Heinrich's sire is questioned. The interchange that precedes the famous lines, "Wo gehn wir denn hin? Immer nach Hause," is as follows: "Wer war dein Vater? Der Graf von Hohenzollern. Den kenn' ich auch. Wohl mußt du ihn kennen, denn er ist auch dein Vater. Ich habe ja meinen Vater in Eysenach? Du hast mehr Eltern" (p. 373).

53. Zulimas queries: "Wer weiß, ob nicht auch ein unbegreiflicher Einfluß der ehemaligen, jetzt unsichtbaren Bewohner mit ins Spiel kommt" (p. 283).

54. Lucien Dällenbach, *Le récit spéculaire: Essai sur la mise en abyme* (Paris: Seuil, 1977), 93.

55. The theme of the cave as the interior of an interior runs throughout *Heinrich von Ofterdingen*. After progressing from one cavity to the next, the party led by the miner in chapter five reaches the abode of the hermit. In the inlaid Atlantis tale, the cave marks the scene of the lovers' consummation. In Klingsohr's tale, Fabel descends to that world within a world—the realm of the fates.

56. The tale of Hyacinth and Rosenblüthe offers us an example of the dream-within-the-*Märchen* construct. Novalis writes that Hyacinth falls asleep because only a dream can lead him into the holy of holies (p. 218). The narrator never tells us when Hyacinth awakens. Is the reunion with Rosenblüthe then only dreamt? Is the journey away from her also perhaps imaginary? We can further speculate that Heinrich never awakens from his dream and that the rest of the novel is its continuation—or at least the effort to recall, recapture, or repeat the initially dreamt experience of gratification.

57. Cf. "Hyacinth und Rosenblüthe," in which the stranger comes from foreign lands (1:215).

58. Mähl sees images of centrality and interiority here, which he calls "der Weg nach innen" (*Die Idee des goldenen Zeitalters*, 412): "Wir befinden uns in der magischen Verzauberung der poetischen Innenwelt, . . . das dem Zustande einer höheren Welt entspricht" (p. 410).

59. Contrast Mähl: "[Heinrich] erhebt sich zu jenem 'echten Bewußtsein'" (p. 410).

60. This is distinct from thematic foreshadowing. Cf. Samuel: "[Der Traum] nimmt die Gesamthandlung des ganzen Werkes andeutend voraus und führt den Helden bis an die Schwelle der Erfüllung" (*"Heinrich von Ofterdingen,"* 269). Mahr similarly writes of "die persönliche Erfüllung . . . im Traum vorgebildet" (*Übergang zum Endlichen*, 63).

61. Cf. 2:601, no. 567; KA 2:169, no. 22.

62. Mahr maintains: "Die Entwicklung Heinrichs von Ofterdingen

zum Dichter steht zwischen dem Bericht eines vergangenen (Arion- und Atlantisgeschichte) und der Beschreibung eines erwarteten goldenen Zeitalters (Märchen von den Wanderungen Fabels)" (*Übergang zum Endlichen*, 264). In the following, I wish to dispute such a progression, especially when it is claimed to culminate in the depiction of the future.

63. Compare their view to the miner's, for whom gold no longer exerts an attraction since it has become a vehicle of monetary exchange (1:291).

64. In the late sketches to the novel, Novalis writes that a person should not depict what he does not completely survey, clearly perceive, and totally master (1:389). The hermit also recognizes the worth of age and experience; only by ample intercourse with others does one acquire independence (p. 303). Such observations sound like an indirect critique of Heinrich.

65. Cf. Ulrich Stadler: "Heinrich soll Jerusalem erreichen; er soll das Goldene Zeitalter wieder herbeiführen. Aber alles, was er tun kann, ist, daß er dieses jeweils für einen Augenblick aufleuchten lassen kann und daß er *immer* nach Jerusalem (oder nach Hause) *geht*" (*Die theuren Dinge: Studien zu Bunyan, Jung-Stilling und Novalis* [Bern: Francke, 1980], 224). Also in contradistinction to Mahr, cf. Jean-Pierre Étienne: "Le roman est la figuration d'une histoire à venir, dans la mesure même où il s'affirme comme utopie régressive" ("Novalis ou le double discours: *Heinrich von Ofterdingen*," *Romantisme* 20 [1978]: 67).

66. Cf. "Variationsreihe" or "unendliche Reihe" (2:419, no. 470; 359, no. 212).

67. Yet the answer cannot lie in further mystifying uninterpretability, as Strack does. He says of this passage: "[Die Sprache] gibt keine sicheren Aufschlüsse, aber einen 'goldenen Schlüssel', der zu vielen Schatzkammern paßt" (*Im Schatten*, 265).

68. Link calls this repetition "Prä- und Postfiguration" (*Abstraktion und Poesie*, 164ff.) but sees it sublating temporality (p. 166). Her other conclusion is more convincing, "daß ein Vor- oder Rückbezug inhaltlicher Art plötzlich auch zu einem Selbstbezug des Werks als Kunstwerk wird. Durch ihn wird das Bewußtsein des Lesers aus der inhaltlichen Illusion hinausgetrieben und auf das Ereignis der Dichtung als solcher verwiesen" (p. 167). Cf. also Ulrich Stadler, *Die theuren Dinge*, 222; and the originator of this reading, Hans-Joachim Mähl, who says, "daß durch die ständige Ineinanderschachtelung der Zeit- und Raumperspektiven . . . sich das Geheimnis dieser inneren poetischen Welt, ihre unendliche Einheit der Zeiten und Räume auftut" (*Die Idee des goldenen Zeitalters*, 410).

69. Birrell, *The Boundless Present*, 76.

70. Cf. 2:282, nos. 123, 124.

71. Compare with the notion of perennial threshold in Jean Paul:

"Vor-Ewigkeit" and "Vorhof der Ewigkeit" (17:95; 13:155). See also in "Die Erwartung": "Vorhöfe des innern Erdenpalastes" (1:300).

72. Cf. pp. 366, 368, 378 and *Hymnen an die Nacht* (1:177, ll. 21–22).

73. Cf. Mähl's "dichterische Vergegenwärtigung des Zukunftszieles" (*Die Idee des goldenen Zeitalters*, 385, 337), or Mahr's "Dichtungen . . . als Vorwegnahmen des Künftigen" (*Übergang zum Unendlichen*, 264).

74. Cf. 2:477, no. 40.

75. Cf. the notion of "retardirende Natur" (2:561; KA 2:139, no. 177).

76. Cf. "Der Roman ist gleichsam die *freye Geschichte*" (2:830).

77. Norbert Bolz has written a good article on the problem of author and authority entitled "Über romantische Autorschaft," in *Urszenen: Literaturwissenschaft als Diskursanalyse und Diskurskritik*, ed. Friedrich Kittler and Horst Turk (Frankfurt: Suhrkamp, 1977), 44–52.

78. Cf. 2:388, no. 22.

79. Lacoue-Labarthe and Nancy, *L'absolu littéraire*, 425.

80. Helmut Pfotenhauer gives Novalis's encyclopedic efforts convincing sociological motivation: "Eben jene Obsession aber, die sich hinter dem Vervollständigungsdrang bemerkbar macht, gibt eher den Blick frei auf die Unerschöpflichkeit des Materials, als daß der intendierte geglückte Abschluß transparent würde. . . . Gemeint ist . . . das Verlangen, sich alles Vergangene und Fremde vertraut zu machen, nicht zuletzt als Entschädigung für die in ihrer Eigengesetzlichkeit dem einzelnen zunehmend entgleitende gegenwärtige soziale Realität" ("Aspekte der Modernität bei Novalis: Überlegungen zu Erzählformen des 19. Jahrhunderts ausgehend von Hardenbergs *Heinrich von Ofterdingen*," in *Literaturwissenschaft und Sozialwissenschaft* 8 [1977]: 128).

81. Cf. Friedrich Schlegel: "Die Unvollendung der Poesie ist nothwendig. *Ihre Vollendung—das Erscheinen des Messias*" (*Literary Notebooks 1797–1800*, ed. Hans Eichner [Toronto: University of Toronto Press], 207, no. 2090). Cf. also KA 18:421, no. 1222.

82. Cf. KA 12:9.

83. See KA 2:159, no. 103.

Chapter 3   Hölderlin

1. Jochen Schmidt writes that "Friedensfeier" is Hölderlin's most consequent model of the future ("Hölderlins Entwurf der Zukunft," *Hölderlin-Jahrbuch* 16 [1970]: 119).

2. For thorough studies on "Mnemosyne" which convincingly interpret the death of memory, see Jochen Schmidt, *Hölderlins letzte Hymnen:*

"Andenken" und "Mnemosyne" (Tübingen: Niemeyer, 1970) and Richard Unger, *Hölderlin's Major Poetry: The Dialectics of Unity* (Bloomington: Indiana University Press, 1975).

3. Unger traces the theme of All-Unity in Hölderlin's hymns, working out decisive changes from poem to poem. In the opening of his chapter on "Mnemosyne," he writes: "The great synthesis attained in 'Patmos' soon proved untenable. . . . ['Mnemosyne'] constitutes a final statement on the now hopeless status of the problem of All-Unity" (*Major Poetry,* 206–7). As I suggest in the following discussion, though, the break between these two hymns is probably not so clean.

4. Thus the same tendency we saw in Novalis criticism surfaces again with Hölderlin: accomplished secularization is exalted. By now we have sighted and diagnosed the problem of such readings enough to refer in passing to its examples. Cf., for instance, two of the major critics on Hölderlin. Wolfgang Binder writes that even a pantheistic history of salvation is nonetheless a *Heilsgeschichte* ("Grundformen der Säkularisation in den Werken Goethes, Schillers und Hölderlins," *Zeitschrift für deutsche Philologie* 83 [1964]: 67). Ernst Müller similarly observes: "Vom kommenden Gotte voll sind die um 1800 entstandenen großen Elegien, und die letzten Hymnen singen vom großen Aufbruch" (*Hölderlin: Studien zur Geschichte seines Geistes* [Stuttgart: Kohlhammer, 1944], 85). Cf. also Peter Howard Gaskill, *Christ and the Divine Economy in the Work of Friedrich Hölderlin* (Diss., Cambridge, 1971) and "Meaning in History: 'Chiliasm' in Hölderlin's 'Patmos'," *Colloquia Germanica* 11 (1978): 19–52.

5. See letters nos. 236 and 240 to Böhlendorff (StA 6:425–28, 432–33).

6. See Martin Brecht, "Zum sozialen und geistigen Umfeld von Hölderlins Jugend," in *Bausteine zur geschichtlichen Landeskunde von Baden-Württemberg* (Stuttgart: Kohlhammer, 1979), 347–56. Cf. also Reinhard Breymayer, "Ein unbekanntes Gedicht Friedrich Hölderlins in einer Sammlung württembergischer Familiengedichte," *Blätter für württembergische Kirchengeschichte* 78 (1978): 73–145.

7. Friedrich Christoph Oetinger, *Biblisches und Emblematisches Wörterbuch dem Tellerischen Wörterbuch und anderen falschen Schrifterklärungen entgegen gesetzt* (1776), 21.

8. *Hölderlins Lehre vom Wechsel der Töne* (Stuttgart: Kohlhammer, 1960), 307. See his footnote 159 for a list of other interpretations.

9. Andrzej Warminski writes: "Caring for the 'veste Buchstab' (that of Holy Scripture) suggests an activity not unlike *dienen* which calls for submission and self-effacement" ("'Patmos': The Senses of Interpretation," *Modern Language Notes* 91 [1976]: 482).

10. See Karlheinz Stierle for the dichotomy *nah-fern.* One wishes Stierle could have developed more fully his notion of the "Gebrochenheit des Diskurses" (p. 62) rather than reconciling the dichotomies in the

hymn ("Dichtung und Auftrag: Hölderlins Patmos-Hymne," *Hölderlin-Jahrbuch* 22 [1980–81]: 47–68).

11. Binder sees this move concurrent with Hölderlin's history of the human spirit: "Dem entspricht der Schritt von Asia wieder nach Westen; denn in Hölderlins mythischer Geographie ist die Ost-West-Richtung das Korrelat des Geschichtsganges" ("Hölderlins Patmos-Hymne," in *Hölderlin-Aufsätze* [Frankfurt: Insel, 1970], 376).

12. This avoidance parallels the trend in current "enlightened" theology to focus on the historical rather than on the glorified or apocalyptic Christ (cf. Reimarus, Herder, and the early Hegel). Hölderlin, though, seems elsewhere more engaged in the mythical aspects of Christ as "Fürst des Festes" and therein displays his Swabian Pietist background. Perhaps Hölderlin's preoccupation with, yet evasion of, the apocalypse betokens the conflict between these two traditions.

13. Cf. Binder: "Für die Dichter, deren Amt das Nennen ist, ist die Gefahr der Vergegenständlichung, die sie verleitet, sich des Göttlichen in positiven Namen zu bemächtigen. Darum zieht sich der Dichter in die Distanz der Dämmerung zurück, worin ihm die Demut eines namenlosen Nennens der Unendlichen erhalten bleibt" ("Hölderlins Namenssymbolik," *Hölderlin-Jahrbuch* 12 [1961–62]: 115).

14. Cf. StA 2:145, l. 119.

15. Binder calls these lines the hymnic pinnacle of the work (*Hölderlin-Aufsätze,* 370). I would prefer to interpret the last triad as correcting the exuberance of this passage.

16. Contrary to readings by Ryan, who speaks of the affinity between poetic and divine creation ("Hölderlins prophetische Dichtung," *Jahrbuch der deutschen Schillergesellschaft* 6 [1962]: 219). Cf. also Hans-Georg Gadamer, "Hölderlin und das Zukünftige," in *Beiträge zur geistigen Überlieferung* (Godesberg: Küpper, 1947), 65. But cf. Jean-Luc Marion for the distancing of God: "Rien de plus proprement divin, que la gloire masquée et l'absence d'immédiate apparition" (*L'idole et la distance: Cinq études* [Paris: Grasset, 1977], 148).

17. At least in "Patmos," the discovery of limits and awareness of distinctions does not, however, lead to silence. Concerning this problem in the late Hölderlin, see Winfried Kudszus, *Sprachverlust und Sinnwandel: Zur späten und spätesten Lyrik Hölderlins* (Stuttgart: Metzler, 1969).

18. Cf. the *fern* compounds in "Patmos": lines 103, 125, 131.

19. For other instances of the central image of night, cf. "Dichterberuf": "Der Vater aber deket mit heilger Nacht, / Damit wir bleiben mögen, die Augen zu" (2:48, ll. 53–54); the first stanza of "Chiron": "wo bist du, Licht? . . . mich / Hemmt die erstaunende Nacht nun immer" (2:56, ll. 2–4; cf. 2:54, ll. 2–4); and, as we shall later see, "Brod und Wein."

20. In "Brod und Wein" the accomplished sign (*fernhintreffende Sprüche*) flashes (*leuchten*) like lightning (2:92, l. 61).

21. For interpretations of "Wie wenn am Feiertage," cf. William Arctander O'Brien, "Getting blasted: Hölderlin's 'Wie wenn am Feiertage . . .'," *Modern Language Notes* 94 (1979): 569–86; Martin Heidegger, "Wie wenn am Feiertage . . . ," in *Erläuterungen zu Hölderlins Dichtung* (Frankfurt: Klostermann, 1951), 47–74; Eduard Lachmann, "Hölderlins erste Hymne," *Deutsche Vierteljahrsschrift* 17 (1939): 221–51; and Peter Szondi, "Der andere Pfeil," *Hölderlin-Studien* (Frankfurt: Insel, 1967), 33–54.

22. Cf. Kudszus: "Das Heil Christi impliziert Unheil für den Dichter; denn die Schwingen der Erkenntnis, die Christus über das Land der Sprache erheben, besitzt er nicht. . . . Ihm droht 'tief unter die Lebenden . . . ins Dunkel' geworfen, als 'falscher Priester' gebrandmarkt zu werden" (*Sprachverlust*, 38). Kudszus maintains that this state ultimately leads to the loss of control over language. But, as I want to show here, Hölderlin attempts, at least in "Patmos," to circumvent this danger.

23. Cf. Andrzej Warminski: "Error, then, would not be a mistake or a momentary disturbance but the very condition of meaning: 'der lebendige Sinn' in its purity would be absolutely different, sheer exteriority, and 'der Sinn,' unable to grasp the totality of the truth presented by the living sense, would be an arbitrary imposition" ("The Senses of Interpretation," 495).

24. The poetic persona recognizes the necessity of remaining within the bounds of symbolic night: "Der Vater aber deket mit heilger Nacht, / Damit wir bleiben mögen, die Augen zu" (2:48, ll. 53–54; cf. also last stanza of "Dichterberuf"). The word *bleiben* is often set in opposition to an overpowering parousia: "Darum, ihr Gütigen! umgebet mich leicht, / Damit ich bleiben möge, denn noch ist manches zu singen" (2:129, ll. 111–12), or to blinding light: "aber es sonnen / Die Herzen der Sterblichen auch / An mildem Lichte sich gern, und heften / Die Augen an Bleibendes" (4:115). It therefore signals, usually at the end of a poem, renewed attention to the present: "göttlicher, sei / Am Abend deiner Tage gegrüßet. / Und mögen bleiben wir nun" (2:132, ll. 87–89).

Yet in other instances, *bleiben* forestalls not parousia but senseless temporal change: "Ersehnter Friede, komm und gieb ein / Bleiben im Leben, ein Herz uns wieder" (2:7, l. 43–44); "dieses vesteste Bleiben vor der wandelnden Zeit" (5:268, l. 19). *Bleiben* thus also implies *bewahren* or sustained memory of significant past moments: "Zu wohnen in liebender Nacht und bewahren / In einfältigen Augen unverwandt / Abgründe der Weisheit" ("Patmos," ll. 117–19). Here the notion of *bleiben* is related to the poetic word which captures and holds the past: "Es bleibet aber eine Spur / Doch eines Wortes; die ein Mann erhaschet" (2: 163, ll. 73-74); "Was bleibet aber, stiften die Dichter" (2:189, l. 59). At this point, we recall the closing lines of "Patmos": German song upholds what endures.

25. Cf. Rainer Nägele, *Literatur und Utopie: Versuche zu Hölderlin* (Heidelberg: Stiehm, 1978).

26. Like the apostles after the Crucifixion: "Doch trauerten sie . . ." (l. 91).

27. On the paradoxical nature of silence in language, see Maurice Blanchot, "La Parole 'sacrée' de Hölderlin," in *La Part de feu* (Paris: Gallimard, 1949), 118–36.

28. Cf. Jochen Schmidt for a lengthy footnote on *fest* as a token of the late Hölderlin's frenetic desire to fasten onto something secure and controllable. Such security, though, would betoken a slackening of the poet's vigilance (*Hölderlins letzte Hymnen*, 9).

29. Rainer Nägele writes of "die Fixierung auf das 'Angesicht' des Herrn, auf die einmal, geschichtlich erfahrene Gestalt, als Moment der Innerlichkeit selbst." He also speaks in this context of fetishism ("Fragmentation und fester Buchstabe: Zu Hölderlins 'Patmos'-Überarbeitungen," *Modern Language Notes* 97 [1982]: 565).

30. Nägele's *MLN* article on "Patmos" is a welcomed exception, as is the conclusion to his *Text, Geschichte und Subjektivität in Hölderlins Dichtung – "Uneßbarer Schrift gleich"* (Stuttgart: Metzler, 1985). In both cases Nägele interprets the emendations as expressing splintered subjectivity.

31. Cf. 2:186, l. 160.

32. The poetic subtleties of this elegy have been discussed at great length in a number of close readings. The interested reader should consult Richard Unger; Manfred Frank, *Der kommende Gott;* Jochen Schmidt, *Hölderlins Elegie "Brod und Wein": Die Entwicklung des hymnischen Stils in der elegischen Dichtung* (Berlin: de Gruyter, 1968); Theodore Ziolkowski, *The Classical German Elegy, 1795–1950* (Princeton: Princeton University Press, 1980); and Jochen Hörisch, "Dichtung als Eucharistie: Zum Motiv 'Brot und Wein' bei Hölderlin," in *Invaliden des Apoll: Motive und Mythen des Dichterleids,* ed. Herbert Anton (Munich: Fink, 1982), 52–77.

33. Wolfram Groddeck, "Die Nacht: Überlegungen zur Lektüre der späten Gestalt von 'Brod und Wein,'" *Hölderlin-Jahrbuch* 21 (1978–79): 209.

34. Cf. ll. 68–69.

35. Kudszus's commentary on "Der Vatikan" appropriately fits our example from the late Hölderlin's writing: "denn dort, wo er sprachlich differenziert, erscheint Drohendes, und nur dort, wo er fast gänzlich auf 'Unterschiede' verzichtet, breitet sich Ruhe aus – freilich eine totenstille" (*Sprachverlust,* 71). Concerning paratactic listing in the late Hölderlin, cf. also Eric L. Santner, "Sober Recollections: Hölderlin's De-idealization of Memory in 'Andenken'," *Germanic Review* 60 (1985): 16–22; and his "Paratactic Composition in Hölderlin's 'Hälfte des Lebens,'" *German Quarterly* 58 (1985): 165–72.

36. For the sake of honesty it should be said that Hölderlin does not

consistently make the same changes throughout the poem: reference to the heavenly ones is indeed retained in lines 55, 81, and 88.

37. Schmidt perceives here a reference to Dionysus at his birth (*Hölderlins Elegie*, 205–6).

38. Groddeck's position is the former, whereas Schmidt sees Hölderlin consolidating the earlier version with more precise formulations (*Hölderlins Elegie*, 184).

39. Cf. Laplanche: "Au lieu de subir passivement la dialectique narcissique qui le fait passer sans transition du Même à l'Autre, le sujet prend sa distance en tentant de concevoir ce qu'on pourrait nommer *la différence de la différence et de la non-différence*. . . . Ainsi se trouve ouverte la distance illimitée d'un *Zwischen:* non pas tant un 'entre-deux' qu'un 'entre' pris absolument" (*Hölderlin et la question du père* [Paris: Presses Universitaires de France, 1961], 112, 131). For a response to Laplanche see Stanley Corngold, "Hölderlin and the Question of the Self" in *The Fate of the Self: German Writers and French Theory* (New York: Columbia University Press, 1986), 21–53.

40. Roman Jakobson and Grete Lübbe-Grothues, "The Language of Schizophrenia: Hölderlin's Speech and Poetry," *Poetics Today* 24 (1980): 137–44. See also Maurice Blanchot, "La Folie par excellence," *Critique* 7 (1951): 99–118.

41. Contrast Schmidt, who sees in Hölderlin the Kingdom of God as the attainment of a world of inner perfection (*Hölderlins Elegie*, 145). Cf. also Ryan: for Hölderlin, the willful giving oneself up to the passage of time helps to further temporal progress and the march towards perfection ("Hölderlins prophetische Dichtung," 205).

42. Cf. "Die Heimkunft" (2:97, ll. 39ff.) and "Am Quell der Donau" (2:129, ll. 111–12).

43. Michel Foucault, "The Father's 'No,'" in *Language, Counter-Memory, Practice*, trans. Bouchard and Simon (Ithaca: Cornell University Press, 1977), 86.

Afterword

1. In Martin Heidegger, *Gesamtausgabe* (Frankfurt: Klostermann, 1977), 5: 214ff. See also Eugenio Donato, "Divine Agonies: Of Representation and Narrative in Romantic Poetics," *Glyph Textual Studies* 6 (1979): 90–122.

2. Friedrich Nietzsche, *Sämtliche Werke: Kritische Studienausgabe* (Berlin: de Gruyter, 1980), 3:481.

3. J. Hillis Miller, *The Disappearance of God: Five Nineteenth-Century Writers* (Cambridge: Harvard University Press, 1963) and *Fiction and Repe-*

tition: Seven English Novels (Cambridge: Harvard University Press, 1982). Cf. Manfred Frank, *Die unendliche Fahrt: ein Motiv und sein Text* (Frankfurt: Suhrkamp, 1979) and D. A. Miller, *Narrative and its Discontents: Problems of Closure in the Traditional Novel* (Princeton: Princeton University Press, 1981).

4. Cf. the notion of *Reihen* (N 2:543, no. 378; 614, no. 615). In their awareness both of the subjectivity of historical narrative and of the necessity of stratification and serialization, the Romantics approach recent trends in French historiography. I am thinking here of the Annales school, Fernand Braudel, Michel Foucault, and of studies on historiography by Roland Barthes, Michel de Certeau, Paul Ricoeur and Lionel Gossman—to name but a few. Cf. also volume 59 (1980) of *Yale French Studies* on "Writing and History."

5. Cf. the concepts of *Unsinn* (N 2:164, no. 472) and *Irrthum* (N 2:438; 2:622; 2:637, no. 685).

6. A telos is the unrealizable *sine qua non* of any philosophy of history. For a discussion of Schelling's critique of Hegel on these grounds, see Manfred Frank, *Der unendliche Mangel an Sein: Schellings Hegelkritik und die Anfänge der Marxschen Dialektik* (Frankfurt: Suhrkamp, 1975).

A Selective Bibliography

In the chapters on Novalis and Hölderlin I have made frequent reference to critical works on these two authors, trying to indicate the particular bent of each scholar and at what point each diverges from another. The purpose of my bibliography is not to relist these works; and the addition of the few titles I have not dealt with would contribute little to the topic of delayed endings. Instead I would like to direct the interested reader to a number of works on temporality and closure—in relation, first, to narrative theory and Romanticism and, second, to adventism and its secularization. The boundaries, of course, overlap, and there are some works that I would have liked to include in both categories. I have given the English translation of French and German texts, where available.

(Romantic) Narrative Theory

Abrams, Meyer H. *Natural Supernaturalism: Tradition and Revolution in Romantic Literature.* New York: Norton, 1971.
———. *The Mirror and the Lamp: Romantic Theory and the Critical Tradition.* London: Oxford University Press, 1953.
Arendt, Dieter. *Der poetische Nihilismus in der Romantik: Studien zum Verhältnis von Dichtung und Wirklichkeit in der Frühromantik.* Tübingen: Niemeyer, 1972.
Bakhtin, Mikhail. "Epic and Novel: Toward a Methodology for the Study of the Novel." In *The Dialogic Imagination: Four Essays,* translated by Emerson and Holquist, 3–40. Austin: University of Texas Press, 1981.
Barthes, Roland. "The Discourse of History." *Comparative Criticism* 3 (1981): 3–20.
Benjamin, Walter. "Der Begriff der Kunstkritik in der deutschen Romantik" and "Metaphysisch-geschichtsphilosophische Studien." In *Gesammelte Schriften,* edited by Tiedemann and Schweppenhäuser. Frankfurt: Suhrkamp, 1974 and 1977.

Blanchot, Maurice. *L'entretien infini*. Paris: Gallimard, 1969.
———. "La Folie par excellence." *Critique* 7 (1951): 99–118.
———. *Le Livre à venir*. Paris: Gallimard, 1959.
———. "La parole 'sacrée' de Hölderlin." In *La Part de feu*, 118–19. Paris: Gallimard, 1949.
Blumenberg, Hans. *The Legitimacy of the Modern Age*. Translated by Robert M. Wallace. Cambridge: MIT Press, 1983.
———. *Die Lesbarkeit der Welt*. Frankfurt: Suhrkamp, 1981.
Bohrer, Karl Heinz. *Plötzlichkeit: Zum Augenblick des ästhetischen Scheins*. Frankfurt: Suhrkamp, 1981.
———, ed. *Mythos und Moderne: Begriff und Bild einer Rekonstruktion*. Frankfurt: Suhrkamp, 1983.
Bolz, Norbert. "Über romantische Autorschaft." In *Urszenen: Literaturwissenschaft als Diskursanalyse und Diskurskritik*, edited by Kittler and Turk, 44–52. Frankfurt: Suhrkamp, 1977.
Brisman, Leslie. *Romantic Origins*. Ithaca: Cornell University Press, 1978.
Brooks, Peter. *Reading for the Plot: Design and Intention in Narrative*. New York: Knopf, 1984.
Brown, Marshall. *The Shape of German Romanticism*. Ithaca: Cornell University Press, 1979.
Carroll, David. *The Subject in Question: The Languages of Theory and the Strategies of Fiction*. Chicago: University of Chicago Press, 1982.
Corngold, Stanley. *The Fate of the Self: German Writers and French Theory*. New York: Columbia University Press, 1986.
Dällenbach, Lucien. *Le récit spéculaire: Essai sur la mise en abyme*. Paris: Seuil, 1977.
Deleuze, Gilles. *Différence et répétition*. Paris: Presses Universitaires de France, 1968.
De Man, Paul. "Genesis and Genealogy (Nietzsche)." In *Allegories of Reading: Figural Language in Rousseau, Nietzsche, Rilke, and Proust*, 79–102. New Haven: Yale University Press, 1979.
———. "The Rhetoric of Temporality." In *Interpretation: Theory and Practice*, edited by Charles Singleton, 173–209. Baltimore: Johns Hopkins University Press, 1969.
Derrida, Jacques. "Differance." In *Speech and Phenomena, and Other Essays on Husserl's Theory of Signs*, 129–60. Evanston: Northwestern University Press, 1973.
———. *D'un ton apocalyptique adopté naguère en philosophie*. Paris: Galilée, 1983.
———. "The Ends of Man" and "*Ousia* and *Grammē:* Notes on a Note from *Being and Time*." In *Margins of Philosophy*, translated by Alan Bass, 109–36, 29–67. Chicago: University of Chicago Press, 1982.
———. "Outwork, Prefacing." In *Dissemination*, translated by Barbara Johnson, 1–59. Chicago: University of Chicago Press, 1981.

———. "The Theater of Cruelty and the Closure of Representation." In *Writing and Difference*, translated by Alan Bass, 232–50. Chicago: University of Chicago Press, 1978.

Donato, Eugenio. "Divine Agonies: Of Representation and Narrative in Romantic Poetics." *Glyph Textual Studies* 6 (1979): 90–122.

Ehrmann, Jacques. "The Tragic/Utopian Meaning of History." *Yale French Studies* 58 (1979): 15–30.

Foucault, Michel. "Language to Infinity" and "Nietzsche, Genealogy, History." In *Language, Counter-Memory, Practice: Selected Essays and Interviews*, edited and translated by Bouchard, 53–67, 139–64. Ithaca: Cornell University Press, 1977.

———. *The Order of Things: An Archaeology of the Human Sciences.* New York: Random House, 1970.

Frank, Manfred. "Die Dichtung als 'Neue Mythologie': Motive und Konsequenzen einer frühromantischen Idee." *Recherches germaniques* 9 (1979): 122–40.

———. *Der kommende Gott: Vorlesungen über die Neue Mythologie.* Frankfurt: Suhrkamp, 1982.

———. *Das Problem 'Zeit' in der deutschen Romantik: Zeitbewußtsein und Bewußtsein von Zeitlichkeit in der frühromantischen Philosophie und in Tiecks Dichtung.* Munich: Winkler, 1972.

———. *Die unendliche Fahrt: Ein Motiv und sein Text.* Frankfurt: Suhrkamp, 1979.

———. *Der unendliche Mangel an Sein: Schellings Hegelkritik und die Anfänge der Marxschen Dialektik.* Frankfurt: Suhrkamp, 1975.

Fränkel, Hermann. *Wege und Formen frühgriechischen Denkens: Literarische und philosophische Studien.* Munich: Beck, 1968.

Frye, Northrop. *The Great Code: The Bible and Literature.* New York: Harcourt, Brace, Jovanovich, 1982.

Gockel, Heinz. "Friedrich Schlegels Theorie des Fragments." In *Romantik: Ein literaturwissenschaftliches Studienbuch*, edited by Ernst Ribbat, 22–37. Königstein: Athenäum, 1979.

———. *Mythos und Poesie: Zum Mythosbegriff in Aufklärung und Frühromantik.* Frankfurt: Klostermann, 1981.

Griewank, Karl. *Der neuzeitliche Revolutionsbegriff: Entstehung und Entwicklung.* Weimar: Böhlau, 1955.

Hamlin, Cyrus. "The Temporality of Selfhood: Metaphor and Romantic Poetry." *New Literary History* 6 (1974–75): 169–93.

Hamon, Philippe. "Clausules." *Poétique* 24 (1975): 495–526.

Hartman, Geoffrey. "The Poetics of Prophecy." In *High Romantic Argument: Essays for M. H. Abrams*, edited by Lipking, 15–40. Ithaca: Cornell University Press, 1981.

———. *Saving the Text: Literature, Derrida, Philosophy.* Baltimore: Johns Hopkins University Press, 1981.

Herz, Neil. "The Notion of Blockage in the Literature of the Sublime." In *Psychoanalysis and the Question of the Text*, edited by Geoffrey Hartman, 62–85. Baltimore: Johns Hopkins University Press, 1978.

Herrnstein-Smith, Barbara. *Poetic Closure: A Study of How Poems End*. Chicago: University of Chicago Press, 1968.

Hörisch, Jochen. *Die fröhliche Wissenschaft der Poesie: Der Universalitätsanspruch von Dichtung in der frühromantischen Poetologie*. Frankfurt: Suhrkamp, 1976.

Hult, David, ed. *Concepts of Closure*. *Yale French Studies* 67 (1984).

Jauss, Hans-Robert. "Schlegels und Schillers Replik auf die 'Querelle des Anciens et des Modernes.'" In *Literaturgeschichte als Provokation der Literaturwissenschaft*. Constance: Universitätsverlag, 1967.

Kermode, Frank. *The Sense of an Ending: Studies in the Theory of Fiction*. London: Oxford University Press, 1966.

Kesting, Marianne. "Aspekte des absoluten Buches bei Novalis und Mallarmé." *Euphorion* 68 (1974): 410–36.

Koselleck, Reinhart. *Kritik und Krise: Eine Studie zur Pathogenese der bürgerlichen Welt*. 3d ed. Frankfurt: Suhrkamp, 1979.

———. *Vergangene Zukunft: Zur Semantik geschichtlicher Zeiten*. Frankfurt: Suhrkamp, 1979.

——— and Wolf-Dieter Stempel, eds. *Geschichte, Ereignis und Erzählung*. In *Poetik und Hermeneutik V*. Munich: Fink, 1973.

Kudszus, Winfried. "Geschichtsverlust und Sprachproblematik in den 'Hymnen an die Nacht.'" *Euphorion* 65 (1971): 298–311.

Kurz, Gerhard. *Mittelbarkeit und Vereinigung: Zum Verhältnis von Poesie, Reflexion und Revolution bei Hölderlin*. Stuttgart: Metzler, 1975.

Lacoue-Labarthe, Philippe, and Jean-Luc Nancy. *L'absolu littéraire: Théorie de la littérature du romantisme allemand*. Paris: Seuil, 1978.

Lämmert, Eberhard. "Zum Wandel der Geschichtserfahrung im Reflex der Romantheorie." In *Zeitgestaltung in der Erzählkunst*, edited by Alexander Ritter. Darmstadt: Wissenschaftliche Buchgesellschaft, 1978.

Laplanche, Jean. *Hölderlin et la question du père*. Paris: Presses Universitaires de France, 1961.

Les fins de l'homme: A partir du travail de Jacques Derrida. Colloque de Cerisy. Paris: Galilée, 1981.

Lévinas, Émmanuel. *Autrement qu'être ou au-delà de l'essence*. The Hague: Nijhoff, 1974.

———. *De Dieu qui vient à l'idée*. Paris: Librairie Philosophique J. Vrin, 1982.

———. *Totality and Infinity: An Essay on Exteriority*. Translated by Alphonso Lingis. Pittsburgh: Duquesne University Press, 1969.

Link, Hannelore. *Abstraktion und Poesie im Werk des Novalis*. Stuttgart: Kohlhammer, 1971.

Lovejoy, Arthur O. *The Great Chain of Being: A Study of the History of an Idea.* Cambridge: Harvard University Press, 1964.

Manuel, Frank. *Shapes of Philosophical History.* Stanford: Stanford University Press, 1965.

_____ and Fritzie Manuel. *Utopian Thought in the Western World.* Cambridge: Harvard University Press, 1979.

Marin, Louis. *Utopiques: Jeux d'espaces.* Paris: Minuit, 1973.

Marquard, Odo. *Schwierigkeiten mit der Geschichtsphilosophie: Aufsätze.* Frankfurt: Suhrkamp, 1973.

McFarland, Thomas. *Romanticism and the Forms of Ruin: Wordsworth, Coleridge, and Modalities of Fragmentation.* Princeton: Princeton University Press, 1981.

Metzner, Joachim. "Die Vieldeutigkeit und der Wiederkehr: Literaturpsychologische Überlegungen zur Phantastik." In *Phantastik in Literatur und Kunst,* edited by Thomsen and Fischer, 79–108. Darmstadt: Wissenschaftliche Buchgesellschaft, 1980.

_____. *Persönlichkeitszerstörung und Weltuntergang: Das Verhältnis von Wahnbildung und literarischer Imagination.* Tübingen: Niemeyer, 1976.

Miller, D. A. *Narrative and its Discontents: Problems of Closure in the Traditional Novel.* Princeton: Princeton University Press, 1981.

Miller, J. Hillis. *The Disappearance of God: Five Nineteenth-Century Writers.* Cambridge: Harvard University Press, 1963.

_____. *Fiction and Repetition: Seven English Novels.* Cambridge: Harvard University Press, 1982.

_____. "Narrative and History." *Journal of English Literary History* 4 (1974): 455–73.

Nägele, Rainer. *Text, Geschichte und Subjektivität in Hölderlins Dichtung – "Uneßbarer Schrift gleich".* Stuttgart: Metzler, 1985.

Narrative Endings. Nineteenth-Century Fiction (Special Issue) 33 (1978).

Neubauer, John. "Intellektuelle, intellektuale und ästhetische Anschauung: Zur Entstehung der romantischen Kunstauffassung." *Deutsche Vierteljahrsschrift* 46 (1972): 294–319.

_____. *Symbolismus und symbolische Logik: Die Idee der ars combinatoria in der Entwicklung der modernen Dichtung.* Munich: Fink, 1978.

Pfotenhauer, Helmut. "Aspekte der Modernität bei Novalis: Überlegungen zu Erzählformen des 19. Jahrhunderts ausgehend von Hardenbergs *Heinrich von Ofterdingen.*" *Literaturwissenschaft und Sozialwissenschaft* 8 (1977): 111–42.

Poulet, Georges. *Studies in Human Time.* Translated by Elliott Coleman. Baltimore: Johns Hopkins University Press, 1956.

Ricoeur, Paul. *Time and Narrative.* Translated by McLaughlin and Pellauer. Chicago: University of Chicago Press, 1984.

Said, Edward W. *Beginnings: Intention and Method.* Baltimore: Johns Hopkins University Press, 1975.

Scholem, Gershom. *On the Kabbalah and its Symbolism.* Translated by Ralph Manheim. New York: Schocken, 1965.

Sørensen, Bengt Algot. *Symbol und Symbolismus in den ästhetischen Theorien des 18. Jahrhunderts und der deutschen Romantik.* Copenhagen: Munksgaard, 1963.

Stam, James H. *Inquiries into the Origin of Language: The Fate of a Question.* New York: Harper and Row, 1976.

Szondi, Peter. *Poetik und Geschichtsphilosophie I & II.* Frankfurt: Suhrkamp, 1974.

Torgovnick, Marianna. *Closure in the Novel.* Princeton: Princeton University Press, 1981.

Veyne, Paul. *Comment on écrit l'histoire: Essai d'épistémologie.* Paris: Seuil, 1971.

Vietor, Karl. "Die Idee des Erhabenen in der deutschen Literatur." In *Geist und Form: Aufsätze zur deutschen Literaturgeschichte,* 234–66. Bern: Francke, 1952.

Voßkamp, Wilhelm, ed. *Utopieforschung: Interdisziplinäre Studien zur neuzeitlichen Utopie.* Stuttgart: Metzler, 1982.

Weiskel, Thomas. *The Romantic Sublime: Studies in the Structure and Psychology of Transcendence.* Baltimore: Johns Hopkins University Press, 1976.

Wohlfart, Günter. *Der Augenblick: Zeit und ästhetische Erfahrung bei Kant, Hegel, Nietzsche und Heidegger mit einem Exkurs zu Proust.* Freiburg: Alber, 1982.

Writing and History. Yale French Studies 59 (1980).

Yovel, Yirmiahu. *Kant and the Philosophy of History.* Princeton: Princeton University Press, 1980.

Adventism and Its Secularization

Aichele, Klaus. *Das Antichristdrama des Mittelalters, der Reformation und Gegenreformation.* The Hague: Nijhoff, 1974.

Bauemler, Alfred. *Das Irrationalitätsproblem in der Ästhetik und Logik des 18. Jahrhunderts bis zur Kritik der Urteilskraft.* Darmstadt: Wissenschaftliche Buchgesellschaft, 1975.

Behler, Ernst. *Die Ewigkeit der Welt: Problemgeschichtliche Untersuchungen zu den Kontroversen um Weltanfang und Weltendlichkeit im Mittelalter.* Munich: Schöningh, 1965.

Benz, Ernst. *Schellings theologische Geistesahnen.* Mainz: Akademie der Wissenschaften und der Literatur, 1955.

Beyreuther, Erich. *Geschichte des Pietismus.* Stuttgart: Steinkopf, 1978.

Binder, Wolfgang. "Grundformen der Säkularisation in den Werken

Goethes, Schillers und Hölderlins." *Zeitschrift für deutsche Philologie* 83 (1964): 42–69.

Bollacher, Martin. *Lessing: Vernunft und Geschichte: Untersuchungen zum Problem religiöser Aufklärung in den Spätschriften.* Tübingen: Niemeyer, 1978.

Brecht, Martin. "Johann Albrecht Bengels Theologie der Schrift." *Zeitschrift für Theologie und Kirche* 64 (1967): 99–120.

Buber, Martin. "Prophecy, Apocalyptic, and the Historical Hour." In *On the Bible: Eighteen Studies,* edited by N. Glatzer, 172–87. New York: Schocken, 1968.

Bulle, Ferdinand. *Franziskus Hemsterhuis und der deutsche Irrationalismus des 18. Jahrhunderts.* Jena: Diederichs, 1911.

Bultmann, Rudolf. *The Presence of Eternity: History and Eschatology.* New York: Harper, 1957.

Chamberlin, E. R. *Antichrist and the Millennium.* New York: Saturday Review Press, 1975.

Cohn, Norman. *The Pursuit of the Millennium.* London: Secker and Warburg, 1957.

Frei, Hans W. *The Eclipse of Biblical Narrative: A Study in Eighteenth and Nineteenth Century Hermeneutics.* New Haven: Yale University Press, 1974.

Fullenwider, Henry F. *Friedrich Christoph Oetinger: Wirkungen auf Literatur und Philosophie seiner Zeit.* Göppingen: Kümmerle, 1975.

Heiner, Hans-Joachim. "Das 'goldene Zeitalter' in der deutschen Romantik: Zur sozialpsychologischen Funktion eines Topos." In *Romantikforschung seit 1945,* edited by Klaus Peter, 280–303. Königstein: Hain, 1980.

Hermelink, Heinrich. *Geschichte der Evangelischen Kirche in Württemberg von der Reformation bis zur Gegenwart: Das Reich Gottes in Württemberg.* Stuttgart: Wunderlich, 1949.

Janentzsky, Christian. *J. C. Lavaters Sturm und Drang im Zusammenhang seines religiösen Bewußtseins.* Halle: Niemeyer, 1916.

Kaiser, Gerhard. *Klopstock: Religion und Dichtung.* Gütersloh: Mohn, 1963.

———. *Pietismus und Patriotismus im literarischen Deutschland: Ein Beitrag zum Problem der Säkularisation.* 2d ed. Frankfurt: Athenäum, 1973.

Kamlah, Wilhelm. *Utopie, Eschatologie, Geschichtsteleologie: Kritische Untersuchungen zum Ursprung und zum futuristischen Denken der Neuzeit.* Mannheim: Bibliographisches Institut, 1969.

Kemper, Hans Georg. *Gottesebenbildlichkeit und Naturnachahmung im Säkularisierungsprozeß: Problemgeschichtliche Studien zur deutschen Lyrik in Barock und Aufklärung.* Tübingen: Niemeyer, 1981.

Korn, Dietrich. *Das Thema des Jüngsten Tages in der deutschen Literatur des 17. Jahrhunderts.* Tübingen: Niemeyer, 1957.

Langen, August. *Der Wortschatz des deutschen Pietismus.* Tübingen: Niemeyer, 1954.

——. "Zum Problem der sprachlichen Säkularisation in der deutschen Dichtung des 18. und 19. Jahrhunderts." *Zeitschrift für deutsche Philologie* 83 (1964): 24–42.

Lehmann, Hartmut. *Pietismus und weltliche Ordnung in Württemberg vom 17. bis zum 20. Jahrhundert.* Stuttgart: Kohlhammer, 1969.

Lewalski, Barbara Kiefer. *Protestant Poetics and the Seventeenth-Century Religious Lyric.* Princeton: Princeton University Press, 1979.

Löwith, Karl. *Meaning in History: The Theological Implications of the Philosophy of History.* Chicago: University of Chicago Press, 1949.

Mähl, Hans-Joachim. *Die Idee des goldenen Zeitalters im Werk des Novalis.* Heidelberg: Winter, 1965.

Mälzer, Gottfried. *Die Werke der Württembergischen Pietisten des 17. und 18. Jahrhunderts: Verzeichnis der bis 1968 erschienenen Literatur.* Berlin: de Gruyter, 1972.

Marion, Jean. *L'idole et la distance: Cinq études.* Paris: Grasset, 1977.

McGinn, Bernhard. *Visions of the End: Apocalyptic Traditions in the Middle Ages.* New York: Columbia University Press, 1979.

Narr, Dieter. *Studien zur Spätaufklärung im deutschen Südwesten.* Stuttgart: Kohlhammer, 1979.

Nigg, Walter. *Das ewige Reich: Geschichte einer Hoffnung.* Zurich: Artemis, 1954.

Pestalozzi, Karl. "Lavaters Utopie." In *Literaturwissenschaft und Geschichtsphilosophie: Festschrift für Wilhelm Emrich,* 283–301. Berlin: de Gruyter, 1975.

Petersen, Julius. "Das goldene Zeitalter bei den deutschen Romantikern." In *Die Ernte: Abhandlungen zur Literaturwissenschaft,* 117–75. Halle: Niemeyer, 1926.

——. *Sehnsucht nach dem dritten Reich in deutscher Sage und Dichtung.* Stuttgart: Metzler, 1934.

Peucker, Brigitte. *Arcadia to Elysium: Preromantic Modes in 18th Century Germany.* Bonn: Bouvier, 1980.

Peuckert, Will-Erich. *Die große Wende: Das apokalyptische Saeculum und Luther.* Hamburg: Claassen & Goverts, 1948.

Piepmeier, Rainer. *Aporien des Lebensbegriffs seit Oetinger.* Freiburg: Alber, 1978.

Rabkin, Eric, et al., eds. *The End of the World.* Carbondale: Southern Illinois University Press, 1983.

Rowley, H. H. *The Relevance of Apocalyptic: A Study of Jewish and Christian Apocalypses from Daniel to the Revelation.* London: Lutterworth, 1944.

Ruh, Ulrich. *Säkularisierung als Interpretationskategorie: Zur Bedeutung des christlichen Erbes in der modernen Geistesgeschichte.* Freiburg: Herder, 1980.

Schilson, Arno. *Geschichte im Horizont der Vorsehung: G. E. Lessings Beitrag zu einer Theologie der Geschichte.* Mainz: Matthias-Grünewald, 1974.

Schmidt, Martin. *Pietismus.* Stuttgart: Kohlhammer, 1972.

Schneider, Klaus. *Die schweigenden Götter: Eine Studie zur Gottesvorstellung des religiösen Platonismus.* Hildesheim: Olms, 1966.

Shaffer, Elinor S. *'Kubla Khan' and the 'Fall of Jerusalem': The Mythological School in Biblical Criticism and Secular Literature, 1770–1880.* Cambridge: Cambridge University Press, 1975.

Sölle, Dorothee. *Realisation: Studien zum Verhältnis von Theologie und Dichtung nach der Aufklärung.* Darmstadt: Luchterhand, 1973.

Stadler, Ulrich. *Die theuren Dinge: Studien zu Bunyan, Jung-Stilling und Novalis.* Bern: Francke, 1980.

Strack, Friedrich. *Im Schatten der Neugier: Christliche Tradition und kritische Philosophie im Werk Friedrichs von Hardenberg.* Tübingen: Niemeyer, 1982.

Wagar, W. Warren. *Terminal Visions: The Literature of Last Things.* Bloomington: Indiana University Press, 1982.

Wessell, Leonard P. "G. F. Meier and the Genesis of Philosophical Theodicies of History in 18th-Century Germany." *Lessing Yearbook* 12 (1980): 63–84.

———. *G. E. Lessing's Theology: A Reinterpretation: A Study in the Problematic Nature of the Enlightenment.* The Hague: Mouton, 1977.

———. "Lessing's Eschatology and the Death of God." *Lessing Yearbook* 6 (1974): 59–82.

Zimmermann, Rolf Christian. *Das Weltbild des jungen Goethe: Studien zur hermetischen Tradition des deutschen 18. Jahrhunderts.* 2 vols. Munich: Fink, 1969 and 1979.

Index

Lightning Source UK Ltd.
Milton Keynes UK
UKHW012132111019
351429UK00001B/158/P